MESSENGERS

Who We Listen To, Who We Don't, and Why

Stephen Martin and Joseph Marks

PUBLICAFFAIRS

New York

PublicAffairs
Hachette Book Group
1290 Avenue of the Americas, New York, NY 10104
www.publicaffairsbooks.com
@Public_Affairs

Printed in the United States of America

First US Edition: October 2019

Published by PublicAffairs, an imprint of Perseus Books, LLC, a subsidiary of Hachette Book Group, Inc. The PublicAffairs name and logo is a trademark of the Hachette Book Group.

Simultaneously published in Great Britain by RH Business Books

The Hachette Speakers Bureau provides a wide range of authors for speaking events. To find out more, go to www.hachettespeakersbureau.com or call (866) 376-6591.

The publisher is not responsible for websites (or their content) that are not owned by the publisher.

Images reproduced by kind permission of: Rhesus monkey: iStock/Donyanedomam; proud faces: J. L. Tracy and R. W. Robins; facial widths: Robert Ward; 7-up baby: Advertising Archives; American presidents: John Wiley and Sons/Caroline F Keating, David Randall and Timothy Kendrick; Veganuary poster: Veganuary; Christine Keeler: Getty/Hulton Deutsch.

Library of Congress Control Number: 2019946447

ISBNs: 978-1-5417-2438-9 (hardcover), 978-1-5417-2439-6 (ebook)

LSC-C

10 9 8 7 6 5 4 3 2 1

Arguably, a society's most important messengers are its teachers and parents.

We dedicate this book to an example of the very best of each.

To Robert Cialdini. A brilliant scientist, patient mentor, inspirational colleague and warm and trusted friend. The day I met you was indeed a lucky one.

To Hilary and Richard Marks. Thank you for all your support, wise words and good humour over the years. You are two of the best role models a son could ask for.

Contents

CONTENTS

INTRODUCTION

The Curse of Cassandra

On THE SURFACE SHE POSSESSED many of the characteristics of an effective messenger. The daughter of Priam, King of Troy, and his second wife Queen Hecuba, Cassandra had status. She was beautiful, too: tall and elegant, with dark-brown curly locks of hair that coursed gracefully over her slender shoulders. Her eyes, similarly russet in colour, captured others' attention with such a piercing force that they would often be overcome with wonder. But perhaps her most impressive feature was one most people only dream of possessing: the gift of prophecy.

It was said that Cassandra's ability to 'interpret and communicate the will of the gods' was a gift from Apollo, as part of his attempt to seduce her. She predicted soldiers hiding inside a huge wooden horse left outside the gates of Troy. She foretold King Agamemnon's demise. She prophesied that her cousin, Aeneas, would establish a new nation in Rome. She even foresaw her own death. But Apollo's gift to Cassandra was a cursed one that caused her much anguish and, ultimately, led to insanity and death. For although she agreed to pledge herself to Apollo in exchange for this precious gift, Cassandra then rebuffed his advances, so she was punished in the most merciless way. Forcing his lips upon hers, the god spat into her mouth and swore that she would never again be believed by anyone. 'In his struggle to win me,' she sobbed, 'I consented to him. But then I broke my word. Ever since that fault I could persuade no one of anything.'[1]

Cassandra may be a mythical character, but she represents a fascinating paradox. She possessed knowledge and shared it with people who stood to benefit from listening to what she had to say, yet no one paid her any attention or believed her. It is a paradox that we encounter every day. There are plenty of people around who make accurate predictions, whose proposals are carefully based on the evidence available or whose points of view are eminently sensible, but who have the misfortune to go unheeded – even to be mocked. They suffer from what has become known as 'The Curse of Cassandra'.

From Trojan horses to Wall Street bears

In the late 1990s the US stock exchanges were a positively bullish place to be, with financiers shovelling seemingly bottomless pits of cash into dot-coms. It seemed everyone on Wall Street had bought into the idea that riches beyond compare were waiting to be made. Everyone, that is, except for one investor – the *highest*-profile investor. Warren Buffett, the then sprightly sixty-nine-year-old founder and chairman of investment behemoth Berkshire Hathaway, was unyielding in his disdain for what he described as the 'irrational exuberance' of the market. 'After a heady experience of that kind, normally sensible people drift into behavior akin to that of Cinderella at the ball ... Overstaying the festivities,' he remarked, 'will eventually bring on pumpkins and mice.'[2]

Many chastised Buffett for his gloomy commentary and his ominous warnings of 'a bubble about to burst'. The champions of dot-com companies claimed that Berkshire Hathaway's chairman, a well-known technophobe, would miss out on the oceans of profit that stood to be made. For a while the markets agreed. In the late 1990s the company's shares fell. But Buffett remained steadfast, adding a mid-sized energy supplier and a furniture rental business to his company's portfolio, further reinforcing the market's perception that he was a Luddite. Drawing parallels between his pessimistic prophecies and those of Cassandra, investors dubbed Buffett the 'Wall Street Cassandra'.

Of course the markets did eventually pop, with the previously dismissive investors – and not Buffett – suffering the reputational damage. Their 'Wall Street Cassandra' sneer proved unwise. In the long term it also turned out to be inaccurate. Ultimately, Buffett was publicly vindicated and his credibility soared to a level that has remained largely untouched ever since. He ceased to carry the curse of the Wall Street prophet who goes unheeded in their own lifetime.

That dubious distinction belongs elsewhere – to a true victim of the Cassandra Complex whose name almost no one would have heard of, had it not been for the investigative skills of the savvy journalist Michael Lewis.[3]

The real 'Wall Street Cassandra' was a man named Michael Burry, who was born in New York in 1971. He studied medicine at the University of California, Los Angeles, before earning his MD in Nashville, Tennessee. While working as a resident at Stanford he found time to start his own hedge fund and quickly developed an aptitude as a shrewd and successful investor. In 2001, shortly after the dot-com bubble burst, the S&P 500 fell almost 12 percent. That year Burry's investments were up more than 50 percent. Beginner's luck maybe? Yet the following year when the S&P fell by 22 percent, Burry returned more than 15 percent. And even when the stock market began to register a positive turn, in 2003, Burry beat the market hands-down. By 50 percent to 28 percent.

During the mid-2000s Burry shifted his investment focus. He started taking positions against subprime mortgage bonds, at a time when there was no formal way to bet against them (he had to invent his own method). Burry's genius lay in spotting the under-recognised, perilous fault lines underpinning the subprime mortgage market. And shorting them. The message he seemed to be sending to the market was one of an impending apocalypse. It was a message that seemed credible and evidence-based, and it was made with conviction. Burry had skin in the game. He was putting his own money on the line.

Who knew that Burry's astute and perceptive insights would turn out to be the early predictors of what ultimately became the biggest financial crisis in more than seventy years? Very few, in fact. In contrast to those late-1990s investors who heard but dismissed Warren Buffett's forewarnings, Burry's prophecy simply wasn't heard. Not by the media. Not by the financial in-crowd. Next to no one was listening.

Arguably, it was even worse for Burry than it had been for his classical forebear. Cassandra's single great obstacle was an inability to convince anyone of her prophecies. Burry faced other disadvantages, too. He was an awkward communicator. He also had only one eye, having lost the other when he was barely two years old because of a tumour. This physical drawback made simple face-to-face conversations difficult because, in his attempt to line up his good eye, Burry's glass one would appear strangely skewed. This awkwardness had dogged him throughout school and college, where he had made few friends. The fact was that Burry was seen as different. At school. At college. As a resident at Stanford Hospital. And when he arrived on Wall Street. He even dressed differently. In contrast to the industry norms of tailored suits, starched shirts and Windsor-knotted ties, Burry wore shorts and T-shirts to work.

Years after the crash, and despite his fund having made a gross gain of 726 percent, Burry's entirely accurate prophecy remained a largely unacknowledged one. Perhaps the best example of how Cassandra-like Burry was occurred in 2008. Bloomberg News published an article detailing a long list of the foresighted folks who had predicted the financial crash. Conspicuous by its absence was the name of Michael Burry. No one called to hear his story. No one sought out his predictions for the future. Even the Financial Crisis Inquiry Commission – a bipartisan group set up by President Barack Obama to examine the causes of the financial and economic crisis – weren't interested in speaking to him (at least at first).*

They called the journalist Michael Lewis instead.

Why would officials from the Financial Crisis Inquiry Commission choose to contact Michael Lewis for an account of the warning predictions that were made before the crash? Surely it would have made more sense to talk directly to one of the principal sources of those predictions – Michael Burry. Michael Lewis is a very fine journalist, but he could scarcely be said to have possessed Burry's practical expertise.

A possible answer emerges when viewing the Financial Crisis Inquiry Commission's actions through the lens of what cognitive scientists refer to as *focalism* or, more commonly, the *focusing illusion*.[4] When judging the relative worth of a messenger, there is a natural tendency for audiences to assign undue levels of importance and causality to the most salient and prominent messengers. Often such people possess characteristics that provide them with a veneer of credibility, even though these characteristics may have no bearing on what is actually being said. The messenger just happens to be well known. Or charismatic. Or rich. Or dominant. Or likeable.

---

* The Financial Crisis Inquiry Commission did eventually interview Michael Burry. They stated at the beginning of the interview that the reason they had decided to speak to Burry was because 'we read about you in *The Big Short*'.

This explains why certain messengers – those in the spotlight – will often be awarded a much larger portion of the credit for any resulting successes or failures than they actually deserve.[5] It's unfair and yet understandable. When judging the relative worth of a proposition, audiences will often face the difficult task of having to process large amounts of information, much of it conflicting, in order to come to a satisfactory answer. Think about it. Questions like 'Which candidate is the best choice for president?', 'Will Brexit really result in a brighter future for the United Kingdom?' and 'Does it make sense to bet against the subprime mortgage market?' are incredibly tough questions to answer. It is surely understandable, therefore, that frequently we tend to judge an idea not on its merits, but according to how we judge the person putting it forward. We fail to separate the idea being communicated in a message from the person or entity conveying it. This commonly overlooked insight – one that is frequently missed by audiences, and results in them ignoring the expert in the room – illuminates a fundamental feature of the effective messenger.

They *become* the message.

Perhaps that is why the Financial Crisis Inquiry Commission chose to listen to Michael Lewis's account of Burry's predictions rather than to Burry himself. Lewis represented a more prominent and accessible messenger.* He may not have been the source of the insights he shared with the inquiry, but he was articulate, intelligent

---

* And he was, at least, a real person. In the 2008 book, *A Novel Approach to Politics*, Douglas A. Van Belle, Editor-in-Chief of *International Studies Perspectives and Foreign Policy Analysis*, noted that 'the most popular Democratic US president in recent memory' had never actually served a single day in the Oval Office. Given the increasing opposition to a number of US foreign policies at the time, it is easy to see why a fictitious president (*The West Wing*'s Josiah Bartlet, played by actor Martin Sheen) might be considered by many American citizens to be the better figurehead.

and an economics-trained journalist who had once worked as a bond salesman at Solomon Brothers. And he was well known. In focusing on these traits, it is easy to see why the Financial Crisis Inquiry board of commissioners saw Michael Lewis as a more effective messenger than the Cassandra-like Burry. They were making a judgement about the quality of the message, based on the quality of the messenger. After all, it's much easier to spot those who are in the spotlight.

But what of the argument that it wasn't Burry being rejected, but rather his message? After all, rumours of an impending implosion of the subprime mortgage market were hardly ideas that many would have wanted to contemplate, let alone believe. Burry could have been the most charismatic man on the planet, but if the message he had to convey was an unpalatable one, it's scarcely surprising that people should have chosen to ignore it. The fact is, though, that that's not quite what happened. Many chose to ignore Burry – indeed, some of his existing investors tried to bale out on him before the subprime market imploded. Others, though, who agreed with his analysis, were able to sell the story more convincingly because they fitted the messenger profile better. Greg Lippman, who was a head subprime mortgage trader at Deutsche Bank, is a case in point. No smarter than Burry, and no more insightful, he possessed a confidence and dominance that Burry lacked. As a result, Deutsche Bank and its shareholders listened to him. Burry was right (and indeed profited considerably from his insight), but he was the wrong type of messenger, so his message travelled only so far. Lippmann was right and was also the right kind of messenger. He, his bank and the bank's investors therefore benefited accordingly. At the end of one particularly successful year, Lippmann was paid a US $47 million bonus.

When someone communicates an idea, an audience doesn't just make judgements about the coherence and validity of that communicator's message. They also make a whole range of judgements about the messenger, too. Does this person appear to know what they are talking about? Do they have relevant expertise or experience? Do they seem genuine, or might they be trying to scam me? Are they tough enough to get the job done? Might they have an ulterior motive? Do I think I can trust them? These are important questions that should be attended to before you jump into bed with someone. Metaphorically *or* literally.

When Burry and Lippmann were attempting to convince investors that betting against the subprime mortgage bond market was a good idea, investors were no doubt asking themselves these exact same questions. Burry and Lippmann were both saying the *same* thing. The subprime market was in a perilous state that would probably bring about a tsunami-like financial crisis. Both men's claims were thoroughly researched and credible, and history went on to vindicate them both. But only Lippmann was able to get the investors to listen.

Michael Burry was the 'Wall Street Cassandra'.*

Messengers versus messages

This is a book that explores why some messengers and their messages are listened to, accepted and acted upon and why others are not.

---

* Burry has said that he believes he may have Asperger's syndrome, and this might help further explain why he finds interacting with others challenging. People with Asperger's are often brilliant at systematising information, yet may struggle with aspects of social intelligence. Being ignored, or being conscious of an inability to control a situation, is linked with depression, and this is something Burry also experienced when investors turned on him and refused to listen to – let alone back – his predictions. The very act of being heard is a crucial component in giving a person their dignity. Sometimes the simple process of airing a grievance to a friend, a concern to a neighbour or a worry to a colleague is all one needs to feel better about things. Being heard also allows us to influence and take control. It is rare for an individual to achieve great things without the help of others.

We define a 'messenger' as an agent – it could be an individual, a group, a media platform or an organisation – who delivers information. That information could be a simple piece of data, like today's temperature, as broadcast by a meteorologist. Or it could be a point of view, such as an op-ed written by a journalist or blogger. It might be a rebuttal, as when a tweet or a Facebook post claims that a news story is fake. Or it could be a sales campaign that uses a paid 'influencer' to promote a product. It might even convey a policy idea, a vision or a worldview that attempts to influence not only what an audience pays attention to, but also what they think, believe and, subsequently, become. We regard an audience as anyone, from a single person to an identifiable group – large or small – to whom a message is directed. And we describe a 'messenger effect' as the change in the level of influence or impact that a messenger's message has on an audience – because they sent it.

Importantly, that influence or impact doesn't have to come about as a result of the content or wisdom of the message itself. Instead it comes about as a result of a trait that the messenger delivering the message is perceived to possess. We will investigate, in detail, eight fundamental traits that, whether real or inferred, reliably impact upon whether or not a messenger will be listened to. Some of these messenger traits will be familiar to readers. What will be less familiar, however, are the subtle, hard-to-detect and frequently missed features that signal possession of one or more of these traits, which so powerfully influence how audiences respond.

It is also important to realise that messengers aren't necessarily the ones who craft a message. Big companies hire actors to endorse products in advertisements. Managers bring in consultants to deliver tough news or to advocate new approaches, prompting a commonly touted view about advisors that 'They don't need to know more than their client, they just need to have a suit, a briefcase and come from out of town.' Large sums are spent on speakers who get junior researchers – or speechwriters, if they are really important – to pen the content. Rivals pass missives through mediators. Divorcing couples pass messages through lawyers. Schoolchildren recruit friends to send out feelers to the girls and boys they like in class. The media pays handsome sums to get a quote from the most interesting messenger for a story, even when there are others who could provide the same soundbites for a much smaller fee.

Regardless of its source, when a message is delivered, something intriguing happens. The messenger becomes connected to the content of that message, in the listener's mind.[6] Even if they did not craft the message themselves. This association can have a dramatic effect on how the messenger and their messages are subsequently evaluated. It helps to explain, for example, the origin of the phrase 'Don't shoot the messenger', which is thought to have originated at a time when warring generals were known to punish scouts and emissaries who brought bad news. Legend has it that when a messenger arrived to inform Tigranes the Great, King of Armenia, that forces under the Roman consul Lucullus were on their way, Tigranes responded by removing the messenger's head. One can only assume that any subsequent information imparted was rather more positive, though it's worth noting that Lucullus went on to defeat Tigranes.*

Messengers weren't only at risk when it came to delivering bad news to their leaders. Royal messengers faced similar danger when delivering a message *from* the monarch. As spokespeople for the

---

* In August 2017 a number of reputable news outlets reported claims that, twice a day, US President Donald Trump is presented with an ego-boosting dossier filled with flattering photographs and good-news stories about himself. Unlike those messengers in Tigranes's Palace, who would clamour to avoid being the bearer of negative news, one wonders whether officials in the Trump White House clamour to be chosen as the one to deliver this positive news to their master. https://news. vice.com/en_ca/article/zmygpe/trump-folder-positive-news-white-house

King of England of former times, town criers were particularly at risk of harm from angry mobs who did not like the messages being passed down from the royal palace. So commonplace were the physical attacks on town criers that laws were passed to protect them. Any harm caused to a town crier was, by association, harm directed at the king. It was treason. And the penalty for treason? Death.[7]

If the link we make between a messenger and their message is such a strong one, then it's important to understand how we make trait-based inferences about the myriad of messengers we encounter in our lives, and which of these traits matter most. How do we decide what a messenger knows? How do we evaluate what skills they possess? How do we judge what sort of person they are?

While we certainly build and modify our views about others over time, through repeated interactions and exchanges, we also form beliefs and opinions about them extremely quickly – sometimes in a matter of milliseconds. The Stanford psychologist Nalini Ambady, who before her untimely death from leukaemia in 2013 pioneered much of the work on *snap-judgements* (single-glance impressions), demonstrated conclusively that humans are actually very good at forming generally accurate impressions based on brief observations.[8] Her work showed that our first impressions of a complete stranger not only tend to match those of others viewing the same stranger for a similarly brief period of time, but are also likely to be in line with the stranger's own assessment of their personality traits.

Such judgements are fundamentally linked to our perception of how accomplished someone is at communicating information. Together with Harvard psychologist Robert Rosenthal, Ambady conducted a study where participants saw a series of video-clips showing thirteen teachers in action.[9] Each clip was only ten seconds in duration and there was no sound. After watching them, each participant was asked to rate how they perceived the teachers, across fifteen dimensions of personality: confidence, enthusiasm,

dominance, warmth, attentiveness, optimism, competence, professionalism, and so on. What Ambady and Rosenthal discovered was
that the participants' ratings were incredibly consistent. If a teacher
was perceived as likeable by one person, they were probably seen as
likeable by most people. But more than that, the evaluations arrived
at by the group of volunteers were remarkably similar to the evaluations given by the teachers' students at the end of the semester. Think
about that. People who had seen ten-second video-clips of teachers
– with no sound, remember – made judgements about their personalities that turned out to correlate closely with how their actual
students, who had sat through months of lectures, would rate their
teaching at the end of term.

It sounds miraculous, but in fact those observing the videos
were simply responding to the physical cues given off by each of the
thirteen teachers. When Ambady and Rosenthal arranged for two
independent researchers to watch the video-clips and break down
each teacher's body language, second-by-second, they discovered
that every time a teacher looked down, shook their head, became
more animated, enthusiastic or simply smiled, their movements
registered with observers and, cumulatively, shaped the perceptions they formed. Ultimately, teachers who seemed animated and
enthusiastic were marked up. Those who frowned were viewed
more critically, as were those who looked down too much and
therefore appeared to lack confidence. Teachers who displayed
these last two forms of behaviour received worse student evaluations at the end of term.

Ambady's studies show that there may be *no more* to how we make
first impressions than meets the eye. We will often infer, from a
scant few moments of observation, who is confident, warm and
enthusiastic, in control, dominant, trustworthy, likeable, authoritarian or expert. These person-perception processes are thought to
be automatic, occurring within fifty milliseconds of being exposed

to a new individual;[10] and, as we will show, they frequently develop very early in life.

Of course there's more to human interaction than first impressions and non-verbal behaviour. True feelings of respect and connectedness do not form immediately, after a single glance. We also build up an understanding of people over time. We develop feelings for them – sometimes positive, sometimes negative, occasionally both – that will also influence how much we are prepared to listen to them. As a general rule, if we respect and feel connected to someone, then we will be more inclined to listen to and follow them (although there are plenty of exceptions to this rule, which will be explored later). We can also learn to manage the signals we send out. A communications coach or media trainer may show us how to alter our speech, expression and manner so that we come across more positively. We may even try to train ourselves by honing our self-presentation skills, although this is certainly harder. What media coaches and self-development activities lack, however, is an understanding of the astonishingly broad and fascinating science that informs the characteristics of successful messengers, and how we are frequently influenced by the most trivial and seemingly inconsequential of cues.

Messengers, hard and soft

In 1982 the respected scholars Edward Jones and Thane Pittman developed a conceptual framework describing five strategies that a messenger might adopt as a means to manage an audience's impression of them.[11] They might choose to appear competent, morally respectable, intimidating, likeable or pitiful. The two researchers also noted that a single approach will not work in all circumstances. A teacher walking into a new class may choose to adopt an intimidating style – say, by sternly warning a student who has been misbehaving – in an attempt to signal that they are not to be messed with. Adopting that same messenger style in a different situation – let's say, meeting a partner's parents for the first time – would likely be self-defeating. Even within a single interaction, it might be advisable to shift from appearing likeable to appearing intimidating, or from competent to pitiful, should the circumstances demand it.

The Jones and Pittman messenger framework is fine as far as it goes, but it is also somewhat incomplete and, of course, has been overtaken by a substantial body of research that has emerged during the last forty years. In this book we offer up a more contemporary and compelling framework, built upon two broad categories of messenger: hard and soft. Hard messengers are more likely to have their messages accepted, because audiences perceive them to possess superior *status*. Soft messengers, in contrast, win acceptance of their messages because they are perceived to possess a *connectedness* with an audience. In the chapters that follow we consider each trait of these two broad messenger types in turn.

In Part One we explore the domain of the hard messenger. The hard messenger possesses, or might claim to possess, elevated status. Messengers with higher perceived status carry greater sway in society, regardless of whether their position has been achieved explicitly through an agreement or has emerged informally, because they are believed to possess power and qualities that may be valuable to those around them. Think of the leader of a political party or the captain of a sports team. Typically, we associate status with hierarchy in the workplace, which makes sense because those at the top of a clearly defined organisational structure are the ones who make the important decisions, control company resources and usually get paid the most. Indeed, the very fact that they do have status may mean that they receive more respect, and are judged as providing more value to their organisation, than perhaps they should. But status hierarchies

16

are not confined solely to the domains of the workplace. They can be found in our schools, family groups, networks of friends and associates, and in our local communities and broader societies, too. We explore four important traits, dedicating a chapter to each, which contribute either individually or in combination to status-driven messenger success: socio-economic position, competence, dominance and attractiveness.

Part Two is devoted to an investigation of societies' soft messengers. Effective messengers are not just rich or famous. Nor are they necessarily expert, dominant or in possession of overpowering levels of attractiveness. The standout feature of soft messengers is their *connectedness* with an audience. Humans are social animals and have a strong desire to form connections, to bond and cooperate with others. People don't always look to experts or CEOs for information. Sometimes they prefer to hear from their friends, those they trust and the people who are 'like them'. In Chapters 5, 6, 7 and 8 we investigate four fundamental factors that contribute – again either individually or in combination – to the softer-driven characteristics of successful messengers: warmth, vulnerability, trustworthiness and charisma.

In the Conclusion to the book we examine the interplay between the various hard- and soft-messenger effects, and attempt to distinguish between those situations where a hard, status-driven messenger is likely to be preferred, and those where a softer, connectedness-driven messenger will emerge victorious. We then turn our attention to the professional, political and societal impact of these messenger effects. If we accept that these messenger effects are so fundamental as to influence the very fabric of society and our place within it, the values we hold, the political parties we follow, who we choose to believe and who we don't, which groups we join and which ones we reject, then what can we do to manage their broader impact on our society? We offer up two principal ideas that could be helpful for a variety of groups, including policy-makers, professionals who design and construct impactful communications, educators and parents. Our ideas are not designed to be deliberately contentious, but rather to start a conversation about the important factors that influence who we listen to and who we do not. For one single reason.

Recognising the traits of society's messengers is crucial because they fundamentally influence not just *who we listen to* and *what we believe*, but also *who we become*.

PART ONE

Hard Messengers

The Champagne Twitterati

THE ALLURE OF TWITTER IS UNDERSTANDABLE. Anyone can share their opinion (admittedly constrained by a limited number of characters) with the rest of the world. It has an organisational quality, too. Tweets can be systematically categorised by topic, according to the hashtags used in messages. People who agree with the views that a user expresses in a message can signal their approval by 'liking' it. They can get involved and engaged by posting a reply. They can share it, too, retweeting messages to the people who follow them. So tweets can spread like a wildfire. Across social networks and social-media platforms, millions of people around the world can see the same message, written by a messenger they otherwise couldn't possibly have had an opportunity to interact or connect with.

It's incredibly democratic.

But Twitter is also notoriously glib. It starts with someone deciding to communicate a message. But that message doesn't necessarily have to be a thought-provoking one. Nor does it need to be heartfelt, poignant, sarcastic, funny or, as we seem to have wearily come to accept, even mildly accurate or true. It just has to be able to grab attention. Even for a fleeting moment. If Twitter had a personality, it would be that of an attention-deficient three-year-old casting aside every toy its exasperated parents offer up, accompanied with an expectant look of 'Is that it? What else do you have? Come on, entertain me.'

In 2017 Harsha Gangadharbatla, at the University of Colorado, teamed up with Masoud Valafar, a software engineer at Twitter.

They wanted to examine how information on Twitter influences beliefs and opinions.[1] The researchers therefore randomly selected 300,000 active Twitter users and tracked their messages, posts and activity over the course of a month, in an attempt see whether Twitter users were being influenced by the mass media – what they were directly consuming on television, in newspapers and online articles – or whether they were just reacting to messages disseminated by certain types of messengers. The latter is what they found. It seems there is a tight-knit community of opinion leaders who tend to follow each other on Twitter, form a set of beliefs and attitudes based on media content they consume, and subsequently post their opinions. These are the posts that other users notice, react and respond to. Rather like a champagne fountain where the saucer atop is continually 'topped up', providing a ready supply to the ones below, selected tweets are cascaded down until everyone's glass is full.

Gangadharbatla and Valafar's research is important because it demonstrates that even on information-sharing platforms that, unlike traditional media, have few barriers to entry, certain messengers have significantly greater power when it comes to communicating a message. Quite simply, those who are retweeted, and have the biggest impact on attitudes and thinking, are not those who are necessarily insightful or funny or clever. Instead they often simply possess some form of status.

One tweet that perfectly illustrates this point was sent at 4.59 p.m. on 12 August 2017 by Robby McHale, who hoped this might be 'the one' that would go viral. Several features of his message were in his favour. First, his timing was pretty good, which it has to be on Twitter for a message to have even the slightest chance of capturing attention; when the tweet appears and the context in which it is posted can often matter more than the content of the tweet itself. Second, McHale's tweet picked up on an issue that millions of people were talking about and paying attention to, not just in the United States, but across much of the rest of the world: the Charlottesville riots. It was a story that was holding people captive. Everyone was talking about it: watching their newsfeeds and discussing them on their Facebook pages. Third, Robby McHale's tweet was a carefully considered one. In a clever twist on President Donald Trump's campaign slogan, he suggested that what America needed to become great again was not hate and division, but understanding and cooperation.

'The people of the US should come to terms, unify, and work together regardless of race to make the country great,' he tweeted. He followed it with #Charlottesville.

Who wouldn't agree with that sentiment?

By Friday 25 August, thirteen days after his message to the American people, Robby McHale had received a single response. One person posted a comment on his tweet. No one had 'liked' his post, nor had anyone retweeted it. Out of Twitter's 330-plus million monthly users, only one of them engaged with McHale's tweet. Nobody was listening. His astute and timely message – one that, doubtless, millions would agree with – was cast aside. Rather like the toys of that uninterested, attention-scarce three-year old.

Just seven minutes after McHale posted his tweet, somebody else posted a message on Twitter that communicated a sentiment very similar to McHale's. It had most of the hallmarks of a tweet that wasn't going anywhere. The context wasn't particularly clear and, unlike McHale, the author, rather than use his own words, instead repeated a line that had first appeared more than twenty years earlier in Nelson Mandela's 1994 autobiography, *Long Walk to Freedom*: 'No one is born hating another person because of the color of his skin or his background or his religion ...'

Despite this, the tweet immediately went viral.

True, this second tweet had one or two features in its favour. The words were eloquent, even if they weren't the tweeter's own. And the tweet was accompanied by an uplifting picture of the tweeter, smiling up at an open window where a group of ethnically diverse children were standing and looking out. But it was the person in the picture who was the decisive factor. By early 2018 former US President Barack Obama's tweet had been retweeted more than 1.6 million times and 'liked' by 4.4 million users. According to a Twitter spokesperson, it was, at the time, the most popular tweet ever posted.[2] It probably still is.

Is it a surprise that a former, and still hugely popular, president's tweet receives the approval of more than 4.4 million people, and counting, while Robby McHale's receives just one? Absolutely not. Barack Obama has 100-plus million followers on Twitter. That's close to 30 percent of all Twitter's registered users who potentially see his messages on their Twitter home page each time he posts. Of course Robby McHale's tweet is going to be crowded out by a former President of the United States of America. It's going to be crowded out by a former president of a Home Owners' Association.

Nor is it a surprise how undemocratic and hierarchical the seemingly democratic and accessible Twitter platform really is. It is true that Twitter is an environment where any messenger can have their say and where all voices have an opportunity to be heard. But it is also true that only a tiny fraction of those messengers are listened to. And that tiny fraction is likely to possess some kind of status.

Status is a 'hard-messenger' effect and is incredibly powerful. Those perceived to possess high status are regarded as having *instrumental value* – that is, they are seen to be in possession of certain features or qualities that have not only helped them to be successful, but could also be of use to others. As a result we assume that these people are worth listening to, and they carry greater sway. It is the primary reason why, when meeting people for the first time, the conversation so often starts with, 'So, what exactly is it you do?'

Knowing a person's status allows us to infer many other characteristics about them – sometimes accurately and sometimes not.[3]

Status allows us to answer a vitally important question: 'Is this person worth listening to?'

In Part One we discuss the four most important 'hard' traits that can lead to a messenger being perceived as possessing high status and, as a consequence, being well placed to win other people's attention. The traits in question are socio-economic position, competence, dominance and attractiveness.

As you will see in the next four chapters, status – not just on Twitter, but in pretty much every societal context and situation that we come across – counts for a lot.

1

SOCIO-ECONOMIC POSITION

Fame, Fortune and Being Recognised
without Being Recognised

FOR MANY PEOPLE the idea of being a celebrity is an appealing one – imagine all that recognition and adulation. For the celebrities themselves, though, it's more of a mixed blessing. In an expletive-filled rant in the film *Funny People*, Eminem laments the pitfalls of celebrity: 'I can't go to Best Buy,' he complains. 'I can't go to fucking Walmart, Kmart. You fucking name it, I can't go there. Everyone in this fucking room is either staring at us [or] wanting to take a fucking picture.' The US comedian Aziz Ansari made a similar point in an interview with Stephen Dubner on the hugely popular *Freakonomics Radio* podcast.[1] He certainly recognised the advantages, suggesting that 'The biggest upside is that random people are really nice to you. People are inclined to be nice to you. Strangers come up to you and they tell you they appreciate the work that you do … They say, "I love your work." I think that's really nice.' But then he dwelt on the downside:

> … at a certain point, if you're walking down the street, you're some-what recognizable and you get stopped all the time. You can either take all those photos – and I used to do that but I started becoming a grumpy person. I would do it and I'd be grumpy about doing it.

29

You're with your girlfriend and every minute you get stopped ... There's some people I know that are famous to the point where they don't even walk down the street anymore. They're always in a black car. Wherever they go, they're in a black car. They don't get to be like normal people. I don't want to lose that. I want to be able to walk around and be a dude, you know? And just be a person.

Ansari seems to be saying that being famous is good, but only to a certain point. Beyond that point it becomes problematic ... for the *celebrity*.

The upside of being a celebrity is obvious. Most people like to be complimented and to bask in the accompanying warm glow that arises from the praise and approval of others. Curiously, research finds that many of us are more than happy to accept compliments even when they have scant basis in truth.[2] Other studies suggest that recipients of such fawning look kindly on their admirers.[3] Presumably this is the reason why one astute commentator on a fanzine website advised always telling the celebrity how much you love their latest work, *before* requesting a selfie. Not afterwards.[4]

When it comes to establishing their influence, the downside of being a celebrity is arguably more revealing. Celebrities are that rare breed of individuals who have been deemed worthy not just of their local group's attention, but of the public's attention (and, usually, admiration) more generally. People are desperate to be in their presence. They are somehow deemed the best of the best. And the more prominence, attention and airtime given to them, the more this belief is perpetuated. When a 2009 UK survey asked ten-year-old children what they wanted to be when they grew up, a large proportion said they aspired to be pop stars, sportsmen and actors. Another UK survey showed that 22 percent of children (again, average age ten) said they would like to be 'rich' when they grew up, and that 19 percent of children said they wanted to be 'famous'.[5] Results like these speak to the incredibly powerful effect that celebrities have on our society. They may dislike the attention that comes with their fame, but it nevertheless gives them a power and influence that extend far beyond the sphere in which they established their credentials.

Given this, it comes as no surprise that celebrities, whether film stars, pop stars, sports stars or the occasional head of state, tend to be powerful messengers: we pay them attention. But it's important to bear in mind that we're not listening to them simply because they're famous. We're also responding to the socio-economic status that is an integral part of their fame. Quite simply, we're prepared to listen to them because they're high up the hierarchical tree: they have status.[6] And status is something that is possessed by many people who are not household names. You don't have to be famous to command attention and respect.

How to be recognised, without being recognised

On a sunny Sunday morning in 1967 Anthony Doob and Alan Gross got into their respective cars and took a drive around Palo Alto and Menlo Park in northern California. Each carried a single passenger, lying low down on the back seat and hidden from view from other road users. These clandestine passengers had in their possession two stopwatches and a tape recorder. Were Doob and Gross about to undertake some kind of college-kid prank (after all, Stanford University was close by)? Actually, no. They were, in fact, attempting to find a scientifically robust answer to an intriguing question. On average, what was the tendency of Californian drivers to honk their horn when delayed at a traffic intersection?

Anthony Doob pulls up to an intersection on a narrow road and, just as he planned, the lights turn red before he has a chance to go through. So he stops in front of the junction. While the lights are red, a few other cars join the queue behind him. A minute goes by and the lights go green. But when they do, Doob doesn't move. He just sits there waiting, with the engine running. Meanwhile Alan Gross is across town, also at the front of a traffic-light-controlled intersection, doing the exact same thing.

Doob and Gross already knew that the lights at their chosen inter-sections stayed green for an average of twelve seconds and that the roads were too narrow for other drivers to pull past them. They therefore knew that any delay on their part would lead to frustration among those behind them. But precisely how many would then vent their irritation by hooting? Doob and Gross's back-seat conspirators, tape recorders activated, had the answer: 68 percent proceeded to honk their horn at least once. A couple of drivers went further and actually drove into their back bumpers instead.

Establishing how many people would honk their horn in such a situation was only part of the experiment, however. Doob and Gross also wanted to find out if people's honking behaviour would differ according to the type of car that was holding them up.

On that Sunday morning they started out with two different makes of cars. One was a new Chrysler Crown Imperial hard-top in black. Washed and polished, it was a high-status car. The second was a rusty old 1954 Ford stationwagon. In fact, the Ford looked so bad that Doob and Gross had to replace it after a few trials, because they worried that drivers queuing up behind it would simply assume it had broken down. So they swapped the Ford for a 1961 Rambler sedan in grey. Scruffy. Unwashed. Unpolished. The Rambler was the low-status car.

Before embarking on their experiment, Doob and Gross approached a group of psychology students at the university and asked them to imagine they had stopped at traffic lights behind either a black 1966 Chrysler or a dirty grey 1961 Rambler sedan. 'The light turns green and, for no apparent reason, the driver does

32

not move. Would you honk your horn?' they asked. They followed up that question with, 'And how long would you wait before sounding it?'

The students were unanimous. And full of bravado. Of course they would honk. And they certainly wouldn't make any distinction between the two cars. Some claimed they would honk sooner at the high-status car. But what actually happened on the road that subsequent sunny Sunday morning told a different story. Whilst overall close to 70 percent of waiting drivers sounded their horns in frustration, the distribution of results was unevenly split between the two cars. Fewer than 50 percent honked at the high-status car; 84 percent hooted at the lower-status car. Not only was a Californian driver's *likelihood to honk* influenced by the status of the car that was delaying them, but their *latency to honk* was influenced, too. When behind a low-status car, people would sound the horn much sooner than when behind a high-status one. Very often, more than once.[7]

As psychology experiments go, this is a quirky one. It's also over fifty years old. Yet findings in other much more recent studies are strikingly similar. For example, in 2014 a team of French researchers found that drivers were much less likely to overtake a slow-moving vehicle if that vehicle also happened to be a prestigious one.[8] It seems that when deciding whether to honk or overtake, some drivers (certainly not all) will be influenced by the status of the car and, by extension, its owner. Perhaps this goes some way to explain why well-known celebrities will often hide their identities by riding in cars with black-tinted windows. Ironically, maintaining their anonymity in these high-status vehicles may actually allow the celebrities inside to achieve what might at first appear to be two incompatible goals. They are able to signal their privileged status, without having to suffer the downsides of the unwanted attention, as lamented by Eminem and Aziz Ansari. The air of mystery created about who is inside boosts the enigmatic quality of the unknown passenger. It is a remarkably efficient way to remain recognisable without having to experience the hassle of actually being recognised.*

Socio-economic position is just one form of status, but it is the most obvious and salient one, because it can easily be signalled by the purchasing and consumption choices that we make. A limousine with blacked-out windows is a single example of 'conspicuous consumption' – a term coined by the Norwegian-American sociologist Thorstein Veblen, who noted how certain members of society would deliberately pay more than necessary for goods and services, in order to impress the rest of society and boost their social power and prestige.[9] Socio-economic position can therefore be bought as much as earned. A Ferrari. A million-dollar wristwatch. A top-floor waterfront penthouse. All purchased to help signal someone's status and wealth and, in doing so, change how others respond to them.

But signals of socio-economic position aren't restricted to what many would regard as ostentatious purchases. Even a humble T-shirt can be effective, when it comes to signalling socio-economic status. In 2011 a pair of Dutch psychologists conducted a set of studies that bore several similarities to Doob and Gross's earlier work, but with T-shirts rather than cars. Approaching shoppers in a busy shopping

---

* It is important to note that a car doesn't always have to be expensive to boost someone's socio-economic position. But it certainly doesn't hurt if it is, especially if the status-enhancing action of buying a pricey vehicle is combined with a universally approved one. In 2006 a US government-sponsored tax break for low-emission cars ended, making the average 'emission-neutral' vehicle $3,000 more expensive to purchase. Rather than falling off a cliff, sales of the Toyota Prius immediately rose by 69 percent. Articles quickly surfaced detailing the number of Hollywood stars who were ditching their Ferraris and driving to film sets in their new Prius instead. Dubbed *competitive altruism*, the signal seemed to be, 'Look at me, I am a friend of the environment and I am willing to pay to be a friend of the environment.' In light of the French study, one wonders if their commutes also took longer, as a result of driving their shiny new blacked-out Prius slower than normal, so that mere mortals could (not) recognise them.

mall, they enquired whether they would be willing to take part in a short research study, after which they would be rewarded with a drink of their choice. Those who agreed were shown one of a series of pictures of a young man wearing a polo shirt and were asked to rate the man's likely socio-economic status. The pictures were all identical, except for one feature – a signal of status in the form of a digitally imposed brand label on the man's polo shirt. Those shown a picture of the man with a premium-brand label on his shirt rated him as having higher status and being wealthier than when he appeared wearing the same shirt, but with either a less prestigious label or no label at all.[10] At Palo Alto traffic intersections, a prestigious car was sufficient to enhance the perceived socio-economic status of a complete stranger. In Dutch shopping centres, it was a Tommy Hilfiger logo.

Recall how Doob and Gross's studies also found that the prestige of a car could influence the amount of time a delayed driver would be willing to wait before sounding their horn. Does the inclusion of a premium logo on a shirt have a similar effect – influencing, for example, people's likelihood to respond positively to a request or message that will hold them up and eat into their time? In the same Dutch shopping centre, other passers-by were approached by a clipboard-carrying researcher, who looked them in the eye and asked whether they would be willing to answer a few questions. Half the time the requester's green jumper bore the Tommy Hilfiger logo, and half the time it didn't. The results were remarkable. Only 13 percent of people agreed to answer questions when the requester wore the logo-free jumper, but 52 percent agreed when their socio-economic status was boosted by way of a brand label. It seems that this effect doesn't just facilitate compliance with small requests for assistance. In a separate study, the same Dutch researchers sent fund-raisers on a door-to-door canvassing mission to collect charitable donations for the Dutch Heart Foundation. Half wore a shirt with a luxury label (this time Lacoste) and the other half a shirt with no logo. Again, people responded to high-status messengers more favourably, with fund-raisers wearing the brand-label shirt collecting twice as many donations.* Notice how, in each case, the message or request never changed. What was different was the perceived socio-economic position of the messenger. Their status became the message.

The buying and selling of status

These 'costly signalling' effects are not limited solely to human society's high-status individuals, like the rich and the famous. They can be found in the animal kingdom, too. Peacocks, for example, are the archetypal costly signallers.[11] The males grow their tails to be as big and beautiful as possible because a large tail sends a signal about

---

* Evidence of how people use subtle signals to infer an individual's socio-economic status has been found in numerous other studies. For example, a team of US researchers found that people were able to accurately predict the personal characteristics of a complete stranger by seeing nothing other than photographs of their shoes. One wonders whether the UK's former prime minister Theresa May had knowledge of this research. As a newly appointed Home Secretary, she became well known for her collection of branded 'power-shoes' from the UK retailer L. K. Bennett. Perhaps some members of the public, unfamiliar at the time with May, formed their first impressions of her by her shoes. If, as the US research suggests, shoes are indeed an important signal of socio-economic status, perhaps they even subtly contributed to May's rise in office. It is certainly the case that her footwear remained a source of fascination for the media during her premiership. In October 2016, during particularly important Brexit negotiations, the BBC was heavily criticised for focusing the camera too much on Prime Minister May's shoes. Perhaps the BBC believed that viewers might be as interested in what her shoes had to 'say' as they were in the words coming out of her mouth. Gillath, O., Bahns, A. J., Ge, F. & Crandall, C. S. (2012), 'Shoes as a source of first impressions', Journal of Research in Personality, 46(4), 423–30.

their good genes to nearby peahens. There's a danger here, of course: rather as with celebrities, whose external costly signalling and conspicuous consumption can expose them to the unwanted attention of stalking fans, nature's costly signalling can place the peacock in jeopardy, too – and a peacock's predators invariably want more than a selfie or an autograph. But it seems that evolution has done the sums and concluded that, even though escape from a potential attack is harder with a grander tail, it is a risk worth taking for a peacock that is attempting to gain the attention of available peahens.

It is easy to understand why Mr Peacock is willing to incur a potentially heavy cost to signal his status. His reproductive success may depend upon it. In humans, the same basic principles apply: a messenger's ability to exhibit wealth or status influences how people view and respond to them. And while some of us may think that such displays are vulgar, that doesn't mean that we are immune to the cues such signals send. Doob and Gross's psychology students thought they wouldn't be swayed by the sight of an upmarket car. Some claimed they would even be hostile to it. But the experiment proved otherwise.

The array of benefits afforded to the high-status individual helps explain why people are often willing to pay a premium for products and luxury items. Their preparedness to pay often bears little relationship to their ability to pay, and is primarily driven by the need to signal socio-economic position, relative to others. Even poor, low-income individuals in developing countries will often be willing to pay a premium for higher-status labels. When researchers offered low-income Bolivian families a choice of two perfumes, whose only point of difference was the label they bore, many were happy to pay more for the Calvin Klein-labelled fragrance than for exactly the same, generically labelled product.[12] Despite their economic hardship and the higher cost of the aspirational buy, when an opportunity to increase their status was offered, they grabbed it. Even in poor communities, where most occupy a lowly status, people are willing to buy status items.

It's true, of course, that not everyone is concerned with acquiring items and badges that enable them to signal an elevated status to others. But many of us are. It's a basic truth that was ably demonstrated by psychologist Brad Bushman in a study that, on the surface at least, looked like a simple peanut-butter taste test for shoppers in a mall, but was, in fact, designed to say rather more about those who took part than they might have realised.[13] Those who accepted the invitation were randomly offered one of four different types of peanut butter – either an expensive or cheap peanut butter, each with either a high-price or low-price label. After tasting a sample, they were asked to rate how much they liked it and to indicate how much they would be willing to pay for it. They were also asked to complete a test that measured their public self-consciousness, by asking how much they agreed with statements like 'I usually worry about making a good impression' and 'I'm concerned about what other people think of me'.

Even when the contents of the jars were the same, most shoppers said they preferred the peanut butter served from a premium-labelled jar. This tendency was particularly marked among the shoppers who scored highest on the public self-consciousness test. Not only were they much more likely to express a liking for the jar labelled premium, but they were also more likely to show a marked dislike for the jar labelled bargain. It would appear that those most motivated to signal their socio-economic status are also those with a heightened sensitivity to their public self-consciousness. They are more likely to fret about how they appear in public and be prepared to pay a premium to signal their status, figuring that it can boost their chances of receiving favourable reactions from others and, consequently, confer greater social influence on them.

If cars, shirts with logos and even peanut butter in a jar labelled premium can boost an individual's socio-economic position, then it should come as no surprise that those harbouring such aspirations might attempt to buy their way in. Some are even prepared to endure momentary embarrassment to secure the status they crave. Research has shown how, when it comes to selling luxury goods, a particularly effective messenger is a pompous, aloof individual who looks down witheringly and with exasperation on a potential purchaser's lack of knowledge about the status-enhancing products they wish to buy.[14] Ironically, the reaction to such disdain and rudeness is not to turn around and march out of the shop, but rather for the untrendy purchaser to experience an increased motivation to buy. This is likely to be especially true for those who score highly on Bushman's public self-consciousness scale. Researchers at Florida State University have shown how salespeople who signal an elevated socio-economic position, such as by wearing branded clothing, being pretentious and behaving snootily, are much more likely to be considered cold and unlikeable by prospective customers. But this is more than compensated for by an increased desire among these customers to compete, and pay, for equal status with the very people they dislike.[15] The widely held perception may be that a customer who likes a salesperson tends to buy and spend more, but this is not necessarily true of customers who are insecure about their status, when it comes to purchasing status-enhancing 'positional' products. Such people have a greater need to signal that they are good enough to receive the salesperson's approval. And the best way to do this is by reaching for their wallets and purses.

Items that signal a person's status are known as 'positional goods' because they serve to elevate that person's position in the status hierarchy, and the stand-out feature of positional goods is, by definition, that they stand out. Certain goods have more positional value than others. This was well demonstrated in 2005 by a pair of US economists, Sara Solnick and David Hemenway, who asked people to consider a variety of situations where they could either be better off compared to others, or better off in absolute terms but less well off than those around them.[16] So, for example, people were asked if they would prefer:

- To live in a home with seven rooms, while other people's homes had ten.
- To live in a home with five rooms, while other people's homes had three.

If people simply value space, then they should primarily be concerned with the absolute number of rooms and so choose option 1. If, however, they are motivated by a positional desire, they may be unhappy with option 1 because, while it gives them more space, it leaves them worse off relative to others, and they may therefore prefer option 2. In the event, when Solnick and Hemenway ran their experiment, they found that about one-third of participants said they would prefer to live in the smaller house, as long as other people were worse off than them. When asked a similar question that related to preferences for absolute versus relative increases in their income, respondents were split 50–50.

Not only are people's attitudes to positional goods relative, but they also vary according to what is at stake. Solnick and Hemenway's work demonstrates, for instance, that people exhibit more positional concerns for income than they do for leisure. Workplace benefits, such as salary, title, position in the hierarchy, all offer an opportunity to boost one's positional qualities and may, therefore, make the individual a more effective messenger. Back in 1883 the French socialist thinker Paul Lafargue wrote in his *The Right to be Lazy* that the machine 'will be the saviour of humanity, the god who shall redeem man from working for hire, the god who shall afford him leisure and liberty'.[17] It was an idea that would be taken up by most other futurologists, and by the twenty-first century there would indeed be more leisure time for those living and working in advanced economies. But such is the status we still think work gives us that, when it comes to positional concerns, we place far more emphasis on it and on the money, title and our position in the hierarchy that comes with it than we do on leisure pursuits. Work is worn, rather like a prestigious logo, as a sign of our socio-economic position.

Purchasing choices and conspicuous consumption aren't the only ways a messenger signals their socio-economic position. They also do so via the kinds of food they eat, the establishments they frequent, the activities they engage in and the social groups and clubs they belong to.[18] These all send out cues that are picked up by others almost instantaneously. Volunteers in one study who were shown a series of Facebook profile pictures were able to make remarkably accurate assumptions about the messenger's socio-economic characteristics, including the subject's early and current household income, social class and even parental educational background.[19] They did so not by examining such factors as their physical attractiveness (also a cue that people use to infer socio-economic position),[20] but by taking account of what was in the background. Where was the photograph taken? Who else was in it? Such tiny signals spoke loudly. It's not surprising that research has revealed that frequently looking at other people's pictures on Facebook, and the natural tendency to make social comparisons that goes with that, can lead to feelings of envy and what is increasingly referred to as 'Facebook depression'.[21]

It is even possible to infer someone's status by watching how motivated they are to interact with strangers. Those lower down the socio-economic scale often tend to be very sociable. But once people feel accepted and held in esteem, their desire to affiliate and connect with new individuals and groups wanes dramatically – presumably because their social needs are already sated – and they become less willing to engage with strangers.

This was nicely demonstrated by Michael Kraus at Yale University's School of Management and Dacher Keltner at UC Berkeley, in a study that involved filming pairs of participants from different economic and social backgrounds who had been seated together in a waiting room and left to chat to each other while they waited for an experimental task to begin. In fact the actual experiment was already going on, because what Kraus and his team were interested in was how these strangers would behave when they assumed no one was observing them. Time after time the researchers discovered that those with a higher socio-economic position, measured in terms of their affluence and schooling, showed less affiliative behaviour. Those with a lower socio-economic position were more likely to look in their conversation partner's direction to see what they were doing and were typically friendlier. They were also more likely to nod in agreement and chuckle at their partner's jokes. The more privileged volunteers, by contrast, spent more time looking at their phones, doodling and 'self-grooming'. Kraus and Keltner suggested that such disparate behaviour principally reflected the differences in each individual's motivation to connect and gain approval.[22]

When a new group of volunteers were then shown short clips from these videos, they were very quick to pick up on the socio-economic status of the people they were watching, even though the clips were silent and the new volunteers were not allowed to consult one another. Quite simply, they inferred relative socio-economic position from who was making an effort to engage and who wasn't. Lower-status people wanted affiliation and approval. Higher-status people didn't need either.

This doesn't mean that those with a higher socio-economic position are necessarily less warm by disposition. Rather, because their social and status needs are already being met, they don't feel the need to engage in the way that those further down the pecking order do. The common intuitive paradox applies: people who come across as too keen to make friends and impress others often end up achieving the opposite. The reason is not simply that their neediness is unattractive, but that it inadvertently signals a diminished status.

Status hierarchies

Why are we such slaves to hierarchies that we naturally shape our behaviour to fit them? A good way to start tackling this question is to ask why people are so often willing to accede more readily to requests from those who signal their high socio-economic position, through the clothes they wear and the flash cars they drive (or, more likely, are driven around in), than to ones from those who lack these attributes. Surely those who can afford these luxury items have less, not more, need for help? While strictly true, this thinking rather misses the point. The purpose of status hierarchies is not to provide a boost to those at the bottom; it is to motivate effort and provide rewards to those who make it to the top; to ensure that the individuals with the most impressive physical, mental, material and social resources – those with the most instrumental value – receive more attention and deference from their subordinates; and, ultimately, to prevent conflict and reduce the costs of repeated contests. We need people to make strategic decisions, set group norms, teach others and contribute to a community or group's superordinate goals. And, of course, we want the best people in charge of fulfilling these duties.*

* Understandably, there has recently been a lot of attention paid to the widening inequalities in society: claims of CEOs earning more than 200 times the salary of one of their average workers; reports of the world's richest 1 percent owning close to half the world's assets and wealth. This is hardly a modern-day

43

Hierarchies exist in almost all domains – socially, at work and even in sport. When a basketball player is lining up a pass with the purpose of making a three-point shot, they may well pass the ball to the team's most expensive or most well-known player rather than the one who happens to be performing best at that moment in time. In other words, they are responding to that player's status rather than their skill. The same is true in organisations. Those with a higher profile, infamy within their industry or grand-sounding titles will often be afforded more influence when it comes to making decisions. These high-status individuals are more likely to have their opinions heard and valued. They are also more likely to be awarded more respect, recognition and importance than those lower down the chain. In short, as messengers they command greater attention and are listened to more often.[23]

Although status-seeking and deference to status are human universals, there are individual differences in how much hierarchy people want in their societies, and cultures do vary in how egalitarian they are.[24*] For example, humans living in modern hunter-gatherer

---

phenomenon. When Khufu, the Egyptian pharaoh, built the Great Pyramid at Giza, he could lay claim to the greatest concentration of resources available on the planet at the time. Measuring a base area of 230 square metres and close to 150 metres tall, the building required more than two million sandstone blocks, each weighing 2.5 tonnes, and more than 80,000 labourers working for twenty years. The pyramid was possible because at Khufu's disposal was the entire territory and civilisation of Egypt, then the greatest country on Earth. It has been estimated that it cost the equivalent of approximately $10 billion today. In 2560 BC only one country possessed the necessary resources to build such a monument. In 2005, thirty-five individuals were reported to have the necessary resources to repeat such a feat; at the time of writing, there were eighty-one individuals.

* Primates also vary in how hierarchical they are, and in how they maintain status hierarchies. Some species primarily engage in aggressive conflicts to establish their rank positions. Others rely more on bluster, preferring to display their physical prowess than engage in a physical struggle that may cause them harm. Like

44

societies such as the Aborigines in Northern Australia have much flatter social structures. The role that leaders in these groups play is more of a facilitator than CEO. Rather than directing and commanding, they are more likely to orchestrate the meeting and metaphorically write everyone's ideas on the whiteboard. They may put forward their own opinions, have a disproportionate influence over the group's decisions and facilitate discussion between the members of the group, but they won't overrule or put their own interests before those of others. To do so would risk revolt and exclusion. It is an arrangement that is thought largely to mirror how our ancestors lived around 13,000 years ago during the Pleistocene era. Only the emergence of additional organisational complexities that coincided with the invention of agriculture and larger human communities necessitated leaders being given more power and resources.[25]

Another reason why socio-economic position has such a powerful messenger effect is because people like to believe that society rewards talent and hard work – that the world is a just meritocracy. It's therefore commonly believed that individuals who occupy high-status positions are deserving of them. The American social psychologist Melvin Lerner has conceived a 'Just-World Hypothesis' to explain this.[26] At its core, the hypothesis posits that people believe those at the top – by virtue of the fact that they are at the top – deserve their high position, and the heightened attention, respect and deference that go with it. In the parlance of this book, they deserve to be more powerful messengers. Those further down deserve the blame and social punishment that accompany their presumed lack of effort, skill and initiative. There is evidence to suggest that conservatives and individuals who already occupy a high socio-economic position

most humans, chimpanzees will kiss and make up after episodes of conflict. De Waal, F. B. & van Roosmalen, A. (1979), 'Reconciliation and consolation among chimpanzees', *Behavioral Ecology and Sociobiology*, 5(1), 55–66.

are especially likely to make assumptions about a person's competence from cues given about their societal status.[27]

The 'Just-World' mindset is created very early on. Children are taught 'The Rules' as soon as they are able to grasp them: to share and take turns; to give back to others; to play fair. They also learn that hard work and effort lead to just rewards. What's interesting, though, is that such messages may only be reinforcing what they intuitively already understand.

In a 2012 study, nineteen-month-old infants watched interactions between two animated puppet giraffes, while the researchers observing them measured their eye gaze – a common method used in developmental studies to assess infants' expectations and levels of surprise. In the first version the puppets performed a show and at the end were each given a cookie. The average eye gaze across the nineteen-month-olds was measured at 13.5 seconds. In the second version one puppet was given both the cookies and the other none. Now the infants' average eye gaze lasted six seconds longer. Kids who hadn't reached their second birthday were surprised that despite both puppets being equally deserving, only one puppet received all the rewards. Even to toddlers, that's not a Just-World![28]

These findings were confirmed and expanded upon in a follow-up study, this time involving twenty-one-month-olds who were asked to watch two children playing with toys. After a few minutes an adult entered the room and told the children that it was time to tidy up. In one version, both infants obeyed and helped. In the second, one child did all the work while the other slacked off. In both scenarios, both children were awarded a sticker. The question was: would the watching infants notice the unjustness in the second version? Absolutely. Their eye gaze was a whopping twenty-eight seconds longer when the slacker was given the same reward as the hard-working child, compared to when both children had shared the task equally. Our intuitive knack for identifying examples of a Just-World seems strongly bound to us from an early age. In general, we expect rewards to be distributed on the basis of merit, rather than some measure of social equality. And because we expect this, we tend to assume that those who enjoy higher status deserve it.

That said, we are sufficiently sophisticated to make certain distinctions. It's well known, for example, that people with higher socio-economic status – aka the rich and famous – make for highly desirable romantic partners. But how they made their money does have a bearing on how their prospective partners view them. When men and women have been asked by researchers to make a choice between a partner who had earned their money and one who had acquired it another way (inheritance, lottery win and embezzlement were some of the options offered), in nearly every case self-made millionaires were preferred over lucky or lawless ones. Especially by women.[29] And the self-made millionaire also scored particularly highly over the lucky lottery winner when participants were asked to consider their relative attractiveness as a long-term partner, as opposed to their attractiveness as a one-night stand. When it comes to which rich messengers we like most, it seems that we typically prefer those who earn the money themselves, through hard work, grit and determination, over those who have acquired their money in other, nefarious or less effortful ways.*

---

* Several lottery winners offer examples of how a newly acquired, but not earned, fortune can lead to their downfall – particularly if they try to buy socio-economic position with their new-found wealth. In November 2002 Michael Carroll, a refuse worker, won £9,736,131 in the UK's National Lottery, leading to a short period of celebrity status during which he revelled in being labelled a 'Lotto Lout' by some of the British media. His behaviour seemed only to encourage public disdain. He declared himself 'King of Chavs' – a phrase that he even printed on his high-status, black Mercedes van. *(One wonders how many honked at him.)* Despite

Through the lens of a Just-World, someone who has earned their own money is also likely to possess other desirable traits and skills. There is a reason why they are in the position they are in. In addition to money, they are also likely to possess other attributes that provide instrumental value, such as intelligence, assertiveness, tenacity, ambition and drive. These are factors that single them out as a better long-term partner, not just a rich one. Furthermore, if the money were to ever dry up, those same attributes should make them better equipped than most to restore their bank balance to its earlier levels. Their proven track record of accumulating wealth acts as a pretty good signal of their likely future success, should it ever be required. Conversely, if a perception arises that a messenger's socio-economic position is an illegitimate one, the link between their status and their effectiveness as a messenger can collapse. Any messenger who is awarded status beyond what is deemed deserving can cultivate feelings of envy, even malicious resentment.[30] Rather than yielding the stage, the audience might well knock the messenger off their pedestal.

The status that wealth and fame give people, then, is not an absolutely fixed one. It can be shaped by a number of factors. Nevertheless, in general terms – and thanks to our inbuilt subservience to hierarchies – it has an impact on us so strong that it transcends the immediate qualities that such people possess, which gave them their wealth and fame in the first place. Quite simply,

---

saying that he would avoid needless and lavish spending, Carroll went on a 'conspicuous consumption' course of monetary-destruction. While we are not claiming it was his attempt to buy status that was solely responsible for his downfall – poor decision-making, unwise investments and a nine-month prison term for affray hardly helped – it was probably a contributory factor. His reversal in fortune was completed in 2010 when he reportedly applied for his old job at the local council. https://www.thesun.co.uk/news/8402541/how-national-lottery-lout-michael-carroll-blew-9-7m-pounds/

they become immensely powerful messengers – so powerful that others can be quick to infer that their status will have a reliable value in entirely different situations, which have little to no relevance whatsoever.

Monroe Lefkowitz's classic jaywalking experiment demonstrates this perfectly. He was interested to see whether or not pedestrians' willingness to follow a man jaywalking across the road (against the red light, against the traffic and against the law) might be influenced by what that jaywalker happened to be wearing. What he found was that three times as many pedestrians were happy to follow the man across the road when he wore a suit than when the same man was dressed in denim.[31] The message 'It's safe to cross' was always the same. All that differed were the clothes the messenger was wearing. It goes without saying that while wearing a suit might indicate an involvement in business, and so perhaps an ability to climb the rungs of an organisational ladder, it has no bearing on the wearer's ability to cross a road safely at a red light. But the status signal that the suit sends out is sufficient to persuade others that because someone has (possibly) achieved success in one area of their life, they must also possess expertise in road-crossing.

Lefkowitz's experiment is by no means a one-off. In a 2008 study by Maner, DeWall and Gailliot participants had their eye movements tracked while they were shown pictures of different men and women on a computer screen – some wearing suits, others in casual clothing. In the first four seconds – after being presented with the images, and before the participants had had time to process each picture consciously – their eyes darted towards the pictures of men (but not women) in high-status clothing more often than those of men in casual clothing. This suggests that even before we can deliberate and decide which messengers we should give attention to, automatic cognitive processes exist that make sure those of higher status are attended to and processed first.[32]

Would you take plumbing advice from your doctor (or vice versa)?

Lefkowitz's insight – that once a messenger is perceived as possessing an elevated socio-economic position, audiences might infer that they possess value in other entirely unrelated domains – may help to explain, in part, the result of the 2016 US presidential election. Naysayers at the time argued that Donald Trump faced the seemingly insurmountable barrier of possessing little to no understanding of the legal and moral complexities involved in running a country. However, this message seems to have been crowded out by Trump's near-constant practice of reminding people of his wealth and business successes. From the perspective of socio-economic position, there seems little doubt that his overt signals of status contributed, at least in part, to his final vote tally. He is scarcely alone in this. In early 2018 health officials in the Chinese government had to scramble to contain a rumour regarding the effectiveness of the influenza vaccine, after Cantopop singer Kay Tse On-kei claimed on WhatsApp that 90 percent of people who received the vaccine then caught the virus.*[33] Her status as a performer was sufficient to crowd out the expertise of medical professionals. Having to deal with the negative impact that a famous but ill-informed messenger may have is not uncommon – and not just in the medical sphere.

The influential celebrity is a well-known phenomenon, and their power has long been acknowledged. This has been particularly so among advertisers and marketers, who have been using celebrities to endorse their products and services for the last 150 years. It may seem paradoxical that to lure the majority into handing over their

* Kay Tse On-kei pointed out that she had not intended the WhatsApp message to go public or influence opinion.

50

hard-earned cash, advertisers and marketers will give, free of charge, their expensive products to a select minority who are also the group most easily able to afford them. But to marketers, celebrities *are* the gift that keeps on giving. Companies seem only too willing to spend increasingly large sums on them, as evidenced by the growing number of ads that feature celebrities.

The persuasive pull of celebrities isn't solely limited to selling products and services. Celebrities are also deployed as messengers to deliver the campaign messages of politicians, public-health policy-makers and non-government organisations (NGOs), who similarly recognise the extraordinary power such high-status messengers possess. Billions of dollars are spent on celebrity endorsements every year. It is estimated that celebrities feature in approximately 25 percent of all advertisements in the United States. In Japan, that figure is estimated to be between 40 and 70 percent.[34]

The celebrity endorser achieves two things. They get the attention that goes with their socio-economic position, and, like the jaywalker in the suit, they get people to follow them: their star status 'rubs off' on the brands with which they associate. Indeed, viewers of advertisements have often developed unidirectional relationships with the endorsing celebrity, displaying emotions very similar to those experienced in day-to-day relationships. But as with all relationships, there are nuances. There are some celebrities we like and others we dislike. To the marketer tasked with matching their message to an effective messenger, the skill is to figure out who their target audience's favoured celebrity is and then link them with their product, service or political figure. Such an approach will be far more successful than simply engaging a random celebrity to promote a random product, however famous that celebrity might be.

At the same time, it is important to note that this dynamic is not a one-way street. In the same way that positive associations between high-profile figures and products can enhance consumer attitudes, so negative connections can devastate a brand. In 2011 Anders Behring Breivik, a thirty-two-year-old Norwegian, went on a rampage, slaughtering seventy-seven people, including sixty-nine teenagers on the island of Utoya. In subsequent media coverage of the tragedy, the killer was often shown wearing the distinctive crocodile logo of Lacoste. The unwelcome association understandably prompted the French fashion brand to lobby Norwegian police with a request that they ban Breivik from wearing their clothing. The French newspaper *Libération* reported: 'This situation is clearly a nightmare for one of France's most distinguished clothing companies.'[35]

What is important here is congruency. A message is generally much easier to process if its link with the messenger is an unforced one. An attractive model tends to be a better messenger for beauty products than, say, an equally famous singer or sports star. That is not to say there has to be an exact fit. After all, Trump's vaunted business success beat Hillary Clinton's political experience. But it's important, at the very least, to avoid overt dissonance. Interestingly, too, celebrities who *implicitly* endorse a brand, rather than explicitly tell an audience why they prefer it, tend to be more effective messengers. That's why it is not uncommon for advertisements to focus attention on a celebrity's association with (rather than advocacy for) a product. The twenty-first-century crowd may be savvy to the monetary rewards available to celebrities who make paid endorsements, but they are also an overwhelmed crowd – that is, they find it hard to be sufficiently alert to the unconscious associations being made in their minds when viewing celebrity product placements and other implicit messages. Cue, therefore, a plethora of films and online videos of the rich and famous appearing at all manner of events with their omnipresent brands, sipping coffee in a local café, checking into certain hotel chains or drinking their 'favourite' brands of beer at a sporting event.

Of course not even the highest of high-status messengers are immune to losing influence. While we're swayed by their position in the hierarchy, we will certainly start to question it if they deviate too far from the behaviour we expect from them, or if they suffer a particularly spectacular fall from grace. Kanye West is a case in point. By any measure, West is a huge celebrity: he's a successful rapper and social-media heavyweight, who has sold more than thirty-two million albums and won twenty-one Grammy awards. Yet despite these admirable qualities, the public has revelled in putting him down. One notable show of antagonism occurred in 2015 on the Pyramid Stage at Glastonbury, one of the world's best-known music festivals. It was a big crowd and the gig was going well. Halfway through his set, however, someone in the crowd raised a flag with a screenshot of a leaked sex tape of West's wife, Kim Kardashian, performing a sex act on her former partner, Ray J. Accompanying the image were the words 'Get Down, Girl, Get Head Get Down'. The words weren't a random afterthought. They were a play on lyrics from Kanye's own song 'Gold Digger'.

Given that a person's socio-economic position generally leads to admiration and greater deference, why didn't all the other concert-goers leap to Kanye West's defence and admonish the stunt? After all, that's surely what would have happened if someone had pulled a similar stunt on McCartney or the Rolling Stones? There would have been a riot. But the insult to West went unchallenged. Why?

A potential answer emerges if we consider the insults West received that Saturday night in Glastonbury, in the light of his well-documented history of deviating from two key norms of the celebrity world. The first is the imperative to accept the result graciously when a fellow artist is recognised at an award show.* West, famously, has a

---

* There are even website pages that helpfully inform newly minted celebrities about how to adopt what is known as the 'Oscar Loser Face'. Unfortunately for Samuel L. Jackson (*Pulp Fiction*), the service was not available in 1994 when he lost out on the

reputation for not doing so. When his song 'Touch the Sky' did not win Best Video at the MTV Europe Music Awards, he got up onto the stage anyway and publicly announced that he should have won. He made a similar spectacle at the 2009 MTV Video Music Awards when, as Taylor Swift was accepting her award for Best Female Video, West again took to the stage, uninvited, to claim that Beyoncé's *Single Ladies (Put a Ring on It)* was a much better video.

Kanye West's other breach of celebrity etiquette is to be openly boastful about his intellect and status. 'I realise that my place and position in history is that I will go down as the voice of this generation, of this decade, I will be the loudest voice,' he stated in a 2008 interview with the Associated Press.[36] His 2013 album *Yeezus* features a song entitled 'I Am a God' and, speaking to *W* magazine, West explained, 'I made that song because I am a God ... I don't think there's much more explanation.'[37] In an interview with Jon Caramanica of *The New York Times*, Kanye made clear that he not only believed he was a world-class rapper, but also that he possessed superior intellect and ability: 'I will be the leader of a company that ends up being worth billions of dollars, because I got the answers. I understand culture. I am the nucleus.'[38]

There are several ways in which such behaviour could be characterised. Clearly West is somewhat narcissistic.*[39] But it's not just simple narcissism that makes people react to entitled outbursts with hostility. It's more fundamental than that. When a messenger

Best Actor award to Martin Landau (*Ed Wood*). In fairness to Jackson, his understandable reaction (easily found via a quick online search) came nowhere close to Kanye West's in violating one of Hollywood's most treasured norms.

* A core feature of narcissism is that a grandiose self-image is often coupled with a belief that the individual in question is entitled to special treatment because they consider themselves to be ... special. Research shows that people who score highly in tests of narcissism are also more likely to actively seek opportunities to enhance their already self-elevated status. They seek excessive recognition for their accomplishments, conjure fantasies about fame and glory, and are highly motivated to

breaks an accepted standard of conduct or is seen as being incompetent, inferior or just stupid – and, therefore, undeserving of their elevated status – the privilege their socio-economic position previously afforded them can quickly be withdrawn. Kanye West's over-entitled outbursts appear to have led many to view him as a joke who needed to be put in his place. And when a mob feels this way about a messenger, that messenger quickly loses their 'worthy' status. That's the message Glastonbury delivered to West that Saturday night in June 2015. Even former President Barack Obama called him a 'jackass'.

The hottest fires make the finest steel

It's important to bear in mind that socio-economic position is just one type of status. Some groups and cultures award status to individuals who possess characteristics like humility and generosity. Others – perhaps those with a history of frequently engaging in warfare – may prefer to determine status according to someone's physical prowess. In many religions – Buddhism is a good example – status derives from the notion that individuals should strive to overcome any egocentric desires they may harbour and should instead engage in selfless, charitable and compassionate actions. In such societies the features that signal increased status elsewhere (and subsequent increased messenger effectiveness), such as money and luxury goods, are often seen as the root of all evil. It follows,

adopt dominant positions and increase their perceived power. They also appear to be less concerned with other more human-centric qualities such as warmth and humility, and will even adopt behaviours that are argumentative, brusque, insensitive and even offensive – explaining why other people are often irritated by their interpersonal style. It is almost as though the character of narcissists is perfectly designed to promote and enhance their socio-economic position.

therefore, that an important factor that will determine which messenger characteristics are associated with high status in a given society is the ideology to which that particular society subscribes or the culture that underlies it.

Status, more broadly, is the relative standing someone has in a group, based on the degree of importance, attention and respect that is given to them by others, as well as the influence they have over resource allocation, conflict-resolution and group decision-making. As we have shown in this chapter, those with high socio-economic position are, indeed, typically held in high esteem by those around them. They are presumed to possess superior skills and knowledge, to have control over valued resources, and, therefore, to have the ability to inflict costs and endow benefits onto others. Consequently, when the right celebrity or high-class messenger is selected to deliver the right message in the right way, the outcome can be powerfully persuasive. It's surely no coincidence that on the biggest days of the advertising calendar – for example, the day of the US Super Bowl – at least half of the advertisements will include a celebrity.

In 2011 that celebrity was Eminem. He didn't appear in an advert for Best Buy. Or Kmart or Walmart, either. Given his recent outbursts about the difficulty he faced going to those venues, that's perhaps not surprising. Instead he featured in an ad for the new Chrysler 200. A higher-end automobile. Black. Hard-top. Made in his home town of Detroit. Where the hottest fires make the finest steel. Blacked-out windows, naturally. Perfect for the rich and famous to drive around town in, being recognised, without being recognised.

2

COMPETENCE

Expertise, Experience and Why Potential
Beats Reality

IF THE PERCEIVED SOCIO-ECONOMIC POSITION of a messenger – whether gained through fame, fortune, a black-tinted window or a fancy logo – can affect and exaggerate the impact of their message, often regardless of its wisdom, then the same is true of a messenger's perceived competence. Again the important word here is *perceived*. It clearly makes sense to listen to people who know what they're talking about. But just as we have a tendency to defer to the messenger who exudes an elevated socio-economic position, so are we all too ready to defer to those who signal that they are experts. And as the following medical case colourfully illustrates, this can occur regardless of whether or not their message makes any sense.

The Institute for Safe Medication Practices (ISMP) is a US-based not-for-profit organisation whose central goal is to reduce the number of medical errors that occur in hospitals and medical centres. It started life in 1975 as a regular written feature that appeared in a journal for hospital pharmacists, and which provided a forum for physicians and pharmacists to describe (anonymously) any gaffes and blunders that had occurred in their hospitals and health centres, so that colleagues and peers could learn from their mistakes. The modest little column gained a reputation for being both informative and trustworthy, and, as we shall see, often alarming. Such was its popularity that its editors quickly gathered enough examples to turn it into a textbook.[1]

Entitled *Medication Errors: Causes and prevention,* the book was curated by Michael R. Cohen, the Institute's president, and his pharmacist colleague Neil Davis. It was first published in 1981 and has since been revised and updated – evidence, perhaps, of both the value of this type of publication and the number of errors that occur in hospitals. The latest volume describes, across 700-plus pages, case upon case of medicines being prescribed, dispensed and administered in ways counter to recommended practices and protocols. Some errors are more common than others. For example, many patients will be prescribed the wrong drug. Although worrying, that is also understandable. Drug names can be confusing – even to highly trained, competent, yet frequently overwhelmed medical staff. On the ISMP website there is a 'Confused Drug List'. It's an inventory of medicines whose names look or sound very much like those of another drug. There are more than 600 entries. Take Bidex and Videx. They may sound alike and, at a quick glance, may even look alike. But that's where the similarity ends. Bidex is an expectorant used to treat common breathing conditions like bronchitis or a severe case of the common cold. Videx is a nucleoside reverse transcriptase inhibitor. It is used in the treatment of HIV and AIDS. A commonly cited cause of drug prescription errors is the physician's poor handwriting. So it is comforting to learn that hospitals increasingly encourage prescribers to type rather than hand-write drug names on prescription charts. However, that might not be enough for Bidex and Videx, given that on a QWERTY keyboard the letters V and B are right next to each other.

Another common medical error concerns patients who are administered the right drug, but at the wrong dose. Sometimes the drug and the dose are prescribed and administered entirely correctly, but to the wrong patient. In fact there are four common mistakes that tend to be made. In addition to the wrong drug, wrong dose and wrong patient, Cohen and Davis describe a fourth kind of error, called the 'wrong route' error. The drug prescribed is an appropriate one. The dose is of a recommended and approved strength, and it is dispensed to the correct patient. The error occurs in the administration route that is used.

Perhaps the most curious example of a 'wrong route' error concerns a rather alarming entry in the journal's column headlined 'rectal earache'. The contributor described how a doctor had been asked to visit a hospital inpatient who was complaining of a painful right ear. On examination, the doctor correctly noted that the patient's inner ear was indeed inflamed and, also correctly, prescribed a course of anti-inflammatory drops. Nothing unusual at all in this sequence of events. Except that instead of fully writing the words 'drops to be placed in the patient's Right Ear' on the prescription chart, the doctor abbreviated his instructions so that they read 'drops to be placed in the patients R.Ear.'

Requesting that the patient roll onto his side, raise his knees towards his chest and adopt the 'position', the duty nurse duly carried out the doctor's instructions, dispensing three drops into the patient's rectum. Given the patient's known condition, this made no sense at all. At no point, however, did the nurse question the doctor's instructions. Nor did the patient question what the nurse was doing. The message became an irrelevance, because it had been superseded by the messenger(s). As the renowned social psychologist Robert Cialdini astutely points out in his timeless work *Influence: The Psychology of Persuasion*, 'in many situations in which a legitimate authority has spoken, what would otherwise make sense is irrelevant'.[2]

This may be a fairly trivial example, but history is full of cases where high-status individuals have failed to recognise the disproportionate influence they exert over subordinates, and where the perception of expertise – and the deference that was therefore paid to it – has ended in disaster. The KLM / Pan Am airline crash of 1977 on the island of Tenerife and the 1982 Air Florida disaster in Washington DC are just two instances where a person with high status (in each case the captain) made an incorrect judgement that went uncorrected by someone of lower status (the co-pilot). In the case of the Air Florida crash, for example, the pilot in charge failed to activate the engine's internal ice-protection system during a snowstorm prior to take-off, causing the aircraft's pressure-ratio indicators to provide false readings. Despite the first officer remarking, several times, that the instrument readings didn't seem accurate, the captain dismissed his concerns. The plane struggled to take off, managing barely thirty seconds of airborne travel before crashing into Washington DC's 14th Street Bridge. Similarly, medical problems far more serious than the 'rectal earache' case have followed when one qualified person (say, a nurse) has failed to question someone who appears to be more highly qualified (a doctor or surgeon). The perceived difference in status can be sufficient to drown out what is in fact a poor judgement call. Hence the reason Michael Cohen and his colleague Neil Davis are able to fill 700 pages of their book with a catalogue of medical errors.

If one route to a messenger being listened to is their perceived socio-economic status, then another powerful one is the status that derives from presumed competence. Messengers who are seen as competent or expert have *instrumental* value: they are deemed to possess the know-how, experience, skills and knowledge that will help them – and potentially the wider community – achieve their goals. They are also in a position to pass on these attributes to others (through a process known as 'cultural transmission').[3] Their role in society is therefore a crucial one. It also helps to improve efficiency. We could all try to acquire a basic level of knowledge of everything in order to successfully navigate life's complexities and challenges, but it clearly makes far more sense (and is certainly far easier) for us to defer to individuals who have developed a particular talent or specialised knowledge. We need farmers and plumbers and mechanics, and doctors and accountants, to help us where we lack the knowledge, not just to save us time. As the Roman poet Virgil said 2,000 years ago, we should 'believe an expert'.

There is something else going on, too. When someone is motivated to make a decision themselves, and has the ability and capacity to do so, as well as access to the appropriate and relevant information, the need for an expert messenger is reduced. But many of life's decisions are tough ones that require us to make significant investments, in terms of our mental and physical resources – thinking time, comparing options, asking the right questions, calculating possible outcomes – in order to arrive at, we hope, the right conclusion. When faced with such challenges, the easy option is to seek out the advice of competent others and defer to those messengers who appear to possess expertise. It involves less mental and physical effort.

This simple fact was tellingly demonstrated in an experiment that involved placing volunteers inside an fMRI scanner – magnetic resonance imaging equipment that measures changes in blood flow in the brain – to see what happened inside their brains when they were asked to make a series of financial decisions that required them to weigh up the value of accepting a guaranteed payment versus waiting for a potentially larger, but much less certain amount at a later date. Those who had been left to do the calculations themselves, without any outside help, exhibited a pronounced increase in activity in parts of the brain linked to probability weighting. On the other hand, those who had been randomly assigned to receive advice from a messenger, introduced to them as a financial expert, displayed far less mental activity in these brain regions. Consequently, in the majority of cases they made the decision to go along with what the 'expert' had told them to do.[4] Their brains were, metaphorically, shutting down and letting the expert do the work for them. This is hardly surprising.* With modern-day life offering up so many more exciting places to expend our limited attention – YouTube videos and cat-memes, for example – it can be hard to motivate ourselves to attend to arguably more important but often more mundane matters. In this context, the messenger who is perceived to be competent remains a universally reliable go-to.

Again, the key word here is *perceived*. One feature of today's information overloaded, fast-paced world is that we rarely have the time and resources to fully investigate whether a messenger's expertise is genuine and relevant. Instead we have to be content with following the counsel or suggestion of the communicator who merely *appears* to be competent. To do otherwise would be to consume valuable time and resources that we would rather direct to other priorities. But how do we assess whether someone *appears* to be competent, particularly when, as so often these days, different people who claim to be experts are striving to get our attention?

Dressing up, looking down

One answer is that, as with assessing those who occupy the higher socio-economic positions, we look for immediate and simple cues, this time signalling they are an expert in charge. Clothes and

---

* What may be more surprising are studies showing that when a task is less difficult, and the participants don't know that the advisor is an expert, they usually rely too much on their own (much less accomplished) competence, a phenomenon known as 'egocentric discounting'. Yaniv, I. & Kleinberger, E. (2000), 'Advice taking in decision making: Egocentric discounting and reputation formation', *Organizational Behavior and Human Decision Processes*, 83(2), 260–81.

position, once again, can convey very powerful signals – factors that go some way to explaining the alarming behaviour documented in Stanley Milgram's now-infamous studies of obedience.[5] Milgram demonstrated that seemingly ordinary folk would be willing to administer electric shocks of up to 450 volts to another research participant, who could be heard crying out in pain and pounding on the wall for them to stop, simply because a Yale University scientist told them to. The victim was not in fact in any actual pain, or even danger; the pleas for help and cries of pain were all pre-recorded and the whole experiment was staged; but this didn't make the results any less startling to Milgram and the rest of the scientific community.

Milgram's experiments, which were designed to better understand why people would make such horrifying decisions, and the contributory factors that a researcher's white lab coat and position at a prestigious university had on those decisions, have featured widely in both the scientific and popular press. What has been reported less widely, though, is another set of experiments, similar to his first, that were conducted in a run-down inner-city office building, where participants were told the research was being conducted on behalf of a commercial research firm, not a university laboratory. Those environmental changes made a big difference. When expert scientists were replaced with market researchers, participants were far less willing to deliver electric shocks. Notice that – in keeping with the central theme of this book – the message never changed. Only the messenger. What power the scientist's white coat wields.

It's not only clothes that exert this kind of influence. Accessories can work in precisely the same way. For example, patients are more likely to remember health-beneficial messages delivered to them by a medical professional if the practitioner concerned has a stethoscope draped over their shoulders than if they don't.[6] Whether or not the doctor uses it is irrelevant. The patient uses the stethoscope to decide upon the medic's expertise.

It's a similar situation with the array of clocks registering the time in capital cities around the world, which one often finds in office reception areas. Quite how genuinely useful they are is questionable: it seems very unlikely that the average visitor to an office in, say, New York or London urgently needs to know what time it is in Jakarta or Hong Kong. But that's not really why they are there. They are there to impress upon visitors the message that the organisation has global reach and significance, and therefore to signal status and expertise. Time-telling is secondary. These clocks ensure that people know this is an organisation that knows what it is doing.

The same is true of the folders and important-looking papers that executives clutch as they walk purposefully around their offices. Of course it's always possible that these are relevant to the work in hand. But given that people have been observed walking to the water cooler or the restroom with them, it's clear that's not always the case: executives want to enhance perceptions of their importance, and this is a very easy way to achieve their goal.[7] In the sitcom *Friends*, Chandler, arriving home from the office one day, briefcase in hand, exclaims, 'Y'know, I forgot the combination to this about a year ago? I just carry it around.' He is aware of the need to broadcast his instrumental value, and thus his status.

But clocks, uniforms and other associated tools-of-the-trade – a doctor wearing a stethoscope, a business person carrying a briefcase, a builder with their van and tools – aren't the only signals that can increase the perceived competence of a messenger. Competence also has a face.

The face of competence

Usually, when we think of facial cues, we think in terms of emotional signals. For instance, if someone displays a genuine smile, characterised by a tightening of the eyelids and crinkling around the corners of the eyes, we recognise that as registering happiness. (It's a type of smile known as a *Duchenne* smile, after the French neurologist Guillaume Duchenne, considered by many to be a founding father of modern-day neurology.) We can also recognise when someone is angry: their eyes bulge, their eyebrows lower and their lips are typically pressed firmly together. Fear is another emotion frequently written onto faces, characterised by the wide-eyed, open-mouthed look that people often find quite funny – especially when the fear is misplaced.[8] Faces, in short, provide a wealth of information for observers to decode, and we are therefore constantly drawn to them. But it's not just moods that we infer. We also make judgements about personality and character traits. We even use facial cues to assess competence.

Computational modelling techniques have led researchers to conclude that the competent face is mature-looking and attractive. It is typically less round than the average face, with higher cheekbones, a more angular jaw and a shorter distance between the eyebrows and eyes. These principles hold true for both males and females.

Why do people use these facial cues to infer competence? It's thought that children quickly come to learn that mature-looking adults are more competent than softer-faced children. Stereotypes about the physical features associated with competence then become fixed in their minds, and are relied upon when judging adults whose facial maturity is unrelated to their actual competence. This is not just a quaint psychological quirk; these ill-informed evaluations based on facial competence often have significant downstream consequences.

One such consequence was well demonstrated in a study in which people were given fifty photographs of CEOs to examine – half of them were CEOs of the twenty-five highest-ranked companies listed on the Fortune 1000; the other half were drawn from the twenty-five lowest-ranked organisations – and were then asked to infer their personality characteristics. The results were astonishing. The faces rated by the volunteers as the most competent tended to head the more profitable and successful organisations, while those judged to be less competent tended to be in charge of the less financially successful companies.[9] This held true both for male and female CEOs.[10] And, of course, it raises an interesting question: are the CEOs in the top jobs there because they deserve to be, or are they there because they *look* as though they deserve to be? They would, of course, argue – reasonably enough – that they wouldn't be able to hold on to their jobs if they merely looked the part. But one can't help wondering whether there are superb potential CEOs out there who don't make the cut simply because their appearance is against them. By the same token, it's tempting to believe that some less impressive CEOs hold the position they do only by virtue of their physical appearance.

Given the assumptions people are so ready to make about those they perceive to be senior management material, it should come as no surprise to learn that a similar mindset operates when it comes to deciding which people they are going to vote for. Here again, the 'if someone looks competent, then they must be competent' belief holds worryingly true. And it takes hold extraordinarily quickly.

When participants in a Princeton University experiment were asked to look at pictures of politicians – whom they were unlikely to be able to identify, and who had run or were running in gubernatorial election races in the United States – and then provide an intuitive competency rating for each, not only did their impressions correlate very closely with the actual election results, but they were formed in a mere 100 milliseconds. A glance at the faces of candidates running for election was all that was needed to make an informed, and largely accurate, estimate of who would (and indeed did) win.[11] Other studies have shown how these results are replicated when citizens of one country make judgements about politicians from another, with whom they are extremely unlikely to be familiar. For example, the competence ratings made by five-year-old Swiss children accurately predicted the outcome of the 2002 French parliamentary elections.[12] Interestingly, when people are given extra time to review the candidates' pictures and deliberate about their decision, their ability to identify the winners is dramatically reduced, suggesting that the capacity to predict the most likely winner in an election from their facial appearance originates in our guts rather than our heads.* It seems that voters replace the question 'Who is the most competent candidate?' with an easier and more intuitively formed one: 'Who looks like the most competent candidate?'

Confidently competent

Intuitively, it makes sense that the messenger who possesses *competence* is also likely to appear more *confident*.[13] Interestingly, this dynamic also appears to work in reverse. The messenger who simply appears *confident* is often presumed *competent*, even if scant evidence of their actual expertise exists. Confidence is the degree of belief that a person holds in their own abilities, skills and knowledge. Those who exude confidence are therefore projecting an assumed expertise: they strongly believe what they are saying is correct. In the absence of evidence to suggest otherwise – for example, that they are misguided or, worse still, delusional – an audience may well take them at face value and assign greater importance to what they are saying than may be deserved.

Consider, for example, the results of studies where people take what is known as the *Paulhus Over-Claiming Questionnaire* (OCQ).

---

* Unless, of course, the study participants happened to be previously familiar with the extant literature on the influence of competent faces.

This is a quiz of sorts, cleverly designed to measure confidence across a range of subject matters and topics. Respondents are asked to rate their knowledge of and familiarity with a long list of items – historical characters, famous people, brand names, current events – many of which are genuine, but some of which do not actually exist. Those individuals who claim knowledge of the latter, so the thinking goes, are exhibiting classic overconfidence because, of course, they are laying claim to an understanding of things that don't actually exist. It should come as no surprise that the test reveals that many people have exaggerated views of their own levels of knowledge. What is remarkable, though, is the impact their assumed wisdom has on those around them: in the absence of evidence to the contrary, others infer from their fellow participants' confidence that they know what they're talking about; and because they assume the confident individual is also competent, they confer on them elevated status and greater influence.[14] There is a lesson here for all of us. Beware those individuals in a group who confidently speak up, particularly in the early stages of debates. They will often, and automatically, be awarded increased status, and their opinions may consequently appear more relevant, regardless of the merits of what they may be saying.

Given our tendency to expect confidence and competence to go hand-in-hand, it is no surprise that we look to this pair of factors when deciding who we might follow. Naturally we want those at the top to sound as though they have the answers that will guide us safely through the perilous, uncertain and volatile environment that is the modern world. Leaders who lack confidence come across as weak. Uninspiring. Replaceable. Incompetent even. Not just in politics, but in business too, where the messenger needs to convey their confidence in order to communicate effectively their ideas, inventions and innovations. A sceptic might reason that overconfidence masks a lack of imagination or blinkers people, making it harder for them to see alternatives to their expected success. The sceptic is right, of course. Most start-up businesses fail within a few years. But a messenger who conveys anything less than complete confidence risks losing the interest of sceptical audiences, who are looking for signs of fault lines and weaknesses in their proposals. No surprise then that many messengers will primarily be concerned with conveying the level of confidence they hold in their idea, rather than any substance that underpins it. And many audiences, seeing that confidence as a signal of competence, will place greater credence in their claims. This is especially so when that audience is unsure either about a messenger's knowledge or, more worryingly, about what the right thing to think or do is.

So is it always a good idea for messengers to communicate their message confidently? Not necessarily. Those whose confident claims turn out to be inaccurate will suffer reputational damage, in the form of reduced credibility, and will subsequently wield less influence. How, then, should a messenger decide whether or not to convey their message with confidence? The answer is that it very much depends on their current situation. If they're not currently being listened to, but believe their ideas have merit (first-time entrepreneurs, rooky candidates, and so on), or are primarily trying to temporarily quell uncertainty, they need to present their message with more confidence than they might feel appropriate, in order to win over their audience. If, on the other hand, they're well established and so already carry sway, or are more concerned about the accuracy of their statements than about reducing uncertainty, they have less need to overstate their claims. The gains that will accrue to them from appearing very confident are negligible. The losses they will experience, if they are proved wrong, are considerable. They are therefore much better off adopting a more cautious approach when pitching their latest suggestions and ideas.[15]

A suggestion of fallibility on their part carries another advantage, too. A set of studies conducted in 2010 showed that when an expert is prepared to express minor doubts about their advice and opinions, their audience actually buys into their views more, particularly if their views concern a question for which no single, objectively clear answer exists.[16] It works something like this. When a messenger already perceived as competent expresses uncertainty, the audience tends to think, somewhat paradoxically, that if they are confident enough in their analysis and judgements to admit that uncertainty, then they must be reliable. Perhaps the time has come, 2,000 years on, to update Virgil's sage advice. Rather than 'believe an expert', it should perhaps read 'believe an uncertain expert'.

The self-promotion dilemma

All the signals of competence we have described thus far – a specific skill, expert knowledge, a previous accomplishment, clocks on an office wall, a purposeful stride or a confident performance – can, either individually or in combination, increase a messenger's perceived instrumental value and status. But there are limits. Those who overplay their hand run the risk of turning people against them. Both messengers and audiences alike appear to implicitly understand that these signals should be displayed in an understated or covert way, rather than in an overtly boastful manner. That doesn't mean some messengers won't thrive on a diet of self-promotion. But it's generally safer to signal competence more surreptitiously. The effective messenger may casually drop into a conversation at the appropriate moment mention of a skill or attribute they possess; they may lightly season a discussion with a relevant example or two of their current responsibilities and previous achievements. Some may attempt to achieve the perception of competence by adopting a strategy that has remarkable similarities to that of celebrities who get transported around town in blacked-out cars so that they can be recognised without being recognised. Dubbed 'humble-bragging', this approach involves camouflaging self-aggrandising statements with self-deprecation: 'I recall how silly I felt that morning I forgot to set my alarm and almost missed my meeting with the minister.' Humble-bragging, though, is a dangerous strategy. It can make people seem insincere. Worse than that, it can make them come across as less likeable.[17] What the humble-bragger gains by signalling their competence is offset by their corresponding lack of warmth and trustworthiness.[18]

Straight boasting can be equally dangerous. Greg Lippmann, the Deutsche Bank mortgage trader who successfully convinced a number of investors to bet against the subprime market before the financial crash, and whom we met earlier (see p.9), provides a good example of this. The story goes that he would go around brazenly informing audiences how he was going to 'short' the subprime bond market and how he was 'going to make "oceans" of money' as a result.[19] He would then bait his hook like a skilled fisherman, informing potential clients of an upper and lower monetary boundary between which he claimed his salary lay, and inviting them to guess which was closest to the truth. When they bit, he would inform them, in true 'fisherman's tale' style, that their assessment of his earnings didn't come anywhere close to the size of the rewards he considered himself to be worth. To some, such a performance made him appear a man worthy of admiration and trust. But to others, he simply came across as unlikeable and less credible. Someone who worked near Lippmann was reported to have referred to him as 'the Asshole known as Greg Lippmann'.

One company Lippmann had dealings with, FrontPoint Partners LLC – a Morgan Stanley-backed hedge fund – was desperate to believe his pitch because it aligned perfectly with their own view of the subprime mortgage market. But they were also suspicious that Lippmann's attempts to persuade them to buy his credit default swaps masked a hidden agenda. Michael Lewis, *The Big Short* author, describes how FrontPoint, concerned by Lippmann's wholly transparent self-interest, demanded that he return to their offices on three separate occasions to restate his pitch. Perhaps they thought that Lippmann would slip up in some way and reveal something untoward. During one particular meeting, a FrontPoint executive reputedly looked Lippmann in the eye and stated bluntly, 'Greg, don't take this the wrong way. But I'm just trying to figure out how you're going to fuck me.' It seems Lippmann's constant self-promotion meant that he had to battle incredibly hard to demonstrate his trustworthiness to FrontPoint, who saw him as the stereotypical Wall Street scumbag.

So what's going on here? If we have a tendency to take people's claims to expertise at face value, why will we suddenly become sceptical if these claims are pushed in a very false-modest or brash way? We've already seen how confidence can act as a powerful proxy for competence. So surely the more overtly confident a messenger is, the more we should believe them? Life, however, is not quite as simple as that. It's true that humans naturally tend to defer to those they perceive as possessing a higher socio-economic position, or to follow the advice of a messenger who bears nothing more than a trapping of expertise, such as a white lab coat. However, as we will discuss in more detail later, modesty and humility are also highly valued human qualities. Egocentric or conceited attempts to enhance one's status can backfire and result in diminished connectedness. Signalling competence offers immense upsides. But overt self-promotion can crowd out and destroy its message.

That said, there is a way to avoid the pitfalls of self-promotion: remove the self from the promotion. Stanford Business School professor Jeffrey Pfeffer, Christina Fong, Robert Cialdini and Rebecca Portnoy have shown that when a messenger's intermediary makes positive comments about them, others no longer regard this as an act of self-promotion.[20] At first glance, this hardly appears surprising. After all, people will often be receptive to a recommendation or endorsement from a third party. What is extraordinary, though, is that they're receptive even when they know that the third party is not a disinterested bystander, but an advocate. It would appear that people are not good at spotting the element of vested interest that might lurk at the heart of what an advocate has to say. They tend to take whatever message is being transmitted at face value. In other words, they might be cynical about self-promotion, but they don't spot *delegated* self-promotion.

Shortly after becoming aware of these studies, one of us was able to put what was so elegantly demonstrated in Pfeffer's Stanford laboratory to the test in the real world, having been invited to study the world of property management and real estate.

As with many industries, those who work in real estate face a daunting challenge. Because their competitors are doing exactly what they're doing, it's very difficult to stand out from the crowd. Most estate agents deliver a similar service for around the same sort of fee, and the experience for the client is largely the same, regardless of the firm chosen. So given that one estate agent's message will largely be similar to that of others, regardless of who they are and whom they represent, what might happen if arrangements were made to introduce their competence via an intermediary?

The answer is: quite a lot.

When potential customers of an independent, London-based property sales and letting firm got in touch to ask about selling or renting their properties, their first contact would typically be with the firm's receptionist, who would enquire about the nature of their call, before transferring it to an appropriate colleague. This happened seamlessly, in no more than a matter of seconds, and at no point did the receptionist make any mention of their colleagues' competence, expertise or experience. Then, at our suggestion, they made a slight tweak to this process by first drawing potential customers' attention to their colleague's competence, before transferring the call. 'Selling your property?' the receptionist was instructed to say. 'Let me put you through to Peter, our head of sales. He has twenty years of experience selling properties in this area. He's certainly the best person to speak to and get advice from.' The results were immediate and impressive. The company registered a near 20 percent increase in the number of enquiries that were converted to valuation appointments. The number of contracts the company was able to close also received a healthy boost: a 15 percent increase overall.

There are four notable features of this strategy. First, everything the receptionist told customers about their colleague's experience was true. Peter was indeed that branch's head of sales and did have a couple of decades' experience. But for Peter to have informed potential customers of this fact himself would have immediately undermined his position. He would instantly have been marked not as competent, but as conceited. It is the classic messenger conundrum. The upsides gained by taking a 'hard' messenger position will often be more than cancelled out by the downsides of not adopting a softer one. By arranging for their competence to be introduced by a third party, the messenger was able to neatly dodge this dilemma.

The second point is that even though the receptionist at the estate agency could hardly be viewed as an impartial third party, at no point did it seem to matter to customers that the recommendation they were receiving came from someone who was clearly connected to the agent and who was likely to benefit from the strategy themselves. Like the nurse paying such attention to the doctor that she unquestioningly dispensed ear drops into a rectum, so the would-be property sellers attended to a single feature of the receptionist's message – their familiarity with their colleague's work.

This kind of delegated self-promotion is not uncommon, particularly in the political arena. Why else, during presidential debates and conventions, would candidates almost invariably be introduced to voters by the individuals arguably most closely connected to, and most self-interested in, those candidates' success? Their spouses. And yet it works. According to research by the Politics and Public Affairs Department at Princeton University, a spouse possesses a familiarity that enables them to 'go personal' more than any other introducer. In her book, *On Behalf of the President*, Lauren Wright showed how Melania Trump's appearances at her husband's rallies led to more favourable support for her husband, especially amongst independent voters.[21]

Finally, the fourth and arguably most appealing feature of the introduction strategy is that in most cases it can be implemented virtually for free.

Potential versus reality

However impressive the results we measured in the real-estate office, there is an obvious challenge that people may encounter when trying to use this introduction strategy. What happens if a messenger lacks experience? It is easy to create an impressive-sounding introduction for the professional who possesses decades of experience, extensive training and hundreds of sales successes. It's rather more challenging to do so for the person who has yet to achieve an elevated position or a long list of past successes. All is not lost, however. In fact there are circumstances when a messenger who merely possesses potential can outcompete the messenger who has more tangible experience and evidenced competence.

Sport provides plenty of instances of players, with little to no experience, who are signed for multimillions on the basis of their promise. Similarly, young artists and musicians get earmarked as being destined for 'big things' and 'bright futures'. In the political sphere, too, those with little experience can seem more appealing than those with proven track records. The election of Emmanuel Macron as President of France in May 2017, still seven months shy of his fortieth birthday, came despite the fact that he was a virtual unknown (the inexperienced new president was also the Republic's youngest). Similarly, Canadians were seduced by the promising potential of the youthful Justin Trudeau, who took office as prime minister in November 2015 (although it could be argued that, as the eldest son of former Prime Minister Pierre Trudeau, he possessed both potential and at least a connectedness to experience). Reality TV star Donald Trump might not possess Macron's and Trudeau's youth, but for many – particularly those who felt disenfranchised by contemporary American politics – it was his potential, rather than his experience, that counted for him.

These may seem like cherry-picked examples based on casual speculations. But studies by Stanford's Zakary Tormala and Jayson Jia, along with Michael Norton of Harvard Business School, have shown that potential can indeed often trump demonstrated achievement. In one of their experiments, for example, information was provided to recruiters about two candidates who had applied for a senior position in the finance division of a large corporation.[22] Each came from a similar background and had the same set of qualifications. The difference between them was that one candidate had two years' prior experience and scored highly on a *leadership achievement* test, while the other had no experience but scored highly on a test of *leadership potential*. After being shown information about each of the candidates, the recruiters rated the candidate with potential as being much more desirable and interesting than the one with experience. Achievement, at least in temporal terms, is something that has already passed. Achievement is history. Our attention is ready to move on and seek its next fix. That's when potential becomes the drug of choice. It's like head candy, stimulating greater interest and increased mental processing because of its uncertainty and ambiguity.

The researchers found similar results when looking at social media. Facebook users were shown a series of advertisements for an upcoming show featuring a comedian. Half saw an advertisement that communicated a *potential focus*: 'Critics say he could be the next big thing' and 'By this time next year, everyone could be talking about [this guy].' Other ads described a *reality focus*: 'Critics say he has become the next big thing' and 'Everyone is talking about [this guy].' Those exposed to the advertisements that communicated the comedian's potential showed much greater interest (as measured by click-rates) and liking (as measured by 'likes' on fan pages) compared to those who saw and heard about the comedian's actual achievements.

So powerful is the tendency to favour potential that it operates even when the object of evaluation is not the messenger themselves, but something they created. When participants were asked to report how much they liked particular works of art, after learning that one artist had great potential and the other had notable achievements to his credit, they expressed a preference for those painted by the artist in the potential category. Art works, of course, are static and cannot change over time. People's judgements should therefore have been shaped by what was in front of them. Yet their assessments were skewed by the thought that one artist might go on to greater things.

What is true of individuals is true of organisations, too. In April 2017 the financial press was awash with news that Tesla's market value had just surpassed that of General Motors, by more than US $1 billion. This was despite the fact, first, that General Motors had been manufacturing cars since its incorporation in 1908 (in other words, about a century longer than Tesla); second, that in the previous quarter Tesla had sold just 25,000 vehicles compared to General Motors' 2.3 million; and third, that even though Tesla's stock-market valuation was greater than General Motors', Tesla had made a profit in only two quarters of its fifteen-year history. The misalignment between Tesla's performance and its share price led tech analyst Walt Mossberg to write on Twitter, 'this is the billionth example of why stock market valuations don't reflect reality'.[23] Mossberg was right. They often overweight potential.

This doesn't necessarily mean that people *always* believe uncertain potential to be preferable to certain achievement. But it can lead them to assign a greater level of attention and interest to messengers who have potential. In elections, like many one-off competitions that produce an outright victor, that greater attention and interest might just be enough to tip the balance. In 2016 Republicans and Democrats alike would have said that Hillary Clinton was the most experienced and qualified presidential candidate – not just then, but arguably ever. In stark contrast, Donald Trump had never worked a day in public office in his life. During the election campaign the incumbent president, Barack Obama, famously warned that Trump was 'woefully unprepared [to serve as president]' and 'doesn't appear to have basic knowledge around critical issues'.[24] Clinton could, with legitimacy, point to her numerous past achievements. Trump could only point to his potential.

Arguably, that made him more interesting.

Listening to competence

When a messenger signals a cue of competence – whether via their appearance, a persuasive introduction, their potential, a confident manner or simply a suitable title – this can dramatically change how others will respond to them. The KLM / Pan Am airline crash of 1977. The 1982 Air Florida disaster in Washington DC. The qualified nurse who failed to question a ludicrous instruction made by a doctor, even when she believed the doctor could be mistaken. In each case it was the messenger, not the message, that influenced the result, via the unquestioning compliance of a lower-status colleague to a directive made by the higher-ranked one.

To be clear, the competent messenger does not need to hold positional power over their audience to be effective, although often the influence of competence and positional power work in harmony because the high-status messenger is deemed to possess both. This pair of considerable forces can easily crowd out what, in their absence, would otherwise make no sense whatsoever. Ear drops are inserted into a patient's rectum. And Michael Cohen and his colleague Neil Davis are able to fill 700 pages of their book with a seemingly endless catalogue of medical errors.

Nor does the competent messenger necessarily seek to best others or rule by force. The status assigned to competent messengers results from their superior skills, wisdom and experience. Or, at least, the *perception* that they possess such qualities. They carry sway because they are respected for their talents and are seen as a source of useful knowledge and 'copy-worthy' information. Competent messengers *inform* their audiences. They do not *demand* that people should listen to them. Those who demand attention are very different animals: they exert *dominance.*

3

DOMINANCE

Power, Superiority and When Command
Trumps Compassion

During the first 2016 presidential debate, the Republican nominee Donald Trump interrupted his Democrat opponent Hillary Clinton fifty-one times.[1] That averaged out as an interruption about every fifty seconds while Clinton was speaking. In subsequent debates Trump not only persisted with this tactic, but sought to dominate her physically, too. On several occasions he literally stalked her across the stage, looming ominously over her.

Why would a modern democratic country elect a domineering candidate who, during the primaries, had already demonstrated an aptitude for insulting, disrespecting and trying to control those around him? Surely a sophisticated society can reasonably expect their president to be ... *presidential*? Charming. Cooperative. Modest. Someone skilled at turning adversaries into allies. Not someone who thrives on creating the former, at the expense of the latter. Surely in a modern-day society those whose goals are simply to dominate others can't be taken seriously? But this way of thinking masks a sad truth. When it comes to those to whom we listen, the messengers perceived to be dominant or who display dominance over others can enhance their perceived status and, accordingly, will often be afforded an advantage.[2]

Dominance as a route to status

Hard messengers get their messages accepted by first establishing that they have status. And, like socio-economic position and competence, dominance is a path to achieving status.[3] However, unlike socio-economic position and competence, which tend to exist in a continuum, dominance is more binary and absolute. It is most often associated with a single recordable outcome. In genetics, one form or variant of a gene (known as an allele) will be either dominant or recessive. In peas, for example, the presence of two dominant genes (the R *allele*) will lead to round-shaped peas, whereas the presence of two recessive genes (the r *allele*) results in more wrinkled peas. However, when one each of the R gene and r gene are present, R prevails and produces round-shaped peas. In peas, R is completely dominant and r is entirely recessive. The R *allele* wins. It is a zero-sum gain, where if one wins, the other loses.

So it is with humans. While the structure of a social group may be complex, many of the individual relationships come down to who is dominant and who is submissive, and across social groups there will therefore tend to be leaders and followers. Social dominance can be defined as an individual's rank or position in a group, which is formed on the basis of their ability to prevail over others in a competitive situation or encounter. Therefore dominance is gained when a person asserts himself or herself, sometimes in a self-interested manner and very often at the expense of others. It may be in the pursuit of winning a contest. Or to take something they want. Or to ensure theirs is the voice or opinion that is the loudest or most frequently heard. The central goal of the dominant messenger is to triumph over others.

This clearly applies in sport and competitions. Think of Liverpool Football Club in the 1970s and 1980s. Michael Jordan and the Chicago Bulls in the 1990s. Roger Federer in the 2000s. The Patriots in the 2010s. The All Blacks rugby team for pretty much all these periods. When a person or team beats another, especially in a convincing manner, they are said to have dominated their opponent. Simultaneously their opponents lose dominance, or have their lowly status affirmed, both in the eyes of the victor as well as in the eyes of those audiences who witness the defeat.

But dominance is not just a behavioural outcome. It is also a personality trait. Individuals who possess a tendency to act competitively and assert themselves, perhaps aggressively, can be considered dominant by disposition. So, too, can those who harbour a desire to control and hold power in every situation they enter. These dominant personalities adopt the philosophy 'winning is more important than how you play the game'.[4] Messengers who possess dominant personalities are combative rather than friendly types. They are not predisposed to empathy or caring, because their primary concern is focused on self-interest, accruing gains and maintaining social dominance over others. And if their goals can be accomplished at the expense of a competitor or challenger, so much the better. That's the icing on the dominant messenger's cake. In fact, should we ever witness an otherwise dominant person engaging in friendly, polite behaviour, we actually perceive them to be *less* dominant.[5] They can be tough-minded and determined in their conquest for power and can endorse non-egalitarian ideologies that put certain groups at the top and other groups at the bottom.[6] Some personality profiling tools and assessment scales refer to people with these characteristics as 'D-type personalities'. Dominant. Demanding. Direct. Decisive.

Deep-rooted dominance detection

Social dominance, as a form of status hierarchy, evolved long ago to serve an important function: to encourage hierarchical cooperation and so help ensure the avoidance of the unnecessary and repeated costs of conflict.[7] It remains the primary path to status in non-human primates. Rhesus macaque monkeys afford a good example. Often referred to as the monkeys of the Old World, they are charismatic, intelligent, curious creatures that can be found living in close proximity to humans in many of the heavily populated cites of India, Pakistan and Afghanistan. They live on roots, nuts, seeds, bark and cereals. They particularly love fruit, and fruit juice. And they're highly social – and hierarchical – animals.

A rhesus macaque in Jaipur, India.

In one study, a group of thirsty* male rhesus macaques that had been living in small groups were split up and placed, one by one, in front of a large screen.[8] Each monkey soon discovered that it could

---

* Access to fluids was limited to them in the lead-up to the experiment.

earn different quantities of fruit juice according to which side of the screen it orientated itself towards. If it looked to the left, a generous glug of delicious juice was the reward. However, if it looked right, it was shown a picture of another monkey and received a different amount of juice.* The question was: would the macaques choose to pay a higher price (as measured by how much fruit juice they were willing to forgo) in order to view pictures of their peers?

Part of the answer should hardly have come as a surprise: male macaques were willing to give up a considerable amount of juice in exchange for a glimpse of a sexually receptive female's genitalia. But what was perhaps more remarkable was that they were also prepared to sacrifice juice for a glance at a more dominant, higher-status male. At the same time, they demanded a 'juice premium' in exchange for having to look at a lower-ranking male. In other words, depending on their own relative status, they were prepared either to pay a price or to demand payment, according to the relative dominance of the monkey they were viewing. Such hard-wired behaviour, it need hardly be added, is not unique to macaques. Their human cousins are not dissimilar. Parents who despair when their own little monkeys won't come to the supper table because their attention is taken up looking at a screen of their favourite pop stars will recognise that all of us, in some form or another, indulge in Monkey-Pay-per-View.

Humans and monkeys use very similar cognitive mechanisms to navigate certain social environments. These processes are evolutionarily adaptive and would have allowed our common ancestors to selectively acquire information about the most important individuals around them. The processes do more, however, than simply provide guidance about who to look at. They also help us to make

* What we have described here is a simplified version of the actual experiment.

good decisions. Subordinate chimpanzees, for example, will track whether the group's more dominant members have noticed where food is hidden, so that they can decide when it is safe to approach an area to retrieve it. In the same way that a victim of the school bully might retreat to the library or caretaker's cupboard to avoid their lunch being stolen by a tormentor, subordinate chimpanzees are more likely to retrieve food when their dominant peers are unaware of its location.[9] In the case of both the schoolboy and the chimp, these mental processes enable steps to be taken to avoid potential conflicts that they are likely to lose.

Cues of dominance, and the responses that arise, are so deeply embedded in humans that they can be recognised by children as young as ten months old. In one set of studies, a couple of dozen toddlers were shown a short video where two animated shapes played the leading roles. One shape was a brown triangle with eyes and little button-nose. It walked over to a small house and sat inside and seemed quite happy until another shape – a blue circle, also with eyes and a nose – appeared and tried to push the triangle out of its house. The triangle initially resisted, but the bullying blue circle prevailed. The infants were then shown a second video. In this film the same two shapes were seen running around, collecting up objects falling from the sky, rather like apples falling from a tree. In the final scene, the two characters moved to pick up a final remaining object. Like a pair of English gentlemen drawing pistols in a 'matter-of-honour' duel, brown triangle and blue circle faced-off before one finally took the prize. However, two different versions of this ending were presented to the infants. In one, the previously dominant blue circle picked up the last object while the previously submissive brown triangle yielded. In the second version, the roles were reversed. The previously submissive brown triangle asserted its dominance and picked up the object, leaving the previously dominant blue circle to yield.

Using eye-gaze length to measure surprise – a technique we mentioned earlier (see p.46), which helps researchers to assess how surprised an infant is by what they are seeing – the researchers found that the toddlers who saw the unexpected ending stared for significantly longer at the screen than those who watched the dominant shape get its way.[10] That such young children were not only able to recall which character was more dominant, but could then use that information to form an expectation about the outcome of a future conflict, is impressive. The research hasn't stopped there. Another set of studies showed how infants are also able to make transitive inferences about the relative dominance of different messengers. For example, after seeing Person A triumph in a conflict over Person B, and Person B beat Person C in a similar competition, ten-month-olds were able to infer that Person A should triumph over Person C in a contest.[11] Other studies, such as those conducted by Stanford academic Elizabeth Enright, using looking-time measures, show how infants register surprise when resources are shared equally between a dominant and submissive pair, as opposed to when the dominant character receives more.[12]

It is clear, then, that from an astonishingly early age a deeply embedded expectation resides in us all. To the victor go the spoils. As humans, we are hard-wired to detect dominance, use it as a cue to navigate our social environment, and reward it with increased attention and status. It should come as no surprise, therefore, that the dominant person will frequently be an effective messenger.

Non-verbal signals of dominance

We typically associate dominance with a certain form of character. Assertive. Possibly brash. Even aggressive. Although perhaps surprising on the face of it, these traits can be quite appealing. Evidence has shown that men who post photos of themselves adopting expansive and dominant postures often fare better on dating apps, like Tinder, than their less expansive, meeker-looking counterparts.[13] In this context the reason why images of Russian president Vladimir Putin, shirtless and dominant, astride a horse,[14] are so widely circulated is hardly a mystery. In the same way that a dominant-looking guy might win in the online dating market, Putin wins the election market with displays of masculinity. There's rather more to social dominance, though, than crude and rudimentary displays of manliness.

When people interact with each other, there is usually a tendency for them to adopt complementary body postures.[15] The dominant person, however, tends to adopt more expansive postures and make more open gestures. They will take up more space. Indeed, it is not uncommon for someone wishing to signal dominance to literally take ownership of their surroundings by resting their limbs on the furniture. When he was Senate majority leader, Lyndon B. Johnson had a well-earned reputation for giving his political adversaries 'the treatment', in the form of domineering body language and posture. Rather than delegate lobbying responsibility to aides, he would seek out and corner law-makers in Senate corridors, leaning in so close that they would feel his breath on their faces. A 1966 book about Lyndon Johnson described how he 'moved in close, his face a scant millimeter from his target, his eyes widening and narrowing, his eyebrows rising and falling'. The move was said to put his targets into an almost hypnotic state, rendering them stunned and helpless.[16] It was classic dominant body language. By contrast, and in response, a more submissive partner will do the opposite. They will cross their legs and physically contract their posture, making them appear meeker.

We are all alive to such signals, even if we don't register them consciously. Studies have shown how accomplished people are at figuring out which employee holds the higher rank, when shown an image of two employees engaged in a workplace conversation. They don't need to see multiple images or videos. A single picture, taken against a neutral background, is enough to provide them with the cues they need.[17] Even children as young as three years old share this ability.[18] By taking in body posture, eye gaze, head tilt, age and physical positions, they too can swiftly identify 'who's the boss'.

Such gestures will often be associated with the messenger's inner emotional state: dominant poses indicate a feeling of pride; submissive poses are indicative of shame. In his work *Mere Christianity* the British writer and theologian C. S. Lewis suggested that 'Pride gets no pleasure out of having something, only out of having more than the next man.'[19] In essence, Lewis claimed that pride is primarily a competitive emotion. Evolutionary theorists tend to agree, suggesting that pride (and its antonym, shame) have evolved, in part, to convey an individual's social ranking compared to others'.[20] Just as a dominant chimpanzee will adopt an expansive posture, puff out its chest and tilt back its head after defeating a rival, so will humans display similar postural behaviours. Shame results in the exact opposite: a submissive stance, head tilted downwards, shoulders slumped and chest narrowed. In common with other primates, human pride and shame are outwardly evident. And, fascinatingly, these physical manifestations of an emotional reaction appear to be innate.

In an intriguing set of studies conducted by psychologists Jessica Tracy and David Matsumoto, the spontaneous non-verbal behaviours of athletes who had either just won or lost a judo match were examined. Win or lose, the telltale signs of victory or defeat were palpable. Winners stood tall, chest out, expansive posture, with a hint of a proud smile. Losers, in contrast, appeared crestfallen, shoulders slumped, head bowed.[21]

A prototypical pride expression, identified by a systematic analysis of the behavioural movements relevant to pride. The expression includes a small smile, slight backwards head tilt, expansive posture, and arms akimbo with hands on hips.[22]

How can we be so sure that these reactions were innate and not learned? After all, surely one could argue that winners and losers have watched how previous victors and runners-up have reacted in such situations and simply copied them? Tracy and Matsumoto's judo studies show that this is not what is going on, because all the athletes they studied were Paralympians who had been congenitally blind from birth. At no point in their lives had they been able to observe the postures struck by winners and losers. They could not possibly have learned to emulate others and match particular emotions with particular movements. Theirs were deep-wired reactions.

Not only is the prototypical expression of pride an automatic process, but so too is an audience's reaction to it. When we see pride, our minds – with little need for conscious deliberation – quickly make associations with dominance and status. Research conducted using the Implicit Association Test (IAT) – a common test used by psychologists to measure the strength of associations between different concepts – demonstrates this very powerfully.[23] Study participants were asked to react to photos of people who sometimes displayed pride and at other times a different emotion, such as surprise, fear, shame or happiness. While viewing these pictures they were also shown and asked to sort through a series of high-status words like *commanding, dominant, important, prestigious*, and low-status words like *humble, minor, submissive* and *weak*. What the researchers discovered was that when two congruent stimuli were presented together – such as a photo that displayed pride and the word *dominant* – it was easy for people to sort them quickly and accurately. But when stimuli were categorised incongruently – say, pride and the word *weak* – people had to force their minds to overcome the associations they naturally made, in order to deliver correct responses. It was the mental equivalent of rubbing their stomachs while patting their heads. Importantly, these tests were not only conducted with Western, homogenous groups. Similar results were found when the study was repeated with inhabitants of a small Fijian community. An expression of pride on the part of one human is universally linked by others to presumed status.[24]

Pride covers two very different emotions. There's the authentic pride that accompanies achievement. This is pride that is earned. Think of an Olympian who, following years of training, dedicated practice and sacrifice, wins Gold. Then there is hubristic pride, which comes from a self-inflated, arrogant view of oneself.[25] The person displaying hubristic pride might believe they have earned the right, but the awarder and recipient of the honour are one and the same. Authentic pride allows the holder to experience genuine self-esteem. Hubristic pride generates an internal view that others can be treated as inferior, and results in behaviour that it is often aggressive, coercive, selfish and manipulative. Despite the huge differences, to the casual observer these two varieties of pride superficially look much the same. In essence, they are emotion's identical twins. Nevertheless, while their outward manifestations may look the same, people can intuitively pick up on the different messages they send. We seem to know when a messenger is proud of something they have done or when they are merely feeling superior to us, and our reactions vary accordingly.

This was well demonstrated in a study where students had the levels of cortisol – a hormone released in response to stress – in their saliva measured while they gave a presentation via webcam to a watching audience. Periodically during this presentation the students were provided with non-verbal feedback in the form of one of three 'smiles', which – unknown to the presenters – were pre-recorded. The different types of smile used were: a rewarding smile that signalled the presenter was doing well; an affiliative smile that signalled no-threat; and a hubristic, dominant smile that signalled that the evaluator felt a sense of superiority over the presenter. Compared to those who received affiliative or rewarding smiles, presenters who were the recipients of a dominant smile experienced dramatic increases in stress, as measured by the levels of cortisol present in their saliva – levels that did not return to normal until about half an hour after they had finished.[26] If, after being smiled at, you have ever been left with an uneasy feeling of stress or nervousness, the chances are that you have been on the receiving end of a hubristic smile delivered by a domineering character, rather than the authentic smile of a genuinely proud and pleased character.

It's not just their posture and body language that give away the dominant individual. Dominance has a face, too, and it's a look that is common across different cultures and societies. Dominant faces have squarer jaws, more prominent eyebrows, bigger noses and a larger facial width-to-height ratio than average. Think Sylvester Stallone, Babe Ruth, Xi Jinping, Vinnie Jones. These facial characteristics are not tenuously associated with dominance: studies have shown that a person with a larger facial width-to-height ratio will frequently be perceived as being more formidable and dominant. Nor are these characteristics random. People from multiple and varying cultures have all been shown to possess a remarkable ability to accurately infer physical strength from faces.[27] Research has even shown that a man's facial width-to-height ratio is a valid predicator of how aggressive he is likely to be. For example, Canadian researchers found a correlation between the width-to-height face ratios of a selection of professional ice-hockey players and the number of minutes those players lost in penalties because of their overly aggressive in-play behaviour in previous seasons.[28] Similarly, facial width-to-height ratio is a valid predictor of a fighter's likely success in combat competitions, such as the Ultimate Fighting Championship.[29] Possession of a higher-than-average width-to-height-ratio face can even help in business. One study showed how squarer, angular-jawed men aggressively negotiated higher signing-on bonuses for themselves, compared to their longer-faced, round-jawed peers.[30]

Such cues are picked up at a very early age. In one experiment a team of Harvard and Princeton researchers showed hundreds of three- to four-year-olds photographs of faces that had been digitally manipulated, and then asked them questions like 'Which of these people is very mean?' and 'Which of these people is very nice?' Almost invariably, the children picked out faces that were dominant (that is, squarer and with a higher width-to-height ratio) as

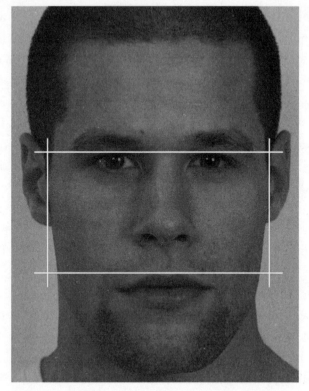

An illustrative example of how facial width-to-height ratio is assessed.[31]

being 'meaner' and those that were rounder and with a lower width-to-height ratio as being 'nicer'. In fact their hit rate was close to 90 percent.[32] Much the same results were recorded with older children and adults, providing further evidence that humans continue to use these rudimental physical cues as they grow older.

It's not just a certain type of face or postural display that signals dominance. Height does, too. This is perhaps not surprising when one considers the societies of our ancestors, where physical strength was a survival essential. But the association between height and dominance is so fixed in us that it extends even to modern-day roles where physical power in itself is not required. For example, all else being equal, taller leaders tend to get elected more frequently than their shorter challengers.* Of course there are exceptions – Napoleon, Churchill and the like – but they are anomalies who deviate from the general rule.[33]

Even in everyday, mundane situations the idea that someone's relative height can lead to perceived dominance, which, in turn, can lead to assent, occurs both predictably and routinely. This was tellingly demonstrated by one team of Dutch psychologists, who observed shoppers negotiating an entrance to a supermarket where only one person could pass at a time. Checking the relative heights of shoppers, using chalk marks they had placed on the passageway walls, the team noted that when two people approached at the same time, and one therefore had to yield to the other, the shorter person yielded 67 percent of the time to the taller one. The finding held true both for pairs of men and women, and was replicated in follow-up studies of more than a thousand pairs.[34] It could just about be argued, of course, that such willingness to yield to a taller person is a Dutch cultural practice. But other research doesn't bear this out. In another research project, ten-month-old infants were shown a video of two characters passing each other in a confined space. They registered much less surprise in their eye gaze when the shorter character gave way and the taller one triumphed.[35]

The fact that pre-verbal infants make dominance attributions based on height would seem to confirm that we are predisposed to associate 'big and strong' with 'gets their way'. And the behaviour of Dutch shoppers suggests that this mindset remains with us throughout the rest of our lives. It influences us in all manner of important decisions. The way in which we select our business leaders is a case

---

* Anyone who has ever thought about the benefits of electing officials on the basis of a public duel might find this extraordinary 1984 music video relevant to this point: https://www.youtube.com/watch?v=K2QAMqTgPKI

in point. We tend to favour taller ones because, so our reasoning goes, taller, stronger-looking messengers are better equipped to deter other group members – co-workers, other would-be leaders and the like – from stepping out of line. And as with the dominant-looking messenger with the larger width-to-height-ratio face, we believe taller messengers will probably be more assertive when negotiating on our behalf. When the psychologist Aaron Lukaszewski showed study participants photographs of male employees of a business consultancy, all similarly clad and with their faces masked, the participants tended to view the taller men more positively, perceived them as stronger and reported that they appeared better equipped to ensure team members complied with their instructions. They also believed that the taller men would better represent their team and predicted they would rise to higher positions within the firm.[36]

So deeply embedded is this prejudice in favour of taller employees that they do better financially, too. In a famous 2004 study, Timothy Judge and Daniel Cable, after correcting for age, gender and weight, found that taller people are likely to earn much more over their career than their shorter colleagues. Judge and Cable were even able to quantify the mathematical relationship between height and earnings: for each additional inch in height, earnings increased by between £511 ($728) and £618 ($897) for every year worked.[37] In addition, the duo found that while men generally tended to earn more than women, taller women also earned more than their shorter colleagues. This strongly suggests that the effect of height on earnings functions similarly for both genders.

Verbal signals of dominance

As well as the visual, there is an auditory aspect to dominance. Put simply, we tend to associate high status with lower, more relaxed-sounding voices. In part, this is because, just as a high-pitched voice runs the risk of signalling distress, fear and anxiety – all states that suggest reduced status, in the ears of the listener – low-pitched voices come across as confident and assertive.[38] In part, the reason is biological. A large, thick larynx producing a low sound is not only an indication of how physically big someone is, but also of how much testosterone is pulsing through their body. It suggests greater physical strength and, therefore, greater dominance. The rule appears to apply to women just as much as it does to men. Those with lower-pitched voices will generally be considered more dominant.

Famously, both Theresa May and Margaret Thatcher – to date the UK's only female prime ministers – sought experts to help them acquire and maintain lower-pitched, stronger and more stable voices, with Thatcher receiving her training – which was arranged for by the actor and director Laurence Olivier – at London's National Theatre. At the 1975 Conservative Party conference, she famously took out a feather duster and started cleaning the speaker's podium before giving her speech, and while the current speaker was *still* addressing the audience.* She then rose to speak, not in her natural higher-pitched voice, but in one that was lower and more resonant. The explicit contrast she sought to draw, between the shrill housewife that some people saw her as and the low-voiced politician talking about her vision of a free society and individual acquisition of status, was very telling. Some consider that moment to have been a pivotal one in her journey to becoming the country's first female premier.

Various studies have demonstrated the power of the lower voice. In one, people were asked to listen to speeches made by male political candidates, each of which had been digitally manipulated to be

* https://www.youtube.com/watch?v=cVje4C1nTt0

either higher or lower in pitch. When they were then asked, 'Who would you vote for?', seven out of ten responded that they would vote for the candidate with the lower-pitched voice, even though he was, of course, articulating precisely the same message as the higher-pitched version of himself.[39] The tone employed when a messenger speaks matters, too. Upward inflections at the end of a sentence have the effect of turning statements into questions – hardly conducive to the domain of the dominant messenger whose use of lower, downward intonation might consequently cause some audiences to receive their messages more as a statement of fact.

Casey Klofstad, a Harvard-educated political scientist, adds an intriguing detail to the impact of a messenger's tone and pitch. His work has involved measuring the impact of both male and female voices, manipulated to be either high- or low-pitched, and all enunciating the simple message 'I urge you to vote for me this November.' Not surprisingly, he found that a strong preference was expressed by listeners for the lower-pitched voice of each pair.[40] Interestingly, he also discovered that the preference was particularly strong among women voters judging other women's voices – a finding that suggests that Theresa May's and Margaret Thatcher's largest return on their voice-coaching investment may have come from female, rather than male, voters. Other research has found the preference for deep-voiced leadership candidates to be typically more pronounced among Republicans than Democrats.[41] The reasoning is that conservatives typically judge the world as more competitive and threatening than do liberals, and therefore prefer candidates who appear capable of standing up for their followers and prevailing in conflicts. As a result, a low-pitched, dominant-sounding voice is a more relevant and impressive feature for voters on the right, when considering election candidates, than for those on the left of the political spectrum.

It would be absurd to claim that in real-life political contests a deep voice invariably wins the day. There are many other factors in play. But the work of a team of Croatian researchers does suggest that pitch has more of an influence than we would perhaps care to admit. They reviewed more than fifty pairs of presidential candidates' debates, sourced from different countries, that had been posted on YouTube. And what they found was that those who possessed deeper (more dominant) voices than their rivals won more often. Not just that. Lower-voiced winners tended to enjoy a wider margin of victory than was the case with the smaller number of higher-voiced candidates who ended up being the victors.[42]

Dominance in practice

Those with a dominant disposition tend to be selfish, self-obsessed and far less likely to make sacrifices for others. Evidence suggests this is true even when those others happen to be their nearest and dearest. Dominant partners are much less willing to concede to their spouse's requests and more likely to lob aggressive comments, like verbal hand-grenades, at them. The meeker partner may believe that by being accommodating to their dominant partner's demands they will gradually gain influence in their relationship. The sad reality is that this is rarely true. When dominance is unevenly split in a relationship, it is the dominant partner who tends to have the last word. Moreover, the less dominant partner will often come to adopt the views and emotions of the more dominant partner.[43] There is an element of truth in the view that couples come to resemble each other over time, but the greater truth is that the less dominant partner does most of the heavy lifting in the convergence: they will travel further towards the direction of the dominant partner than vice versa. Dominant messengers are less willing to make reciprocal concessions or indulge in give-and-take with those over whom they believe they exercise superior status.

Dominance can also be achieved through more formal, structural mechanisms. Unlike other animals, humans have some unique ways of structuring hierarchies. Gorillas tend not to apply for promotions. Chimpanzees don't seal new deals with signed contracts. Unlike our primate cousins, we will jump through procedural hoops and rings to compete and acquire power over others, believing the resultant control of resources to be a much more civilised route to dominance than straightforward aggression and conflict. That is not to say that the results aren't largely the same, however.

People, like animals, have a tendency to submit to those in positions of status and dominance. Remember how Stanley Milgram demonstrated the willingness of ordinary folk to administer powerful electric shocks to another human, simply because a suitably attired scientist told them to do so? Recall also how compliance dropped when Milgram removed the trappings of competence; namely, the scientists' titles and white coats? But removing signs of competence wasn't enough to neutralise the powerful and pervasive influence of positional power entirely: a substantial number of people in this situation – close to 50 percent – still acquiesced to the experimenter's demands.

Work by the social psychologist Leonard Bickman attests to the effect that positional power can have, even in the absence of presumed competence. Bickman found similar results to Milgram's, when swapping titles and white coats for high-vis jackets and padded vests. Many of his studies would simply involve a researcher stopping passers-by and asking them to comply with a request. Pick up that piece of discarded litter. Go and stand on a specific spot by a bus stop. Give change for a car-parking meter. Every time, both the messenger and the message would be the same. The only thing that changed was what they were wearing. Sometimes they might be wearing ordinary casual clothes. At other times, a security guard's uniform. Once, even a milkman's outfit. In pre-study surveys, most people dismissed the notion that a requester's clothes would influence their reaction. But the results of Bickman's studies told a very different story. He found, for example, that twice as many people were prepared to give money to a complete stranger who happened to be wearing a hired security-guard uniform as they were to the same person wearing casual clothes.[44] The participants in these studies were not listening because they believed the security guard or milkman knew more than them about what to do with litter; they complied because the uniforms provided a signal about who was in charge.

Imagine, for a moment, that you work for a large organisation that researches and develops cutting-edge new medicines and therapies to treat human diseases. Imagine, too, that your company has in its portfolio a drug that works well but also carries a significantly high risk of adverse side effects. How comfortable would you be in supporting the marketing of this drug? According to Arthur Brief, a business-ethics professor at the University of Utah, your response may have less to do with the ethics of the issue than with the influence of an individual in a position of dominance.[45] When told that the chairman of the board was in favour of marketing the risky drug and was taking legal, political and other necessary action to prevent it from being banned, only 33 percent of MBA students reported that they would vote to recall the drug in a board meeting. If, on the other hand, they knew that the chairman was concerned about the impact the drug might have on their customers' welfare and was in favour of recalling the drug, 76 percent said they would vote in agreement.

Dominant executives are often at the heart of company scandals. In 2007, for example, three top Purdue Pharmaceuticals executives – the company's president, its top lawyer and its former medical director – pleaded guilty to charges of misleading regulators, doctors and their patients about the addictive qualities of their drug

OxyContin.[46] Such were the domineering tactics used – including the executives' strategy of having sales staff draw fake scientific charts and distribute them to doctors – that the case was compared by some commentators to Big Tobacco's historical concealment of health risks. The financial industry's 'Purdue Moment' came in the form of the LIBOR crisis of 2014, when a number of individuals at various banks conspired to manipulate the London Interbank Offered Rate – the interest rate used in inter-bank lending. Subsequent investigations into the scandal highlighted the influence of senior staff who, in classic domineering style, were orchestrating moves designed to pressure their more junior colleagues into inputting incorrect data, in an attempt to boost their own status and earnings. 'So yeah, leave it with me, and uh, it won't be a problem' was just one telling remark recorded by investigators looking at the interactions between the LIBOR submitters and senior traders.[47] It was a classic example of the way in which junior employees can be coerced into actions they would normally consider morally reprehensible and off-limits, if they are under pressure from someone above them in the hierarchy. And despite regulations and government bodies, the problem has not wholly gone away.

Submitting to dominance

Despite its ubiquity, dominance is perhaps the most under-recognised route to status in a modern, Western society. The idea that disproportionate attention is awarded to a minority simply because they shout louder and more forcibly than the rest is repugnant to most. We prefer to think that, in a contemporary democratic society, all voices will be given an opportunity to be heard, and those with the best ideas will win out. Whether in a family, network of associates, local community, school, workplace or a whole country, it is tough to acknowledge that the person who speaks the loudest, rather than the person who makes the most sense, so often garners the lion's share of attention – to see that uncooperative, egotistical behaviour is often rewarded rather than punished, and that bullies do often get their own way. Neither do we like to admit that, as individuals, we have a tendency to conform to the will of dominant others. Such an acknowledgement would undermine the pride we take in our own identity. We hate to think that we might be conforming to another's will, because that both reduces our status and enhances theirs. No one wants to be someone else's sheep.

An early study by the social psychologist Robert Cialdini demonstrates the subtle influences that submissions to dominance exert.[48] On the one hand, dominant messengers tend to increase their liking of, and assign higher levels of intelligence to, those individuals who acquiesce to them. Accordingly, a student who calls their professor to request more time to submit an essay might be advised to take a submissive, rather than a dominant, position. On the other hand, those observing a submissive individual tend to judge them much more harshly, inferring from the act of submission that their status is lower. So a student who makes their plea for an extension in front of friends and contemporaries may need to accompany it with disrespectful facial expressions and gestures, if they want to maintain status in the eyes of those around them.

As Cialdini points out, most people understand this arrangement pretty well and therefore take steps to avoid appearing overly conformist. At least in public. Privately, things are often quite different. It is a dynamic that can perhaps explain election and referendum results in countries such as the US, the UK and Brazil, which took many pundits by surprise. In public, people may not have been willing to acknowledge their support of a dominant messenger. But voting takes place in private. And once we've made our decision, it is easy to reassure ourselves with the thought that our actions simply confirmed what was self-evidently going to be the eventual outcome anyway. This unwillingness to acknowledge our susceptibility to dominant messengers doesn't make them any less effective. In fact, if anything, our refusal to acknowledge the dynamics of dominant behaviour enables it to operate under the radar, and makes it even more likely to go unchallenged.

The reluctance on our part to acknowledge the dynamics of dominance helps to explain why one of its most extreme manifestations – bullying – has historically been so underplayed and even today is so frequently misunderstood. In its rawest form, it's most frequently found among children at school. For example, one of us (Steve) was subjected to classic childhood bullying for nearly two and a half years. It started out as a largely harmless, almost playful 'scrum', in which a number of boys would indulge in what resembled a game of rough-and-tumble. Over time these free-for-alls occurred with increasing frequency, levels of harmful boisterousness rose, and the scrummaging became more targeted. Soon a small handful of boys would find themselves singled out for 'special' attention: surrounded by others, they would be subjected to slaps and punches of varying intensity. From there it was a short step to verbal insults and threats, and to physical attacks immediately before a lesson, which meant that the victim had to stifle the pain or risk inviting further ridicule. Even the theft of belongings was not off-limits: earnings from an early-morning paper round, dinner money, football stickers and, most frequently (since bringing sandwiches was a preferable alternative to having dinner money taken), lunch itself. Ultimately Steve would be forced to adopt the sort of behaviour noted among submissive primates: avoiding the dominant members of the troupe wherever possible, looking for safe places where food could be consumed rather than stolen. He was the kid who would retreat to the school library or caretaker's cupboard in an attempt to avoid his lunch being stolen by a tormentor.

Such an experience will be depressingly familiar to many. Almost as depressing is the fact that in the past we had a tendency to misinterpret what is going on here. Early research into bullying suggested that those who routinely dominate others are socially awkward types who lack the ability to regulate their emotions appropriately.[49] They therefore act aggressively and hit out angrily at others, when provoked. More recent research, however, has shown that while aggressive victims do certainly exist, the average accomplished bully is no brutish knucklehead. If anything, they're quite the opposite. Bullying can be a strategic and instrumental tactic to establish dominance. More than that, evidence suggests that those children seen as bullies are, in the main, also quite popular. They are often 'the coolest kids in class' and, when they bully, it tends to be in highly targeted ways. Targeted bullying is proactive. It doesn't come about as a result of prior victimisation, but instead is motivated by reward. Bullies do it because they are seeking dominance and the spoils that come with it – increased status and greater influence.[50] It's a comforting interpretation to think that bullying comes from weakness, not strength. It doesn't make it any less wrong.

By the same token, those likely to attract the unwelcome attention of the targeting, domineering bully are typically submissive, low in confidence and socially inept. Those who possess non-normative characteristics suffer, too: ethnic minorities, the obese and members of the LGBTQ communities. To the bully, the bullied are 'safe targets' lacking dominant characteristics of their own. Sadly, those who are bullied will frequently attribute being targeted to their own perceived weaknesses. It is not unusual for victims to report that they are bullied because they are 'weak'. Victimisation, therefore, can be a cyclical process, where depressive and anxious symptoms are not only predictive features of victimisation, but also increase as a result of that victimisation. While no less difficult to accept, one can maybe understand how someone with an opportunity to acquire social dominance through bullying might see it as a potentially attractive proposition. In essence, there is a cost-benefit trade-off between dominance and morality here, particularly in schools and other contexts where hierarchies are often dominance-based. Those willing to perform antisocial actions gain dominance. What results is a boost to their status. And given that some research has found that the bully possesses a heightened need for approval and control, maybe they really do have more to gain by being a bully. And less to lose.[51]

Thankfully, bullies don't have it all their own way, and bullying isn't the only route available to teenagers who seek social status. The scholars Mark Van Ryzin and Anthony Pellegrini suggest that teenagers considered to possess the profile of 'low-bullying high-status' are more popular than those with a 'high-bullying high-status' profile.[52] The former achieve status through their advanced communication skills, greater desire to socialise and by actively involving themselves in prosocial behaviours. In other words, they seek status through popularity rather than superiority. The archetypal bully who attempts to exert dominance over others has a nemesis who is less hostile, disapproves of bullying behaviour, is emotionally intelligent and uses sociable acts as a means to elevate their status. Anything that schools, community groups and policy-makers can do to propagate and actively encourage more of these characters to rise in prominence – perhaps by engineering hierarchies to form on the basis of prestige rather than dominance – should rightly be applauded for a pair of reasons. First, any activity that leads to any meaningful reduction in bullying is worthwhile. Second, it further promotes the status of messengers in a school's ecosystem for reasons of desirability, and not mere dominance.

Messengers who are dominant by disposition may well be looked up to, or simply looked at. But they are not necessarily liked. The boost they receive in status *over* their audience is likely to be tempered by a lack of connectedness *with* their audience. The dominant messenger rules through fear rather than love, power rather than prestige. They give up the soft-messenger effects of warmth and vulnerability (see Chapters 5 and 6) to achieve the hard-messenger benefits that come from elevated status. Although we wouldn't go so far as to claim that the clear incompatibility between the dominant character and a warm one is a wholly irreconcilable one – we will have more to say about the interplay between the various messenger effects later – it does present a conundrum; not least for many of society's leaders and elected officials, who struggle to impose their will whilst simultaneously attempting to maintain their likeability. This was starkly illustrated for us when we asked colleagues in our two offices to 'name someone in public life whom you regard as both dominant and likeable'. Not only was there no consensus, but there was a distinct lack of names offered that would enable one even to start seeking a consensus.

The need for dominance

In a modern-day society do we really want leaders, bosses and politicians who exude dominance? After all, it's unlikely their success at governing is contingent on an ability to beat a competitor in a boxing match. The answer seems to be that it depends. In calm, surer times warm, harmonious messengers tend to be valued. In times of conflict and uncertainty – when people feel anxious, experience hardship, or fear for their security – the motivation to seek out a dominant leader rises. People are looking for someone who will counter these negative factors and bring certainty. At the same time they assume that a dispositionally dominant individual will be better able to make the tough decisions that are clearly required to

111

deal with a crisis, act assertively and crack the whip to enforce adherence to the group's rules and values.[53]

There's another factor in play, too, which is known as the *Individual Success Hypothesis*.[54] It goes something like this. When considering the respective merits of a shortlist of candidates, evaluators – be they voters, recruiters, sports fans or the like – tend to focus more on how a candidate will fare *on their own* rather than as part of a team. The fact that, in order to be effective, the eventual elected leader will be required to solicit the help of, and cooperate with, numerous others – allies and otherwise – will frequently be ignored. Instead audiences can fall into the trap of thinking that a person's future success is solely within their own gift and capability. This can be especially seductive when a potential candidate has dominated in another field or arena, however unrelated. It's a phenomenon that explains why, for example, world-class sportsmen will so often be appointed to management positions, despite the fact that the skills that enabled them to dominate the stadium as players aren't the same as those required to motivate and manage. An analysis of professional soccer teams in the German Bundesliga finds evidence to support this.[55] Teams with former superstar footballers as the lead coach typically perform worse than those teams whose lead coaches never played at the highest level – a finding that seems to have little impact on the number of high-profile players awarded these roles.*

* This is not the case in every sport, though. In the US National Basketball Association (NBA) former top players do make more successful coaches. But there is a reason. Former soccer stars often enter managerial careers in the top flight. In the NBA, former star players have to work their way up the managerial ladder, usually starting out as an assistant coach in the lower divisions. Consequently, bad managers get found out and never make it to the premier leagues. Goodall, A. H., Kahn, L. M. & Oswald, A. J. (2011), 'Why do leaders matter? A study of expert knowledge in a superstar setting', *Journal of Economic Behavior & Organization*, 77(3), 265–84.

Neville Chamberlain and Winston Churchill offer the classic British example of the differing leadership styles deemed to suit very different circumstances. Chamberlain had been a very successful Chancellor of the Exchequer in the 1930s and was, initially, a popular prime minister. In foreign policy, he may have been mistaken in his interpretation of Nazi Germany's ambitions, but while it looked as though war might be averted, he received much support. Churchill's peacetime record was, at best, patchy. He had proved a poor Chancellor of the Exchequer in the 1920s, and many of his views (for example, on India) were judged to be unduly bellicose and jingoistic.

When it came to the likelihood of war breaking out, however, the balance of messenger influence shifted from the more conciliatory Chamberlain to the more aggressive Churchill. In his dealings with Hitler, Chamberlain misunderstood the rules of the dominance game, wrongly assuming that negotiation and cooperation would work, rather than adopting a tougher approach.[56] Churchill, by contrast, with his 'bulldog' spirit, offered an appearance of strength and certainty that appealed to people who were now facing difficult and uncertain times. On 1 September 1939 Hitler invaded Poland, forcing Chamberlain to accept that his pleas and concessions had been exploited. The following year, Churchill – dominant, defiant and with his legendary determination – took up the baton to fight for the freedom, safety and liberty of his people.

The lesson here is a difficult one. When facing a dominant aggressor, strategies that centre primarily on cooperation and appeasement will frequently backfire. Game theorists understand this and note the advantages of the cooperation/conflict-matching strategy: cooperate only when others cooperate; retaliate when others take a more aggressive stance. That is not to say that tit-for-tat is without its own limitations. Situations where neither side backs down can result in a vicious, unending spiral. Displays of dominance, consequently, have to be calibrated according to the needs of a particular situation. They cannot be absolute.

Who we listen to, put our faith in and follow will therefore depend on situational factors. Imagine, for a moment, that you live in a small-scale tribal society in the jungle. Imagine, too, that your local tribe is under threat from a neighbouring tribe. Tensions have been escalating over access to previously shared hunting grounds, and you have been warned that the neighbouring tribe is preparing an imminent attack on your village. You are then shown two pictures and asked to vote for the person you would prefer to lead your tribe through its present difficulties. The pictures are, in fact, of the same person, but one has been digitally manipulated to appear more dominant: square jaw, mean-looking, an air of hubristic pride, greater facial width-to-height ratio.

Now imagine, instead, that the challenge your tribe faces isn't to do with a neighbour's hostilities, but instead the threat of an imminent flood. Who would you choose in this context? The dominant leader or the one who looks as though they are more likely to encourage collaboration and persuade people to work together to build a dam?

If you are anything like the two groups of participants in a study undertaken by a pair of Danish researchers, you will probably look to the messenger cues that most closely fit the current context and threats facing your group. If it's a conflict with a competitor that you are having to confront, you will go with the dominant-looking leader. If it's an emergency that requires cooperation among your own group, you will opt for the non-dominant-looking leader.[57] This – as studies that replicate the situation have shown – holds true whether you're Danish, Ukrainian, Polish or American.

When these same researchers studied citizens in an actual crisis situation – the 2014 Russian annexation of Crimea – they discovered that Ukrainian citizens' votes for a hypothetical leader were influenced by how geographically close they were to the conflict region. Those who were in close proximity and adopted a 'fight' mentality were more likely to choose the dominant candidate. Those who lived further away and felt safer opted for the more cooperative one. Other studies show how voters place greater weight on strong leadership when the possibility of a terrorist attack looms large in people's minds.[58] As a rule then, while we may like kind, caring and relationship-oriented leaders, we are more likely to elect unlikeable dominant leaders when it comes to saving our hides from the competition. We look to them to take decisive action, uphold law and order, and provide a sense of hope in times of uncertainty and conflict.

The same is true in business. When choosing between two suitably qualified candidates for the role of CEO, decisions made by those on the board of directors who are responsible for recruiting will be heavily influenced by the company's current performance. If the company is doing well, its share price and market share stable, and employees are relatively relaxed and feeling psychologically safe, then a leader who scores lower on dominant-related measures such as self-interest and ego will be favoured. However, if the share price is falling, market share is dipping and employee stress is increasing, the dominant candidate who scores higher on these measures is more likely to be chosen.[59] It seems dominant messengers do particularly well anywhere that conflict, competition and uncertainty are rife.

When the time comes to build bridges, however, self-interested bulldozers make for poor leaders and teammates. In his notes about Winston Churchill, the American writer Ralph Ingersoll suggested that, following the end of the Second World War, Britain would enter into an era of recovery that would be less conducive to Churchill's style. 'No one felt he would be Prime Minister after the war. He was simply the right man in the right job at the right time.

That time being the time of a desperate war with Britain's enemies.'[60] When others are trying to cooperate, there is little benefit in aggression and provocation, and the tenure of the dominant leader is a short-lived one. In fact anthropological records show how context can dramatically change the perceived value of the dominant messenger. For example, Native American tribes choose different chiefs dependent on whether they are at peace or at war.[61] And the author and researcher Leslie Zebrowitz observes how in times of social and economic hardship, actresses with harder, more mature facial characteristics feature more prominently in popular culture. 'But in prosperous times,' she goes on to say, 'we turn our preference toward those with a baby's glow.'[62]

Donning dominance

Aspects of dominance may be innate, but there are ways in which individuals can manipulate an audience, whether deliberately or accidentally. For a start, they can manipulate their physical appearance. Recall the experiments showing how men who adopted a more expansive and dominant pose on an online dating platform received more 'likes' and responses? It is becoming increasingly easy (and popular) to alter photographic images in a way that accentuates the possession of certain dominant-relevant features – upper-body torso and arm muscles, washboard stomach and even a larger width-to-height-ratio head. Perceived height, too, is open to manipulation, and not always by digital means. Relative tallness (and, as a consequence, dominance) can be signalled by the presence in images of other poeple who are shorter, thereby giving the illusion of increased height to the photo's main subject.

Given that voice pitch is also associated with dominance, it is reasonable to assume that some messengers may consider voice-coaching or elocution. As with physical appearance, voices are open to digital alteration. For example, in movies about hostage situations the voice of the ransom-demander is often digitally changed so that it sounds slower and deeper in tone. Faster-talking, high-pitched hostage-takers rarely invoke the level of menace required to assert dominance.

Colours, too, can convey dominance, with red being the colour most closely associated with power and supremacy. For example, a red background on a website can induce a more dominant and aggressive mindset, causing people to bid higher and more aggressively to win an item in an online auction than they would do if the webpage had been blue.[63] Red has also been shown to influence sporting outcomes. A 2005 paper in *Nature* found that contestants randomly assigned red rather than blue outfits in one-on-one Olympic events such as boxing, taekwondo and Greco-Roman wrestling were more likely to win, regardless of the stage of the competition or weight class.[64] However, this red-winner effect seems to influence results only when the two competitors are equally matched in terms of ability. And the popular myth that the politician who wears a red 'power tie' is looked upon more favourably is, indeed, a myth. A study that measured perceptions of the dominance, leadership and believability of politicians, both famous and less well known, after digitally altering the colour of the ties in film clips of speeches they made, discovered that red ties made no difference.[65]

Finally, evolutionary theorists hypothesise that inking one's body, or even piercing it, serves to increase perceptions of dominance and a more robust immune system. Others believe that tattoos and piercings are a sign of free expression and are associated with hard-rock music and dominant cultures. In one study, 2,500 Facebook users were shown photographs of nine shirtless men, who had adopted the same neutral facial expression and pose. Those whose photographs had been modified to include a black tattoo on one arm were much more likely to be rated as dominant, masculine, attractive, healthy and aggressive, both by male and female Facebook viewers.[66] The benefits of such a perception are not universal, however. As our editors astutely pointed out, a doorman with a tattoo may well look intimidating, but that doesn't necessarily mean people will vote for law-makers who resemble bouncers.

4

ATTRACTIVENESS

Cute Babies, Beauty Taxes and the
Upsides of Averageness

In 2016 Nora Danish, an Asian TV host and model, lobbied her country's tax officials in the Malaysian Inland Revenue Board (IRB) to give her a tax break to compensate her for the expense she incurred for having to look beautiful.[1] She argued that being famous obliged her to appear attractive in public and, because the cost of doing so was not tax-deductible, her fame placed her at an unfair financial disadvantage. 'For me and indeed all of my Malaysian countrymen there is an obligation to pay taxes,' she said, 'but I would argue that celebrities should have some exemptions. In the modern day and age we have to pay more than ever to keep our appearances up, otherwise we would not have careers where we could earn money, and this should be something we could factor in as an occupational cost.'

Danish received little public sympathy for her plight, or support from the Malaysian IRB, which rejected her proposal outright. But is there any merit in her argument that attractive people get a bad break? Or is it rather the case that the good-looking are actually afforded a valuable advantage in life, in terms of their ability to appeal to others, their resultant higher status and, thus, their effectiveness as messengers?

It's certainly the case that those deemed to be physically attractive appear to receive the kind of attention that goes with being an effective messenger. Pretty much every well-being magazine, fitness journal and lifestyle periodical is adorned with fit, attractive people. Websites, too, are beautified with images of the handsome, which are invariably linked – sometimes implicitly, but often explicitly – to persuade us of the merits of a particular product or brand. The link between the power of an attractive messenger and the promotion of items that we associate with looks and health is a well-established one. Attractiveness is a key factor in choosing who we befriend, who we get to go on dates with, the jobs we win (and the ones we don't), the politicians we vote for and the people we marry.

It also influences decisions in areas that, on the surface, would seem to have nothing whatsoever to do with physical appearance. Take finance. When making financial decisions, such as whether or not to borrow money from a particular lender, people usually assume that they focus solely on economic factors, such as the interest rate on offer, how a product compares to others on the market and price elasticity. But when researchers at the Booth School of Business in Chicago tested whether this really is how consumers make borrowing decisions, their findings contradicted this understandable assumption. What they found instead was that advertising strategies – which, according to the neoclassical economic view of human psychology, should have no effect on people's thought processes because they have nothing to do with finance – also play a role.

For the purposes of their field study, the researchers teamed up with a consumer lending company in South Africa to mail more than 53,000 people who had received mailshots and advertising material from the lender in the past. Now, these potential customers were sent a new financial offer. Thanks to the researchers, however, the way in which it was couched varied across the mailing, not just in terms of the interest rate advertised, but in terms of the accompanying images: some mailshots included an image of an attractive woman, others didn't; some offered advantageous interest rates, others didn't; and there were different permutations of image and financial offer. The researchers then checked with local branches of the finance company to see what level of take-up the differently styled mailings achieved. The question they were seeking to answer was, of course, whether it was possible to quantify how much a picture of a pretty face on an advertising mailshot was worth, relative to a reduction in interest rates. The answer was: a lot! When the photograph of an attractive female was placed next to information about the offer, it correlated with a higher take-up among prospective customers. Not among women – they were too savvy. But the researchers estimated that, among men, an attractive photograph increased take-up by as much as a 25 percent reduction in the interest rate on offer.[2]

It is important to note that what was at issue here was *physical* attractiveness. In general terms, attractiveness is not solely limited to matters of physical appearance. Attractive messengers can also be those to whom people are drawn because they are likeable, warm and possess a manner that attracts attention and goodwill. These *softer* effects are part of the larger 'connectedness' theme, which we will explore in Part Two. For now, though, we will concern ourselves primarily with physical attractiveness and its impact as a *hard*-messenger effect. As the studies of the Chicago Booth School of Business show, physical attractiveness can have a powerful effect. Not because the attractive messenger possesses instrumental value, such as superior knowledge, skills or power. But rather because they possess *mate value*. That is, they make for desirable reproductive partners and, because of that, they invoke positive responses in others. In consequence, the beautiful are given preferential treatment and awarded higher status and, as a result, wield greater influence than the less attractive members of society.[3] Not that the physically less appealing lose out altogether. Those who associate with a beautiful or gorgeous messenger find that their own status is elevated, too, and they gain greater opportunities for social rewards: invitations to cooler parties, conversations with equally or even more attractive people, and maybe, even, links to the high-status world's ultimate messenger: the rich and famous celebrity.

What does attractiveness look like?

We are able to make judgements of attractiveness in less than 200 milliseconds. When, for example, Alice and Laura walk into a bar and see Tom and Jason for the first time, there will be an almost immediate and implicit understanding about which male and female from each pair is the more attractive. Alice and Laura will both fancy, say, Jason, while Tom and Jason will both be attracted to Alice. We all respond as swiftly, and we all tend to consider the same people attractive. Some of us may prefer brunettes to blondes, or redheads to brunettes, or slender types to hunks – individual tastes are bound to vary – but among men and women, adults and adolescents, and within and across cultures, meta-analytic reviews, which compare findings across multiple studies, have shown that there is broad consensus about who is attractive and who is not.[4]

It is a consensus that isn't only found among adolescents and adults. According to Judith Langlois, a provost professor at the University of Texas and an eminent expert in her field, infants as young as two or three months old intrinsically know the difference between attractive and unattractive faces. In one study, tots were seated in front of pairs of photographs of female faces projected onto a screen. All the faces bore neutral expressions and were framed by medium to dark hair. There was just one crucial difference between them. One in each pair had previously been evaluated – by adults – as attractive; the other one had been deemed unattractive. When the babies' responses were assessed by measuring how long they gazed at each photo in each pair, it emerged that, even at two months of age, they spent longer looking at the 'attractive' faces than the 'unattractive' ones.[5] In another study Langlois recorded what she calls '*positive affective tone*' – a measure of how positively an infant responds to someone, as measured by their smile and tendency to move towards them. She found that even one-year-olds demonstrate greater levels of *positive affect* towards attractive strangers (and dolls) than unattractive ones, and lower levels of withdrawal and distress.[6]

This bias is not a one-way street. Adults shown pictures of cute and less cute babies typically pay greater attention, coo more and exhibit increased levels of affection to more attractive newborns. More remarkably still, the effect seems to hold true for the actual parents themselves. Observational studies of feeding and playing activities with firstborns find that the mothers of less attractive infants are less affectionate towards their children and spend more time interacting with other *adults* in the room. They are also more likely to provide merely 'routine caregiving' to their offspring and less 'affectionate behaviour', compared to the mothers of prettier babes.[7] Pretty babies make for pretty effective messengers. It's a basic truth that was not lost on the advertisers of yesteryear, who regularly used pictures of babies in advertisements to sell all manner of products – even sweet fizzy drinks. In 2018 a Twitter post caused a bit of a social-media storm by circulating an ad that appeared in a 1950s issue of *Life* magazine, featuring an image of a cute baby drinking from a bottle of Heineken.[8] The picture was quickly exposed as a fake by astute commentators, who pointed out that the baby shown in the original advertisement wasn't drinking beer at all ... but 7 Up! It seems that regardless of the suitability of the product being advertised, attractive babies have an attention-capturing quality that is hard to match.

Pretty babies can make for pretty effective messengers.

Thanks to the many data sets available – ranging from information drawn from dating apps to research projects involving sophisticated facial morphing techniques – we have a pretty good idea as to who is likely to be viewed as attractive and who is not. Two key and unsurprising plus points are youthfulness and facial symmetry. A third, though, would seem to be rather less immediately obvious. In addition to looking fresh and possessing a proportional evenness, attractive faces are 'average'.[9] This may seem rather paradoxical: after all, how can people prefer an ordinary or 'prototypical' face if, by definition, attractive faces are rated above average? The truth is, however, that we favour average faces precisely because they *are* average – because they lack the individual striking features that would single them out as different. Striking or unique features can be indicative of potential genetic problems. Average faces indicate health. This fact also goes some way towards explaining why symmetrical faces are seen as more attractive. Symmetry is nature's way of signalling the possession of good genes. Evolutionary biologists argue that because genetic quality cannot be observed directly (asking for a Genome Profile Report on a first date pretty much guarantees there won't be a second), we look to other, indirect cues as a proxy. Signs of youth, symmetry and averageness act as a reliable signal that a potential mate is more likely to survive and pass on their good genes to future generations. In other words, individuals attracted to youthful, symmetrical and average-like features are more likely to end up raising offspring, who, in turn, are also more likely to reproduce.

There's another reason, too, why we tend to perceive average faces as being more attractive. Their averageness makes them more prevalent, and their prevalence makes them more familiar. Familiar faces are attractive to us because they are more likely to have components in common with those of the people we know, share social bonds with and around whom we feel safe and comfortable.[10] So strong is this preference for the familiar that, generally speaking, unless a learned negative association exists, we tend to seek out those who resemble us. Indeed, studies show that people are generally most attracted to photographs and pictures of others that have been morphed to look a bit more like themselves. Other research finds that, in general, people tend to cohabit with and marry partners who are about as attractive as they are and of a similar socio-economic status – a pattern described as *assortative mating*. Whilst it may be true that opposites do attract, it is far more common for birds of a feather to flock together.[11]

But there are some birds of a feather who are extremely unlikely to flock together: identical birds. Although we find those who are similar to us attractive, we do also require a degree of divergence. Norwegian researchers who showed participants pictures of their partner's face that had either been blended to some degree with their own or with an independently rated attractive face, found that the sweet spot of attractiveness was reached when their partner's face was modified to include 22 percent of their own face. But when that element was raised to 33 percent, participants no longer found the face attractive. Incidentally, independent observers rated the 22 percent images as very unattractive.[12] There seems to be a sound biological reason for the basic principle here. Similar features may be attractive to a degree, but over-similarity triggers an entirely different response – namely, a hardened aversion to inbreeding.

Of course heterosexual men and women are not necessarily attracted to the *same* features in each other. Not only do women and men not look the same, but neither do they look at each other in the same way. According to the sexual dimorphism theory of attraction,

128

men are attracted to feminine women, and women are attracted to masculine men.*[13] This is borne out by data from millions of online romantic interactions, ads placed in the classified sections, and outcomes of speed-dating; and it suggests the underlying truth of received knowledge. Women *do* typically prefer athletic men who are three or four inches taller than themselves (so if the woman wears heels, that means their heights will be roughly equivalent). Men generally care less about a woman's height and much more about her age. They *do* tend to go for women who are young, thin and feminine-looking.[14] Men on the Forbes Rich List, who presumably have more choice in whom they date, have wives who are, on average, seven years younger. And their second wives are, on average, twenty-two years their junior.[15] Younger women fare especially well on dating sites and apps, prompting many older and less attractive daters to be tempted to enhance their profile photographs and lie about their age and physical features.[16] And although both genders favour youthful looks, this is particularly so of the way men

---

* In fact, whether women prefer masculine men or not is a hotly contested debate. Overly-masculine men are not usually considered attractive, and those with more feminine facial features are often rated as more appealing. What heterosexual women seem to find most attractive is an athletic, tall man with good genes, who is also reliable, doting and offers long-term compatibility; strong, with kind eyes; someone able to defend and assert control over a situation, but caring and loving, unless pushed otherwise. A 'helpful hunk' of sorts, with an obvious example being a firefighter. As eye-rollingly stereotypical as this is, it does appear to represent reality. In 2016 Tinder began allowing people to include their job title on profiles, offering up a chance to record which professions were most attractive to the opposite sex. Pilots, firefighters and entrepreneurs generated most interest from women. For men, models, personal trainers and nurses came top: http://uk.businessinsider.com/tinders-most-swiped-right-jobs-in-america-2016-2?r=US&IR=T

view women. The evolutionary explanation for this is that the average male is endowed with a greater sexual appetite, and places greater weight on physical indicators of fertility when considering potential mates, than the average female.

Interestingly, high heels weren't originally intended for women, but rather as a form of riding footwear for men. Sixteenth-century Persian fighters, who greatly valued good horsemanship, would wear high heels to ensure their feet remained in the stirrups as they loaded their bows before standing upright to take aim and fire. Women wearing heels is a relatively recent innovation. According to anthropologists, heels not only increase the wearer's height, but force a 'courting pose' of arched back and protruding buttocks – a commonly found mating feature in other mammals. High heels, therefore, serve as an example of a non-biological factor of attractiveness. What they are *not* is practical, or necessarily comfortable.[17]

The upsides of attractiveness

Attractiveness is more than its own reward. People viewed as more attractive than average receive greater attention in the romantic domain. Consequently more options are available to them when it comes to choosing future partners, whichever gender they are. Whether it is responses to personal ads, interest garnered by a profile on an online dating site or phone numbers collected at speed-dating events, a society's attractive individuals will be in demand.[18] What is perhaps more surprising is that attractive people appear to gain advantages in many other areas of their lives, too. As babies move from infancy to childhood and from primary school through to high school, the ones regarded as more attractive will often be treated more favourably by their teachers and viewed as more popular with their peers. In the same way that the attractive baby–parent attention bias works in both directions, so, too, does the teacher–pupil bias. Attractive students receive better grades from their tutors, and attractive teachers typically receive better feedback from their pupils. Children judged to possess higher levels of attractiveness are also much more likely to be rated as having more socially desirable personalities and are more likely to achieve greater levels of personal success later in life.[19]

As teens move into adulthood and attention is directed towards work and career progression, attractiveness continues to play a big role.[20] All other things being equal, those possessing features that mark them out as more attractive are more likely to be offered that crucial first job. And their advantage doesn't stop there. Attractive employees are more likely to gain promotions and progress faster, and further, on their chosen career-advancement trajectory. They are also likely to be paid more. All this despite having the same experience, potential and work ethic as their average-in-appearance colleagues. This phenomenon has become known as the 'beauty premium' and, according to Daniel Hamermesh, a noted US economist, it is possible to put a figure on it: it can be as much as an additional 10 to 15 percent in annual earnings – about the same as the difference in earnings in American labour markets between those of different races and of different genders.[21] Indeed, Hamermesh suggests that the earning disadvantage experienced by African American men is similar to the disadvantage experienced by white, unattractive men. Over the course of a career, a below-average-looking man can reasonably expect to earn anything up to $250,000 (£190,000) less than his more attractive peers. Of course money is certainly not the only contributory influence to an individual's happiness. It is, nonetheless, an important one. Little surprise then that unattractive people have also been found to be less happy, too.[22] It is because of such disparities in earning power and life experiences that some people have called for policies to mitigate the influence of attractiveness. Deborah Rhode, a Stanford law professor, has suggested that in the same way that the United States' Civil Rights Act of 1964 prohibits employment discrimination based on race, colour, religion, sex and nationality; the 1967 Discrimination in Employment Act mandates the same for age; and the 1990 Disabilities Act stipulates that applicants and employees be protected from discrimination based on their disabilities – so legal measures should be taken to prevent workers being discriminated against on the basis of their attractiveness.[23]

The problem is that the attractiveness bias runs very deep. The extent to which we live in a 'casting-couch society' may be a matter of debate, just as it's hard to prove either way the precise truth of the commonly levelled charge that recruitment processes are beauty contests in disguise. But there can be no question that attractiveness gets unduly favoured. This was convincingly demonstrated by a group of Italian researchers, who sent more than 11,000 CVs to a range of employers across a number of industries, in response to job offers that had been posted. Some of the CVs were accompanied by a photograph of the candidate; others weren't.[24] Responses from prospective employers followed a predictable pattern. If a CV arrived supported by photographic evidence of the applicant's attractiveness, the candidate in question would be more than 20 percent more likely to be given a call-back than if they had sent in the same CV but without an accompanying photograph. Résumés with pictures of less attractive applicants faired worst. And while the response rate to attractive applicants was the same regardless of gender, depressingly this wasn't true when it came to the success rate of the unattractive applicants. Unattractive men received call-backs for 26 percent of the jobs they applied for; for women, the figure was just 7 percent. These results are by no means a one-off. Similar findings have emerged from studies in Argentina and

Israel.[25] And a meta-analysis that combined the results of twenty-seven studies found that attractiveness impacts on job outcomes in both academic and professional environments, regardless of employment sector or job level.[26]

Obviously, there are ways in which companies can reduce the potentially unfair advantage afforded to more attractive applicants. They can refuse to accept applications from jobseekers who attach a picture to their CVs. They can ensure that the early stages of candidate selection don't require a face-to-face meeting, perhaps by conducting an online test, giving a written assignment or holding screening interviews, either via telephone or by Skype or Zoom with the video functions turned off. (This may benefit both parties, because the relative attractiveness of a recruiter might also bias the process.) Such small steps can at least help to ensure that a broader range of candidates (and potentially the better candidates) make it to interview. But at some point – like the house-buyer who, rather than relying on an estate agent's description alone, will want to view the home they are thinking about buying – prospective employers will want to meet candidates in the flesh. And that's when those messengers who possess the attractiveness advantage will be able to work their magic. Each candidate will be trying to convey the same message: 'I believe I am the best candidate for the job.' But even after their experience, skills and interviewing technique are taken into account, their relative attractiveness will often still bias recruiters' evaluations.

The labour market is just one area of public and professional life where a messenger's attractiveness can hold sway. The political arena is susceptible, too. A study in the *Journal of Public Economics* reports that a more attractive candidate can – all other things being equal – garner up to 20 percent more votes than their less prepossessing rival.[27] Within the justice system, too, research has shown how juries often form impressions of a defendant's guilt or innocence early on in a trial, based on little more than their attractiveness. A meta-analysis conducted by Yale University researchers found that mock-jurors presented with hypothetical cases were less likely to find attractive defendants guilty, and that when they were asked to comment on appropriate punishments for the guilty, they recommended more lenient ones for more attractive criminals – even when the crimes were serious ones, such as robbery and rape.[28] It seems the standard cues that juries use to infer guilt and inform their punishment decisions, that voters use to elect leaders, and that managers use to hire and promote workers can all be influenced by the attractiveness of the messenger before them.

Boosting attractiveness

Attractiveness may be innate, but that doesn't mean there aren't artificial ways of improving the hand that nature has dealt. Good grooming certainly helps. The French consumer psychologist Nicolas Guéguen and his colleagues have shown how waitresses who applied make-up at the start of a shift received, on average, 26 percent higher tips from male diners than when they didn't wear make-up.[29] Dress can influence perceptions of attractiveness, too. In the previous chapter we described how, all other things being equal, a competitor assigned the dominant colour red in a combative sporting contest will win more often than one assigned blue. But red clothes can also boost perceptions of attractiveness, particularly among women. Studies have shown that female hitchhikers get more rides if they are wearing a red-coloured top, and that diners will give bigger tips to female food servers who wear red T-shirts and apply red lipstick.[30] In each case, the underlying messages 'I need a ride' and 'Gratuities are appreciated' remain the same. What changes is the appearance of the messenger.*

134

If wearing red enhances female attractiveness, might women do so deliberately? Studies suggest this can certainly be the case. But it would also appear that it may often be an unconscious act. Researchers at the University of British Columbia who bluntly asked women, 'How many days since the onset of your last period?' found that those in the fertile phase of their menstrual cycle (when the chance of conception and the biological motivation to have sex is at its highest) were much more likely to be wearing red clothing, suggesting an unconscious link in their minds between this particular colour choice and their reproductive potential.[31] The power of red was also demonstrated by researchers who, having invited women to take part in an experiment at a local university, sent them a confirmatory email that included a photograph of the male research assistant conducting the study, who was deemed to be either attractive or unattractive. On arrival at the university laboratory, the women were informed that owing to unforeseen circumstances, the research assistant was no longer available and that a different experimenter would be taking over. In fact the experiment had already been completed and the results were in. Women expecting to meet the handsome assistant were three times more likely to be wearing an item of red clothing.[32] They knew that red clothing boosted their attractiveness and chose their attire accordingly.

Knowledge that an attractive individual is also likely to be an influential one might tempt some organisations to make a deliberate practice of recruiting good-looking staff. It's certainly the case that they can be effective and productive – especially when they work in departments such as sales, PR and business development, where delivering messages is a key part of the job. It's been demonstrated,

* The wearing of red had no effect on female drivers and diners. Only males were more generous to the ladies in red.

for example, that an eye-catching salesperson is more likely than a plainer one to successfully sell prescription drugs to a physician – even though it is clearly the case that the only criteria that should apply here are efficacy and price, and that highly qualified practitioners must be fully aware of the fact. Yet data from a research study showed that when physicians' written prescriptions were collected and scrutinised, a clear correlation could be shown to exist between the attractiveness of the salesperson selling the drug and the quantity of that drug subsequently prescribed.[33] That said, the eye-catching effect of the striking salesperson may be only a fleeting one. Over time, as the number of interactions increases and the salesperson–physician relationship develops, the glow-of-attractiveness halo subsides. Rather, as with the classic spy honey-trap, the attractive messenger may be particularly effective in the recruitment of new customers. That doesn't mean, however, that they will be able to retain them.

But there are other ways organisations can increase their representatives' attractiveness without engaging in discriminatory hiring practices. Often all that is needed is a smile – for the simple reason that smiling makes people appear more attractive. It is a philosophy that US-based supermarket chain Safeway warmly embraced through their Superior Service policy. The programme advocated that staff make eye contact with customers, where possible greet them by name, accompany customers struggling to locate certain products to the aisles where they were stored and, above all, smile warmly. To ensure compliance, armies of 'mystery shoppers' were recruited to score staff. High performance was handsomely rewarded. Poor performers would be sent to what Safeway workers referred to as 'Smile School'. For the most part the programme was well received. For most customers, a company that places superior service front and centre of its retail strategy is one to be applauded and rewarded with increased loyalty. That said, Safeway's initiative also had some unintended consequences. The *Washington Post* reported how some shoppers read too much into the friendliness of smiley service staff, resulting in many female staff members complaining that male customers would misinterpret smiles for come-ons. Undeterred, Safeway persevered with the programme, ultimately prompting five female employees to file discrimination charges against the company. 'We do not tolerate harassment of our employees,' a Safeway spokeswoman said. 'Unfortunately, customers are people, and they may get out of line on occasion.'[34]

Behaviour that enhances perceived attractiveness may lead to positive evaluation and preferential treatment. But as employees at Safeway found out, attractiveness can be a curse, too. In some instances, it can result in unwanted attention and objectification or, worse, harassment and hostility. Particularly for women. And not just from men.

The downsides of attractiveness

Once, during a radio interview, country singer Dolly Parton told a story about a little girl, probably only eight years old, who was in the audience at one of her concerts in the late Sixties. Parton described the girl as having beautiful red hair, beautiful skin and beautiful green eyes. Looking up at Parton, the little girl asked for an autograph, so Parton asked her name.

'Jolene,' came the reply.

'That is pretty,' Parton said. 'I'm going to write a song about that.'[35]

Parton did write her song. But it turned out not to be about the young girl, but about another redhead, who worked in the bank close to where Dolly Parton lived. 'She got this terrible crush on my husband,' Parton explained. 'And he just loved going to the bank because she paid him so much attention. It was kinda like a running joke between us ... I was saying "Hell, you're spending a lot of time at the bank. I don't believe we've even got that kind of money."

'She had everything I didn't,' Parton went on. 'Like legs ... she was about six feet tall. And had all that stuff that some little short, sawed-off honky like me don't have. So no matter how beautiful a woman you might be ... you're always threatened by other women, period.'

In fewer than 200 words, Dolly Parton's song 'Jolene' poignantly portrays a commonly known effect that social scientists have dedicated volumes to explaining: the hostility that female attractiveness can give rise to, particularly in other women.[36] A Canadian study of more than 2,000 adolescents found that while, for men, attractiveness serves as a protective factor that makes them *less* likely to be victimised by other males, for women the opposite is true: the attractive woman is *more* likely to be bullied by other women.[37] Similarly, psychologist Frank McAndrew has written extensively on how one woman's beauty can bring out the beast in others.[38] They quickly spot how easily men are drawn to her, and so they may well gang up to take steps to undermine her reputation, seeking to reduce her status and make her appear less desirable through gossip and unsubstantiated stories. If they're successful, her ability to establish her own social networks and friendship circles will be undermined and she could well end up in a position of social powerlessness. If verbal attacks don't succeed in bringing about her social exclusion, physical intimidation and assault may occur.*

The case of Samantha Brick, a freelance journalist, who in 2012 gained notoriety for penning an article in a UK national newspaper,

---

* This disturbing video demonstrates, all too graphically, how some groups are willing to serve up retribution for the 'sin' of simply being born pretty: http://www.dailymail.co.uk/video/news/video-1101302/School-bullies-force-girl-drink-puddle-water-pretty.html
Warning: this link contains footage that may be upsetting to some readers.

the *Daily Mail*, in which she lamented the downsides of being attractive, powerfully demonstrates this tendency to pack bully.[39] She had written that although there were upsides to being attractive – free champagne on flights; handsome strangers picking up her bar tab or offering to pay for her train ticket or cab – there were frequent downsides, too: not so much unwanted attention from members of the opposite sex pestering her for her number and a date, but rather from other women. She reported occasions when other women slammed doors in her face, or when female bosses made her professional life miserable, forcing her to leave, or promoting more average-looking colleagues over her. She also complained that despite having numerous female friends, she had never been asked to be a bridesmaid. Whether or not her suspicions and complaints were justified is not germane here. What is, though, is the level of hostility that her article aroused. Thousands of readers wrote in to attack her, many of them vitriolically. Tellingly, the negative reactions were disproportionately posted by women. Perhaps Brick had inadvertently proved her point.

The notion of attractiveness, then, comes with a freight of issues for women. They are more likely than men to be judged by their looks. Those deemed to be attractive can be treated by other women in a hostile way; those deemed unattractive are at risk of losing social value in the eyes of others and therefore of suffering from reduced status. When it comes to issues of weight, for example, while it is true that overweight men are penalised in the labour market (on such job-related outcomes as hiring recommendations, qualification ratings, disciplinary decisions, salary and placement decisions), overweight women are even more likely to struggle professionally.[*40]

---

* Paradoxically, some studies have found that marginally overweight men are actually more positively evaluated in certain domains. See Judge, T. A. & Cable, D. M. (2011), 'When it comes to pay, do the thin win? The effect of weight on pay for men and women', *Journal of Applied Psychology*, 96(1), 95–112.

For men, attractiveness is a plus. For women, it is both a plus and a minus. The inconvenient truth is that when it comes to the rules of attraction, gender still matters.[41]

Beyond the general attractiveness features of averageness, youthfulness and symmetry, what men and women find attractive clearly differs. So, too, does the relative importance placed on attractiveness by the genders. Men on the Forbes Rich List are more likely to date young models, while high-status and physically attractive women are more likely to seek socio-economic position and competence in their male companions.[42] Marilyn Monroe, for example, probably could have had her choice of attractive hunks, but instead fell for the playwright Arthur Miller and was even rumoured to have placed Albert Einstein on her list of potential suitors. The media, patriarchal forces and other social factors also have a role to play. Current beauty ideals stipulate that women, in particular, must adhere to thinness norms to avoid losing social value in the eyes of others. In other eras, different rules applied. The Victorians liked full-figured women. In the 1920s, the gamine was all the rage.

The greater emphasis that society places on female beauty than on male good looks has much to do with evolutionary factors. Males have lower levels of obligatory parental investment than females.[43] The woman carries the fetus, gives birth and then possibly breastfeeds her baby, too. She therefore looks for features in a mate which suggest that he will be willing and able to provide support. The man, meanwhile, may never even know he has a child or may opt to vanish upon hearing the news, so that he can avoid parental responsibilities. As a rule, he tends to be endowed with a greater sexual appetite and places a greater weight on the physical indicators of fertility when considering potential mates.[44] To the male seeking a romantic partner, attractiveness and all that it implies matter a great deal. To the female, attractiveness matters a little less so and other factors carry more weight.

140

From the hard messenger to the soft messenger

In the 1920s and 1930s Western Union faced a crisis. The rapid installation of telephone lines across the US was having a devastating effect on the revenues it had traditionally derived from telegram services. And the rise of radio and television – and therefore of radio and television advertising – threatened the company's previously profitable and popular direct marketing services, which involved employing messenger boys to deliver flyers and samples door-to-door, promoting all manner of products from soap to breakfast cereals. Action urgently needed to be taken.

Among the most successful initiatives that Western Union adopted, as it attempted to shore up its position, was one that leveraged several of the hard-messenger effects we have so far explored. It was known as 'Dramatized Delivery' and it took advertising to a whole new level.[45] The messenger boys who offered the Dramatized Delivery service were frequently described as 'handsome types'. They had all been coached to smile radiantly when handing over samples and brochures to the housewives whom the product manufacturers were targeting. They wore prestigious-looking uniforms – smart double-breasted suits adorned with brass buttons; starched shirts; official-looking caps. They exuded prestige and competence. Their service was suitably pricy, too. If you used Western Union's Dramatized Delivery service you didn't just send a signal about your company's product; you sent a signal about the company itself. You were saying, in effect, 'We have status.'

How successful was Western Union's Dramatized Delivery messenger service? Successful enough for the US Trade Association of Advertising, which represented more than 2,000 firms, to lobby the US Senate to investigate the unfair and dominant position Western Union had attained through their new service. Why was it so successful? Every advertising company was essentially sending the same

141

messages to prospective customers – 'Try this sample', 'Look at our brochure', 'Buy our product'. But only Western Union was considering the messenger, too. By employing hard-messenger effects, such as socio-economic position, competence and attractiveness, they were winning the day.

But the story doesn't end there.

Increasingly the recipients of Western Union's Dramatized Delivery service turned to the same messenger boys to deliver messages of their own. Not to sell samples or deliver brochures. But to share news amongst their friends and neighbours; to deliver invitations to christenings, bar mitzvahs and dinner parties; to relay cakes, flowers and smiles. And this added refinement in its turn afforded Western Union a further advantage that made them even more successful. They had been focusing on what we have called 'hard' messenger effects. Now they were making use of a 'soft' messenger effect, which we will explore in Part Two of this book.

Connectedness.

PART TWO

Soft Messengers

A Murderous Connection

By MOST ACCOUNTS, it took several attempts to kill Grigori Rasputin. The first, involving a cake laced with poison, had little effect. Perhaps it didn't contain enough cyanide. The next, three generously filled glasses of wine, also spiked with poison, similarly failed. So the conspirators sent out for a pistol, and a short time later a gunman returned and shot Rasputin in the chest and the head. For good measure they then wrapped up his body, weighted it and dumped it in a nearby river.[1]

Given the lengths his assassins went to, in order to dispatch him, it should come as no surprise that Rasputin was not a popular man. Despite winning favour with Tsar Nicholas II and his wife Alexandra, who adored him for his seemingly god-like ability to control their son's haemophilia, the 'Mad Monk of Russia' was one of the least likeable people in history. Rasputin was reputed to have been a braggart, a sexual deviant and an arch manipulator, who exercised an entirely malign influence over the royal family and thus over Russia's politics. To most, his brutal death was richly deserved.

No surprise, then, that subsequent generations have tended to take a rather uncharitable view of the 'Mad Monk'. But that's not to say everyone has. When one group of people, born some forty years after his death, were brought together to review his life, most of them, predictably, judged him harshly. There were others, however, who believed him to be at least a little less unlikeable. Even though they had been presented with precisely the same information about Rasputin and his numerous malfeasances as their more critical peers, they felt a sense of connectedness with him – although none of them would have been able to articulate exactly what form that connectedness took.

It was, as it happened, a quite straightforward one. They all shared the same birthday.

Each of us possesses an inbuilt 'need to belong' and a fundamental desire to form connections with others.[2] A shared interest, a common point of view or a hard-to-pinpoint warm feeling towards someone is often sufficient to bring people together. And when we sense that connection – when we feel that we are linked in some way to someone else – we tend to listen more and assign greater importance to what they have to say than if no bond existed. In other words, it's not so much the power of their message that holds sway as their power as a messenger.

This is not a feature of a specific culture or personality type, but a universal phenomenon. All humans are motivated to form social connections with others: to care for each other; to share resources; to cooperate. And when we experience a positive social connection we are rewarded with a hit of happiness. We experience greater feelings of control, improved self-esteem and elevated well-being. Data from the World Values Survey suggests that possession of strong social relationships – or *social capital* – is the best predictor of human happiness, trumping wealth, income and material possessions.[3] Those who fail to achieve this most basic of human needs pay a heavy price. They experience loneliness, an aversive emotion associated with a variety of physical and mental-health problems, including anxiety, depression, low self-esteem, obesity, anger and, sometimes, rebellion.[4] Longitudinal studies of pre-school children demonstrate that social exclusion is predictive of increased aggression and reduced cooperation in children as young as six. Other studies have revealed that adolescents who feel alienated will often respond more aggressively to negative feedback than their better-'connected' schoolmates.

In the workplace, those told that a peer doesn't want to work with them will often react in an aggressive and antagonistic way.[5] In its most drastic form, such alienation can lead to extreme acts of violence: almost every school shooting in the US has been perpetrated by a socially excluded individual.[6]

The impulse to form social connections, then, is a powerful one. Almost all of us want to avoid the social and emotional consequences of isolation. In the same way that a hungry person seeks out food, isolated individuals seek ways to satisfy their emotional appetite by looking to form social bonds with others. So fundamental is the motivation to seek connections that even the seemingly trivial traits or interests that we share with others, like a shared interest or a shared birthday, can be sufficient to create meaningful ties. Hence the reason why those assessing the life of Rasputin – who happened to be students at Arizona State University – reacted according to whether or not they had anything in common with him.

The study, conducted by Robert Cialdini and John Finch, involved asking volunteers to review a three-page document charting Rasputin's colourful history, from his birth to a Siberian peasant family to his religious conversion, and his time at Tsar Nicholas II's court to his ultimate assassination – and then to rate his character on a variety of scales. In each case the account provided was balanced and factually accurate. Accurate, that is, except for the one small detail about Rasputin's birthday, a day that some students were randomly misled to think they shared with him. To be clear, those who came to learn of this connection didn't suddenly elevate Rasputin to hero status. They still rated him in largely negative terms. But their view was much less critical than that expressed by their fellow students who felt no bond at all with the man. As Cialdini noted, 'it seems there is a tendency to boost our evaluations of just about anything, or anyone, that we see ourselves in some way connected with'.[7]

What Cialdini and Finch's experiment demonstrates is how tribal we are, and how susceptible we can be to the merest suggestion that a messenger is on our side and could potentially make for a cooperative partner. If a matter as trivial as a common birth date can cause people to rate a nasty character like Rasputin slightly less negatively, then imagine how the views of others can be transformed by less inconsequential bonds and connections.

It's something we see played out in everyday life all the time. Recruiters – all other things being equal – lean spontaneously towards candidates who possess similar characteristics to themselves. Customers say yes more often to those salespeople who highlight a shared experience. More generally, we gravitate towards those of a similar age, education, background, race, religion, level of intelligence and socio-economic status to our own.[8] Analyses of online social networks show that people are more inclined to 'like' and reshare conspiracy theories and 'fake news' if they are posted by a friend. Particularly those who share their worldview.[9] This squares with research that one of us conducted with Eloise Copland, Eleanor Loh, Tali Sharot and Cass Sunstein, which showed that people were much more likely to consult and listen to a messenger who shared their political views when answering questions about a random, non-political topic, even when another messenger who happened to hold dissimilar political views was much more knowledgeable about the task at hand.[10] Our findings go some way to explaining why 'fake news' and conspiracy theories are so often believed, despite a wealth of evidence to the contrary being readily available. It's not only the message that's viewed contrarily, but also the messenger. It seems some people can be persuaded to believe pretty much anything, when a message is propagated by a similar person or likeable news source.

When connectedness is stressed, the results can be extraordinary. 'This Girl Can' – a campaign by Sport England, designed to get more women engaging in recreational sporting activity – is a good example. Normally one would expect such a campaign to feature inspirational elite sportswomen and stars. But in this case, videos and posters were produced that showcased women of all shapes, sizes and ability. Since the campaign was not run in laboratory conditions, it would be risky to argue that showing sports people the British public could relate to had a causal effect on subsequent take-up, but the numbers are nevertheless suggestive: according to Sport England, some 2.8 million women in the UK reported having done some, or more, activity as a result of the campaign.[11]

The decision to choose a connected messenger, rather than one with status, yielded similarly impressive results for a Zimbabwean sexual-health programme. Just as one would expect a sports star to front a sports agenda, so one might naturally assume white-coated doctors and healthcare professionals to be the best messengers to deliver messages designed to ensure safe sex through the use of condoms. But the programme's strategists chose a different route. They trained women from low-income areas who braided hair for a living to deliver messages about the benefits of using condoms, how to introduce them into a relationship and where to obtain them. The message was precisely the same as one that a trained doctor or nurse would deliver. What was different was the messenger – a familiar person offering advice in a friendly, supportive and safe environment.[12]

It was a clever call. Receiving messages from a healthcare professional, regardless of their competence and expertise, can be embarrassing. Listening to a friendly messenger one has grown to know and trust over time neatly dodges a potential barrier – in this case leaving women feeling freer to talk about their personal issues. A medical expert would, of course, have had status with these women. But the message was the more powerful for coming from people with whom they had a reassuring and pre-existing bond.

The 'Get Braids Not Aids' programme also highlights another notable feature of connectedness: namely, that it does not stem solely from shared characteristics such as birthdays, demographics or attitudes. Connectedness usually develops over time as people become familiar with each other, and sometimes results in the formation of powerful, lasting bonds. Such connections can provide a psychological and physical comfort that other messengers, including the elite, simply cannot.

In Part One we described how the perceived status of a messenger – achieved through signals of Socio-Economic Position, Competence, Dominance and Attractiveness – can alter a listener's response to their message, quite often regardless of its merits. In Part Two we show that there is another route to influence: one that involves stressing connectedness rather than superiority. In contrast to society's *hard* messengers, who seek to win influence by getting ahead of others, *soft* messengers achieve influence by getting along with their fellow humans. They do this via four traits: Warmth, Vulnerability, Trustworthiness and Charisma.

5

WARMTH

Likeable Leaders, Humble Servants and When
Cooperation Defeats Conflict

On Tuesday 19 November 1985 a state court jury in Houston, Texas, returned a verdict that stunned the legal and business world and sent a major oil company to the brink of bankruptcy. Finding in favour of the plaintiff, the Pennzoil Corporation, twelve ordinary citizens ordered that Texaco Oil pay damages amounting to more than $10.5 billion. At the time it was the single largest civil penalty in legal history.[1]

The case stemmed from the ambition of Hugh Liedtke, chairman of Pennzoil, to turn his organisation into a larger industry player. At first it seemed that he lacked the oil reserves needed to compete with the so-called big boys. But then, in early 1984, a potential solution emerged. Rumours had been circulating about a series of meetings taking place between Wall Street investment bankers and one of Pennzoil's competitors, Getty Oil, and also about internal squabbling at Getty, whose executives were reportedly becoming increasingly frustrated at the company's stubbornly low stock price. Liedtke spotted an opportunity. Getty Oil had large reserves. Pennzoil wanted to grow. He therefore reached out to Getty Oil chairman, Gordon Getty, to discuss a potential merger.

The numerous meetings that followed over the next few months were productive, and culminated in Getty and Liedtke agreeing a deal that would have seen Pennzoil purchase Getty Oil. As word of the planned merger spread across the industry, however, rival company Texaco sought to counter the Pennzoil bid with one of their own. Getty Oil, perhaps flattered by this sudden show of interest by one of the industry's dominant players, engaged with Texaco and ultimately agreed to go with their bid. Liedtke was incensed. Claiming that Texaco had illegally encroached on his prior deal, he filed a lawsuit against them. In early 1985 the two sides met in court.

The trial – which lasted five and a half months – centred on how legally binding the initial agreement between Hugh Liedtke and Gordon Getty actually was. Dozens of witnesses were called to give their version of events. Legal scholars were asked to deliver their views on the legal status of a handshake, whether the signature on the informal agreement was legally binding, and how much Texaco knew about Getty's original arrangements with Penzoil. Lawyers pored over 15,000 pages of pre-trial depositions. The trial itself generated another 24,000 pages of transcripts. Such was the extent of the evidence, and the range of interpretations that could be put upon it, that many in the legal profession were dubious about how such a complex case would be settled. So it came as a surprise to everyone when the jury returned a verdict that came down so strongly and decisively against Texaco.

What was it that convinced a group of twelve ordinary civilians, none of whom were likely to have had any experience or formal training in either the legal profession or the oil industry, to decide so firmly against Texaco and punish them so severely? Which of the tens of thousands of pages of information and testimony that they were presented with proved conclusive? Whose expert testimony was it that convinced them that Texaco was so clearly in the wrong? These were the questions that exercised everyone's minds at the time

– and understandably so. It was such an extraordinarily complicated case, fought over such a long period, that people were naturally left asking which particular pieces of evidence had swayed the jury's opinion.

But perhaps they were looking at things the wrong way. Rather than trying to work out which key facts and arguments swayed the jury, they should, arguably, have been considering the general impact of such a mass of highly complex detail. Consider the thousands of pages of testimony generated, the hundreds of technical terms used, and the dozens of petty point-scoring battles fought between rival lawyers during those five and a half months. To twelve members of the public, it must all have seemed overwhelming. So overwhelming, in fact, that much of it simply became irrelevant. They should have been weighing arcane arguments and abstruse points of law. Instead they started focusing on the people presenting them. The messages became blurred. It was the messengers who came to count for most.[2]

In this case, it wasn't the high-status messenger they listened to. Had that been so, they probably would have decided in favour of Texaco. It was the richer company. It was better known, too. While Pennzoil was a regional player, Texaco's name and logo were displayed on forecourts across the country. In terms of socio-economic position, Texaco beat Pennzoil without raising a sweat. Texaco was also more experienced. It had been in the oil business longer than Pennzoil. It employed lots of experts who, during the trial, were able to call on yet more experts. And it was dominant. After all, it had managed to persuade Getty Oil to ditch Pennzoil in its favour. 'No one beats us,' its executives must have thought as they swooped in, all guns blazing. 'We should be the ones benefiting from this attractive proposition.'

But sometimes the hard messenger loses, despite their powerful status, and the soft messenger prevails. This is what seems to have happened here. Shortly after the trial, James Shannon, a jury member in the case, was asked by a local reporter why the jury had acted in the way it had. Shannon recalled that he and his fellow jurors thought Texaco's principal attorney had atrocious manners. He also remembered a number of occasions on which Texaco witnesses didn't bother to look at the jury. And he mentioned that he found a top Texaco corporation vice-president to be pompous. The Pennzoil legal team, by contrast, were far more likeable, in his view. This highly technical and complex case turned, it would seem, not on who was right, but on who seemed the warmest and most human.

Be warm and likeable

Warmth is an important messenger trait because it signals care and kindness. Warm messengers do not seek to demonstrate high status but, rather, benevolence. They avoid displays that could be interpreted as hostile and are careful to select words that won't hurt others' feelings. Such is their desire to avoid conflict, or evoke a sense of guilt, that they may well let others get their own way.* They show respect, friendliness and an interest in others and, in doing so, bestow importance onto their listeners rather than themselves.[3]

Being in the company of a warm person is a rewarding experience. Little surprise, then, that they make for particularly effective messengers. 'Be warm and likeable' is essentially the central message in Dale Carnegie's 1936 classic *How to Win Friends and Influence People*. 'Don't criticize, condemn, or complain,' Carnegie advises. 'Give honest and sincere appreciation ... Become genuinely interested in other people.'[4] John Gottman, a clinical psychologist best known for his uncanny ability to predict accurately the likelihood of

---

* Guilt is a fundamentally social emotion; it stops people harming others and motivates them to repair relationships if they do.

couples divorcing, finds that the four most reliable predictors that a marriage will fail are signs of criticism, defensiveness, stonewalling and contempt.[5] Each of these behaviours acts as a kind of socio-emotional nemesis to the superpower of warmth.

Being able to detect warmth is so integral to social functioning that even infants as young as six months exhibit a disposition to prefer the prosocial messenger over the antisocial or neutral one.[6] Once they can move their limbs, they will reach out to and engage more with puppets they have seen 'help' another puppet open a box, climb a hill or retrieve a dropped ball than ones that have hindered progress or have not helped at all. The ability to distinguish the good guys from the bad confers great benefits – reduced conflict, increased cooperation – so we have evolved to interact preferentially with, and favour, those who demonstrate affiliative intent. The factors that swung a Texan jury to favour Pennzoil over Texaco are likely hard-wired from birth.

Adults embed warmth into everyday language to help smooth social interactions. One only has to compare the way people speak to computers with the way they talk to other humans to appreciate how engrained this trait is. No one closes off an interaction with Siri, Alexa or Cortana with 'You take care now!' But we will almost invariably use polite words and phrases in everyday conversation with other humans, to maintain civility and signal our likeability. That's why new conversations usually begin with 'How are you?' If we don't start in that way, others will assume that either we have something more urgent to say or that we're being rude. And if the former turns out not to be the case, they will assume the latter.[7]

It's not just opening remarks that signal warmth. The way we 'sugar-coat' requests does so, too. Whether we're seeking directions from a stranger, interrupting a conversation between colleagues to find out something quickly or simply getting a family member to do something, we soften our demands into questions to avoid appearing unnecessarily needy, bossy or demanding. Even in situations where compliance to a request can generally be assumed – such as asking a dinner companion to pass the salt – we are careful to confer status on that person by acknowledging that they are not subservient to us. We don't say, 'Pass the salt', but 'Could you pass the salt?' Such *conversational postulates* allow the person we're asking a façade of autonomy, despite the fact that they're very unlikely to refuse. Although the prevalence of such niceties varies around the globe – Japan is highly sensitive to them, Israel less so – they exist in languages that range from Tzeltal (a Mayan language spoken in Mexico) to Tamil (spoken in South India and Sri Lanka). In every culture that uses them, they allow messengers to perform a sometimes-tricky social man-oeuvre: signalling that they care about someone, yet still wish to impose upon them. They achieve the latter by ensuring that the messenger doesn't appear heavy-handed or solely interested in their own immediate instrumental value.[8]

Such cues are given and observed in the course of daily interactions, but our response to the warmth that we pick up from others is actually far more immediate. In a recent study, neuroscientists and sociologists at Columbia University used an fMRI scanner to scan the brains of students at the beginning of a nine-week intensive summer course as they looked at photographs of other course attendees. Towards the end of the nine weeks, after the group had broken up into small cliques and tight friendships, everyone's brains were scanned again. What the researchers found was that neural activity measured at the very beginning of the course, as each participant examined photos of the other students, was an excellent predictor of who that individual would end up liking and who they wouldn't get on with.[9] It was as though their brains had pre-determined who they would, and would not, ultimately feel close to, before they even had a chance to get to know the other people taking the course. This is an intriguing finding. But the truly mind-blowing discovery was that those running the experiment could also predict at the outset whether Bill would turn out to like Jim, by looking at *Jim's* brain activity while he viewed a picture of Bill. That's right: it is possible to predict whether you will like a stranger in nine weeks' time by measuring how that person's brain responds when the two of you first meet. We make friends with people based not just on our first impressions of how likeable they are, but also on how much they like us. If a course attendee had a gut liking for someone and detected immediate reciprocal warmth, the two ended up becoming good friends during the nine-week programme.

Displays of warmth – and, by the same token, the absence of warmth – can have a transformative effect. Humans by no means have a monopoly in this regard. Studies in rats show that rat pups that receive little grooming and licking from their mothers (yes, that's licking, not liking) react far more negatively to stressful situations in adulthood than those whose mothers behave warmly towards them.[10] Given that a lack of parental affection has a similar effect on humans, it is hardly surprising that people are drawn to those who provide the warmth and affirmation we so badly need for a mentally healthy life.[11]

This basic human requirement was well recognised by the influential psychologist Carl Rogers, who therefore adopted an approach to therapy that placed warmth at its core. In contrast to other more objective and diagnostic schools of thought, Rogers suggested that therapists who show their patients open-hearted understanding and sympathy are more effective than those who seek to help through, say, reaching into someone's subconscious to analyse feelings of stress or anxiety. Remarkably, he found that even patients suffering from schizophrenia – a condition generally thought to have genetic and biological causes – could experience improved treatment outcomes after receiving his warm, 'client-centred' therapy.[12]

Rogers believed such unconditional positive regard and under-standing from others are fundamental building blocks in the development of a healthy self-identity, and that providing them is the job of the client-centred therapist. Most children, he argued, receive this kind of affection from parents and their extended family when growing up, and are therefore likely to build resil-ience and be at ease with themselves in adulthood. But those who have lacked this most basic of human requirements may need to seek it out from an alternative source later in life. The warm char-acter and sympathetic ear of the client-centred therapist neatly fills the gap.

In fact many professionals consider the building and maintaining of a relationship with patients to be the first and most crucial step in their treatment, regardless of the therapeutic approach being adopted. Not just that, but the evidence suggests that the benefits that accrue extend to the professionals, too – not just in terms of improved patient outcomes, but in how the patient perceives the person helping them. In extreme medical cases, such a bond has even been shown to reduce the risk of litigation. In one study, people were asked to listen to ten-second clips from audio recordings of doctors speaking to their patients, assess how warm or hostile they thought each medic to be, and judge whether they spotted any traces of anxiety and apprehension in their voices. When their rankings were then compared with the professional records of the doctors whose voices they had listened to, a strong correlation between the more dominant voices and cases of malpractice emerged. Compared to an equally competent group of doctors who used a warmer tone of voice, dominant-sounding medics were more than twice as likely to be sued by their patients.[13]

It could, of course, be argued that one should not be surprised to find that sympathetic messengers are better received than their tougher colleagues in a profession, such as medicine, that principally involves caring for others. But evidence suggests that a sympathetic approach works even in situations where, traditionally, a more hard-nosed style has been favoured. Investigative interrogations are a case in point. Accusatorial approaches taken by police and law-enforcement interrogators have long been considered essential – the standard view being that repeated accusations of guilt, accompanied by claims of mounting evidence against the accused, are highly effective techniques when it comes to obtaining a speedy confession and conviction. But such approaches are hardly optimal. A careful examination of 181 interrogations that included those of al-Qaeda-inspired suspects, paramilitary activists and right-wing terrorists found that interviewees who experienced respect, dignity and integrity from their interviewers were much less likely to employ what are known as counter-interrogation tactics (CITs), such as retraction and – the most common CIT tactic of all – silence.[14] Even in the most difficult and emotionally charged of contexts, interrogators who signal their warmth via a gentle tone, gestures of friendliness, disarming humour and cooperative non-verbal body language gain a desirable advantage.

Warmth can provide a healthy boost to financial returns, too. Unlike Greg Lippmann, the self-aggrandising head subprime mortgage trader at Deutsche Bank, whom we met in the Introduction, most salespeople tend not to self-promote and boast to clients about how much money they have earned, to demonstrate their superiority. Their strategy is more subtle and, consequently, smarter. They express warmth rather than grandiosity, and so form a personal connection with clients that is more than its own reward. Sometimes nothing more than a simple compliment is required. Waiters receive bigger tips after approving of diners' choices; so too do hairstylists who compliment their customers by saying, 'Any hairstyle would look good on you'. And warmth can transform the workplace, too. One study found that while roughly 50 percent of employees were willing to assist a colleague at work who asked for help, 79 percent did so if the person making the request complimented them first.[15]

Leaders, who are often thought to be 'harder' messengers, can also benefit from adopting the warmer persona of a soft messenger. Indeed, an analysis of more than two decades of American National Election Studies data by political scientists Lasse Laustsen and Alexander Bor found warmth to be a more important characteristic than competence, when voters came to judge political leaders.[16] It's an insight that arguably goes some way to explain a key difficulty faced by Hillary Clinton in the 2016 US presidential candidate debates. Widely viewed as the most competent and experienced candidate in recent history, Clinton acknowledged that she was rarely considered warm. In April 2018 *New York Times* journalist Amy Chozick published a book claiming that, during debate preparations, Clinton would even go so far as to unleash a 'fuck-laced fusillade' about Donald Trump on aides, so that she might 'keep it all together onstage' and so avoid fuelling the already-negative point of view that many of the electorate held of her.[17] In the event, of course, this didn't pay off. Given that warmth is often perceived as a particularly female virtue, the lack of it in both candidates perhaps counted more against Hillary Clinton than it did against Donald Trump – though it's important to emphasise that we're speculating here. The fact that warmth and likeability, although valued across the political spectrum, seem to be especially cherished by liberals would hardly have helped Clinton, either.[18]

Captains of industry can similarly gain from being perceived as warm. One such is Craig Jelinek, who has been the CEO of Costco since 2012 (having joined in 1984). He is considered likeable, both by those who work in his organisation and by customers and investors. In fact in 2017 he was rated the most likeable CEO of a US quoted company. Once, when speaking to a group of business students at Seattle University, Jelinek cited a number of factors that he believed were instrumental to leadership success: patience; helping people to grow and succeed; being connected to employees; and 'putting on my pants one leg at a time like everyone else'.[19] The fact that he selected qualities more associated with humanity and modesty than with ruthless success helps to explain why so many believe that these have been integral to Jelinek's own achievements, and those of Costco, in a market prone to constant disruption by new players and innovations.

Jelinek's warmth provides a notable contrast to the busy boss who answers emails or talks on the phone during meetings, and who spurns interactions with employees in order to attend to 'more important matters'. Actions like these make it less, rather than more, likely that such bosses will preside over a productive workforce. A recent study found that employees of managers easily distracted by their smartphones – a concept known as 'phubbing' (phone-snubbing) – not only feel unappreciated, but also feel less confident in their own abilities, with the result that their performance suffers.[20] Conversely, according to data from sixty-five US and Belgium-based organisations, CEOs who genuinely attend to their employees end up with a workforce that feels more valued, with a more effective top management team and with enhanced financial performance.[21] If a CEO believes they lack the charismatic skills of the prototypical successful leader, they are far better advised to adopt a warm manner than a forced and inauthentic visionary approach to which they are not suited.

Turning up the warmth

So how exactly do warm leaders connect with followers, CEOs with their employees, salespeople with their clients, interrogators with their interviewees, and therapists with their clients? The answer is that various factors seem to be involved, the first and foremost of which is positivity. In one Australian study, participants were shown videos of supervisors (in fact played by actors) conducting performance appraisals with their staff. Some were encouraging – 'I'm pleased to hear that you're reaching your performance goals.' Others were less so – 'It is disappointing that you've not been reaching your performance goals.' When 'supervisors' delivered the message with a positive and warm demeanour, observers rated them as more effective leaders, regardless of whether the feedback itself was positive or negative.[22] Such is the appeal of a positive messenger that they can help soften bad news, just as a negative messenger can make good news seem less welcome. Obviously there are limits to this – delivering bad news with a smile is not a good idea – but provided there is emotional congruence that preserves a bond of trust (see Chapter 7), the good-natured messenger is the least likely to be shot.

In work situations, they are also more likely to be judged favourably by supervisors and co-workers. Interviewees who display positivity stand a better chance of being shortlisted for a job, especially if they smile during the interview. Employees who maintain a consistent air of positivity are likely to experience increased levels of cooperation from their colleagues, boosting their success, career trajectory and, ultimately, their earnings.[23]

Another way to signal warmth is through social reward. In *The Taming of the Shrew* Shakespeare suggested that a 'mad and headstrong humour' could be killed with kindness – in other words (and in contemporary parlance), that social rewards can be more powerful than threatened sanctions, when it comes to countering bad behaviour. Modern-day psychologists would call this 'rewarding with kindness'. Field research finds that it can have a powerful effect.

In one such study, conducted by Duke University professor Dan Ariely, and subsequently described in his book *Payoff: The Hidden*

Logic That Shapes Our Motivations, employees at a semiconductor factory in Israel were randomly assigned to receive a text message offering them one of three bonuses for their work assembling computer chips.[24] One group was promised 100 Israeli new *shekels* (about £22 / $30). The second was promised pizza. The third was promised appreciation in the form of praise from the boss. A fourth, control group, wasn't promised any reward at all. It should come as no surprise that all the incentives motivated the employees to some degree. At the end of the first day, the groups promised pizza and compliments assembled 6.7 percent and 6.6 percent respectively more semiconductors than the control group. Cash worked, too, although at 4.9 percent not quite as well as pepperoni or praise. But as time went on, those offered the financial incentive actually became *less* productive than the control group (a result that might shock a neoclassical economist). In contrast, those given pizza and praise sustained their productiveness. It seems that financial incentives, while initially boosting productivity, may ultimately reduce internal motivation.* Praise and gifts, by contrast, do not produce this backfiring effect. It wasn't the socially rewarded who experienced a post-carb (*or post-compliment*) slump at the semiconductor factory. It was the financially rewarded, who suffered a post-cash one.

Ariely's conclusions are very much of a piece with other research, such as that conducted by organisational psychologists Adam Grant and Francesca Gino, who have shown how a simple expression of gratitude can increase both liking and performance.[25] When fund-raisers in a call centre were genuinely thanked by a senior manager, the number of calls those fund-raisers made the following week increased by 50 percent. Assuming that the quality and success rate of calls remained constant, such a result represents an easy

---

* Owing to the employee rationalising, 'I'm only working this hard for the extra money, I don't really care about the work itself.'

win – not only for charities and fund-raisers, but for any workplace that offers social and not just monetary rewards to staff. Similarly, we found in a recent study that one of us conducted with US bus operators that drivers given a warm send-off by their supervisors at the start of their shift, such as 'Stay safe out there' and 'We appreciate the hard work you do', experience fewer accidents and avoidable incidents on the roads. It seems that an occasional and well-deserved pat on the back doesn't just boost productivity. In some jobs, it can even save lives.

If positivity and social reward are two elements of the warmth equation, then a third is compassion. Put simply, the messenger able to show compassion for their listener's suffering (or, more commonly, their complaints) increases their own likeability. This basic rule is so strong that it applies even if the messenger in question isn't responsible for causing the bad mood or ill feeling in the first place. A classic instance of this is seen in the preliminary words that President Bill Clinton added to a speech he delivered on 25 August 1995, in front of the Old Faithful Inn in Yellowstone Park, Wyoming, to commemorate the seventy-ninth anniversary of the establishment of the National Park Service. His overall message was a simple but important one: he wanted to restate the government's commitment to preserve America's natural heritage and environment. But it was what he said first that made the most impact. Breaking a golden rule of speeches, he chose to open with an apology: 'Hi, folks. Well, I'm sorry about the rain.' The formal niceties that followed were swiftly forgotten. That opening, though, stayed in people's minds.[26]

One group of researchers was sufficiently intrigued by this unconventional presidential opening to set up a series of experiments to see what happens when a messenger apologises for circumstances they cannot possibly be responsible for. In one, they got an actor to play the part of a phoneless traveller asking passers-by at a train station on a rainy day whether he could borrow their phone. Nine times out of ten, the response was an outright refusal. However, if the man first apologised for the inclement weather before making his request, 'I'm so sorry about the rain! Can I borrow your cellphone?', then nearly half of the people he asked acquiesced.[27] Social science shows what Clinton intuitively seemed to know. The messenger who apologises for something unpleasant, but out of their control, is perceived as compassionate. This makes them seem warmer, which, in turn, moves people to be more receptive to what they have to say.

Given that an unnecessary apology can be so effective, it should come as no surprise that necessary apologies can turn around the most difficult of situations. They are, after all, immensely powerful social tools, critical to the repairing or re-establishing of relationships. Australian prime minister Kevin Rudd provided a formidable demonstration of this when, in the course of a four-minute speech in February 2008, he issued a public apology for the way in which indigenous Australians had been treated years before he himself had achieved public office. He recognised, he said, that he needed to 'apologise for the laws and policies of successive Parliaments and governments that have inflicted profound grief, suffering and loss on these our fellow Australians'. Rudd's predecessor had refused to apologise, arguing that such an admission of public guilt would open the doors to lawsuits and that, in any case, he did not feel responsible for the behaviour of past governments. Perhaps he should have done. In April, two months after Rudd's apology, the public gave him the highest satisfaction rating of any Australian prime minister, a career-peak rating that is yet to be beaten.[28] Many regard him as the most popular and likeable Australian prime minister of all time.

There is one other element to the warmth equation that should be mentioned here: humility. But it's something of a double-edged sword. 'Appreciative humility' – where someone shows an appreciation and celebration of other people, and thereby exhibits an increased desire to affiliate – is generally positive. When Barack Obama was awarded the Nobel Peace Prize in 2009, he did not boast about his accomplishments. Instead he stated publicly that his accomplishments were relatively trivial compared to those of previous winners of the prize. 'Compared to some of the giants of history who've received this prize – Schweitzer and King; Marshall and Mandela – my accomplishments are slight.' Such a lack of egotism and appreciation of others' qualities is associated with increased prosocial tendencies, openness and a willingness to learn from, and accept, criticism. As a result, Obama came across as warm and likeable, and his effectiveness as a messenger was consequently enhanced.[29] 'Self-abasing humility', on the other hand, results in a lack of status in the eyes of others. Whereas appreciative humility is positive and generally comes from a position of strength, self-abasing humility is driven by low self-esteem. Its practitioners don't have a strong sense of belonging. They feel that others don't respect them. They are meek and submissive. And the messages they choose to send are weakened as a result.[30]

The drawbacks of warmth

As with other messenger signals, then, there are nuances to the exercise of warmth. It can be immensely powerful and persuasive. But, wrongly handled, it can cause the messenger to be ignored and exploited.[31] The messenger who appears too cooperative, expresses guilt too easily and shows too great a concern for how another will react could be viewed as a pushover. They leave themselves open to exploitation by an advantage-seeking opponent. Forced, inauthentic warmth, too, tends to be received negatively by others. Audiences see through the façade and judge accordingly.

There's also a danger that if expressions of generosity or empathy seem disproportionate, they will disconcert others rather than win them over. If Ted tells you that he's planning to give away a lot of his money, without explaining why, you may think he's being very generous, but you may also react negatively, worrying that your friend is being more self-sacrificing than he should be. A study that one of us conducted at University College London with Tali Sharot suggests that both responses are equally possible. People in our experiments who voluntarily chose to give away more than their fair share, when deciding how to split a pot of money with another person, often elicited negative emotions in onlookers. The *hyper-altruist* may be regarded as warmer than those who act selfishly, but their actions can also make people feel uncomfortable.[32] And, in extreme circumstances, that can lead to hostility. Vegetarians who justify their choice of diet to meat-eaters often find that their claims to be sensitive to animal welfare and the needs of the planet are thrown back in their faces. Their message is distorted by a perception that by taking the moral high ground, they are automatically putting others on a lower plane. Most of us want to be viewed as good people, so it hurts our self-esteem if it looks as though that is being called into question.[33]

But the biggest threat that warmth poses is to perceptions of status. We touched on this in Chapter 1 where we described how, when a higher- and a lower-status person meet in a waiting room, the higher-status person will tend to be cooler, less keen to engage, more standoffish, while the lower-status person will tend to be friendlier and warmer. Warmth can thus be an indicator of lower status, and this presents a real challenge for a soft messenger, particularly in the early stages of a social interaction. In the waiting-room experiment, the high-status individual chose to look at her phone rather than interact with the other person in the room. His engagement cues – a smile and the occasional glance in her direction to catch her eye – were not enough to win her over. Ultimately he chose to respond in kind, by taking out his own phone and looking at it. He wasn't going to sit around waiting for her to engage, after she had shown a rude lack of interest. Had he persisted with his attempts at ingratiation, however, his status in her eyes would have dropped even lower.[34]

This dichotomy has a physical dimension to it. Dominance, as we have seen, tends to be associated with a face that has a squarer jaw, more prominent eyebrows, a larger nose and a larger facial width-to-height ratio than average. Competent-looking individuals possess facial characteristics associated with maturity. Warmth has a face that is almost the precise opposite. It's more babyish: rounder, with larger eyes, a smaller nose, high forehead and a small chin.[35] This holds true for both men and women, although women are especially likely to possess these features. On the plus side, single-glance impression research has shown that baby-faced individuals are viewed as less hostile and more honest than average. On the minus side, they are assumed to be less competent and in greater need of protection. A baby-faced negotiator might be perceived by others as less competent than a less youthful-looking, harder one. Baby-faced politicians, too, can struggle when seeking to inspire confidence in those whose endorsement they seek. One study in the prestigious journal *Science* reported that a quick glance at candidates' faces was sufficient to predict the winner in roughly seven out of ten US Senate races.[36] Fresh-faced contenders invariably fared worst. Indeed, when images of former US presidents Ronald Reagan, Bill Clinton and John F. Kennedy were morphed to increase 'baby-facedness', ratings of their perceived dominance, strength and cunning decreased significantly.[37]

It isn't always, or necessarily, disadvantageous to have a baby-face. Because it is seen as warmer and less able, it is often given the benefit of the doubt in situations of uncertainty, and the baby-faced individual may even receive greater levels of kindness from others. As they develop into toddlers and then children, the baby-faced receive

Photographs of US presidents Bill Clinton (top), Ronald Reagan (middle) and John F. Kennedy (bottom) morphed to exaggerate facial maturity (right) or babyfacedness (left)

preferential treatment from parents and siblings, are less likely to be made to do the chores and receive fewer parental punishments.[38] A more youthful appearance in later life can even have surprising advantages in the courtroom. Baby-faced plaintiffs on average receive larger monetary payouts in small-claims courts, while more mature-looking defendants are made to pay more in damages.[39] It seems that people find it difficult to believe that baby-faced defendants – with their warm, childlike appearance – could harbour ill-intentions. Consequently, they are less likely to be found guilty and tend to receive lighter sentences, when they are. And while, as British psychologist David Perrett points out, a crime involving unintentional negligence – like forgetting to inform customers of a product recall that results in a hazardous side-effect or damage – may end in a stiffer-than-usual sentence for the baby-faced law-breaker, they are more likely to be acquitted or receive a lighter sentence if they face charges related to crimes of 'nefarious intent', such as actively falsifying records or carrying out a premeditated attack. It would seem that judges find it easier to believe that a baby-faced felon might be an accidental or negligent wrongdoer, rather than a deliberate one.[40]

The cloak of warmth

On balance then, although in some instances generous or cooperative behaviour can endanger status, warmth typically enhances a messenger's reputation and confers advantages in the form of greater connectedness and influence. People typically want to be seen as warm, caring and generous members of society. And when their self-sacrifices, contributions and efforts to help others are socially rewarded, through reputational benefits and heightened interpersonal influence, they are more likely to repeat such actions again in the future.[41] Wikipedia volunteers who create and edit content for free have, for example, been shown to become even more generous with their time if their contributions are publicly acknowledged. In one study, two sociologists randomly assigned 'barnstar' awards to a number of the most dedicated Wikipedia contributors to test how much these inconsequential, non-monetary rewards would further stimulate their willingness to contribute. Over the following ninety days, those who had randomly received the 'barnstars' increased their productivity by 60 percent, relative to those who were not given the award.[42]

Such conspicuous giving – or *competitive altruism*, as it is sometimes known – is not uncommon. The ultra-rich, from Bill and Melinda Gates to Warren Buffett, to George Soros to Mark Zuckerberg and his wife, have set up foundations to distribute vast sums from their own fortunes. Big corporations pursue corporate social-responsibility programmes and initiatives. Many make generous gifts to charity. Obviously self-interest may play a part here – the tax-deductible element of charitable giving can't be ignored. But neither can the reputational benefits that such public and material statements of compassion provide to the donor or volunteer.

Consider the following two acts of public service.

Since its launch, the Toyota Prius has garnered quite a few unfavourable reviews. Commentators have described it as being less powerful, less agile and less prestigious than an average petrol car of comparable size. They have lamented its relatively high price tag, too. They have also claimed that although it is more fuel-efficient and less polluting than the average car, the positive effect one individual can have on climate change and the environment if they switch to a Prius may be limited. Yet in 2007, 300,000 people paid a significant premium to buy the world's first mainstream fuel-efficient hybrid car, and its sales have now exceeded ten million. Why?

On Tuesday 8 November 2016, over 136 million people voted in the United States presidential election – the highest absolute turnout in contemporary American politics.* People knew that their individual vote would have no meaningful impact on the outcome. They could also have opted to do something more rewarding or enjoyable. And yet, cumulatively, they were prepared to spend millions of hours and travel millions of miles to get to a polling station. Why?

Experimental economists are fond of using public-good games, which simulate common real-world situations, to gain a better understanding of such activities as philanthropy, consumer purchases and voting. Those who participate in these games are given a sum of money and are told they can invest it as they like. They could keep it for themselves. Or they could contribute to a cause that benefits the whole group – although, as the Prius and voting examples demonstrate, collective group action may be required for this to have an impact.

If self-interest alone ruled, people wouldn't buy a Toyota Prius and they would stay at home on election day. They would also recycle a lot less – after all, cleaning out jam jars and yoghurt pots rather than simply throwing them in the bin is a chore – and they wouldn't allow environmental or animal-welfare concerns to prompt them into becoming vegetarians and vegans. But then that's not how humans tick. In the first place, of course, we want to see *ourselves* as warm, caring and virtuous; virtuous behaviour is not just about gaining the approval of others. But when reputational benefits are added to the mix, there are plenty of additional reasons to become other-oriented. Friends, family and co-workers who witness these prosocial actions will probably respect us more, praise our selflessness and show a

* But at 56 percent of the electorate, not the highest percentage turnout ever. This was achieved in the 1960 Kennedy v. Nixon race, when 63.5 percent of the electorate voted. Democrat Kennedy won both the popular vote and the Electoral College.

greater inclination to cooperate with us and maintain connections in the future. Indeed, when the results of investments in a public-good game are shared with other players, so that all can see how much others are donating, concerns about reputation will result in higher donations to the collective good being made.[43] The cynic would argue that people are merely buying approval, but the practical effects of what they are doing still serve the wider group.

This is not just an interesting theoretical finding. Erez Yoeli, a representative of the Federal Trade Commission in Washington DC, together with colleagues from UC San Diego, Yale and Harvard, applied the power of reputational effects to improve outcomes in real-world public-good settings. Working with a major electric utility company in California, Yoeli tested whether leveraging the reputational effects of a messenger would increase the number of households who would sign up to a voluntary 'demand response' energy programme – an initiative designed to reduce the risk of blackouts and environmental damage by restricting access to energy during peak periods of demand. The public benefit was obvious. But there was a private cost to be paid: restricted access meant that on hot days the availability of air conditioning would be severely curtailed.

For the purposes of the study, two quite different proposals were put to residents of a number of home-owner associations. One group received letters containing a unique code that they could write up on a board in their communal area to indicate that they were prepared to sign up to the scheme. Another group received letters that simply asked them to write their name and flat number on the communal board if they wanted to be involved. One scheme, then, was anonymous; the other was public. The difference in take-up rates was startling. Three times as many residents who had to put their names and flat numbers agreed to participate as those who simply had to write down a number. The increased level of participation also exceeded, by a factor of seven, that previously achieved by the offer of a $25 cash incentive. By the researchers' estimations, the individual benefit of a good reputation is priced – at least when it comes to energy-consuming behaviours – at around $174.[44]

The sales success of the Toyota Prius tells a similar tale. Those who care about the environment may be motivated to reduce their emissions when driving. But, since the Prius is more expensive, there is a premium to pay for being 'seen to be green'. A survey reported in *The New York Times* found that the majority of people who bought a Prius did so because it 'makes a statement about me'.[45] An individual's Prius might not have much impact on global warming, but it seems to have quite a large effect on how that person is perceived. Economists have long argued that if demand for green products is to be increased, manufacturers will have to make them less expensive, so that consumers do not need to self-sacrifice when buying environmentally-friendly products. According to Vlad Griskevicius, a noted scholar at the Carlson School of Management, the opposite might be true. What is important is the extent to which self-sacrificing behaviours are made publicly.

One of Vlad's studies involved asking people to make a choice between a green environmentally-friendly backpack and one that was considered more stylish and boasted more features. The green backpack was made from 100 percent organic fibres, had a design that minimised waste in the construction process and came with instructions on how to recycle it. The non-green backpack had a water-resistant coating and eight different storage compartments. To prompt a range of reactions, the researchers asked participants to imagine they were making purchases online, and thus privately, or publicly in a retail store. They also asked participants to read a short story before they made their choices, which, in one version, carried a message about reputation and, in the other, did not. The results showed that those primed to think about their reputation

preferred the luxury, non-green product when they were going to purchase online. But when shopping within the gaze of others, the environmentally friendly green option was preferred. The motivation
to protect the planet and buy green goods, it seems, is in part determined by the amount of social approval one will receive for doing so.[46]

We don't only listen to messengers who possess some form of status. We also hold those who express warmth – through positivity, compassion and humility – in high regard, too. These are the characteristics that seemingly swung a jury in a $10.5 billion lawsuit in the direction of the plaintiff, against a hard, colder opponent.

Being regarded as warm also goes a long way to explaining why Craig Jelinek was voted America's most likeable CEO. Warm messengers gain their influence because people find their company inherently rewarding. In this context, it is clear why this soft-messenger effect can have a big impact on an audience. It is also clear why individuals will seek to increase their perceived warmth by noticeably engaging in helpful, people-oriented behaviours. These are crucial characteristics that audiences attend to, when deciding whether they should form a connection and cooperate with others, and act on what they have to say.

But warmth is not the only way to increase connectedness. Taking a risk and letting others into our world can also connect us to an audience. To do that, however, requires us to signal our vulnerability.

6

VULNERABILITY

Self-Disclosures, Identifiable Victims and
How Openness Can Unlock Closed Minds

Archana Patchirajan, from Tuticorin in southern India, is a technology entrepreneur who has founded several start-ups. One of them – Hubbl – which she co-founded with her partner Kushal Choksi, and which provided business-to-business online advertising via an app, proved pretty successful. In late 2013 she sold the company for just over $14 million. But it could have been so very different. A couple of years before the sale, Patchirajan was forced to do something that would fill any burgeoning entrepreneur with dread. Calling together her staff of twenty-five highly trained engineers, she explained that their seed-funding had run dry and she would have to let them go.

Their reaction was surprising. They refused to leave. Instead, each suggested that they take a major pay cut. Some even offered to work overtime for free.[1]

Would you do that for your boss?

Money, career progression and skills development are of course crucial features of a job for most employees, but there is another that can be equally important. The sense of connectedness they feel with that job and company. Connectedness helps to create loyalty. It can provide people with a reason to turn up to work each day, beyond the obvious financial rewards, and encourages them to do their best work. One study of 5,000 Danish healthcare workers, for example, found that those who felt emotionally connected to their workplace experienced increased feelings of well-being, in addition to a greater commitment to their employer and colleagues.[2] It was a sense of connectedness that prompted Archana Patchirajan's colleagues to promise their continued support even when times were tough.

So, how does an employer create such a strong emotional connection with their employees? Brené Brown – a professor of social work at the University of Houston and author of several well-received books on authenticity and social connection – argues, convincingly, that residing at the core of any social connection is some form of vulnerability. Social connection involves a willingness on our part to put aside the protective mask we often wear and to be genuinely honest and open. In other words, to let our guard down and embrace our vulnerability. 'We love seeing raw truth and openness in other people, but we're afraid to let them see it in us,' she writes.[3]

It is a message that has landed well. Brown's TED Talk, 'The Power of Vulnerability', is wildly popular. Her thesis also helps to explain why Patchirajan's company survived its financial storm. Her employees could very easily have found alternative work: in 2013 computer engineers in the south of India were highly sought-after. But financial considerations that might have persuaded them to leave were trumped by an emotional one that persuaded them to stay. Patchirajan's computer engineers regarded her as genuine, and willing to expose her feelings. They knew that she was honest enough to share both good news and bad; that she was happy to discuss her dreams and concerns, her strengths as well as her flaws. Patchirajan was not the stereotypical hard leader – namely, a tall, smartly dressed, middle-aged man. She was open, frank and prepared to reveal the occasional uncertainty or feeling of vulnerability. And people

182

liked that. Because, as Brené Brown astutely suggests, to be vulnerable is to be human.

The exposure of vulnerabilities – whether the admission of complicity in a misjudgement, a confession of a romantic intent or simply signalling a need for help – requires a degree of bravery. The easier course is to protect ourselves by keeping our mental door (and lips) firmly shut. Revealing our true feelings, needs and desires, and thereby adopting a position of vulnerability, is much harder.

One reason for this is the increased risk of rejection that we face if we do open up to others. Receiving a negative response, after making oneself vulnerable, can be heartbreaking. More so than had we never exposed ourselves in the first place. Yet it turns out that our pessimistic predictions are often made with little foundation. Research by Vanessa Bohns and Frank Flynn has shown that in many situations people typically underestimate how forthcoming help will be, when asked for, because they tend to forget that there is a social cost attached to saying 'no'. Obviously the cost varies according to the nature of the request and the type of relationship to those involved – it's easier to refuse a friend a loan of £1,000 pounds than £10, or to say no to a stranger than to a boss. But the cost is still there and might result in a negative perception of the person saying no, who runs the risk of coming across as uncaring, unconnected, unreasonable or even cruel. They may well sense that themselves, and end up feeling guilty. Saying yes, by contrast, is a more positive and rewarding experience. By making someone else happy, the person who has agreed to help them feels positive, too: they can revel in the shared joy, and additionally feel good about themselves for performing a kind act. Agreeing to cooperate also helps strengthen the level of connectedness between two people. Consequently people are usually far more likely to say 'yes' than we would predict. Bohns and Flynn suggest that we typically underestimate the likelihood of a positive response by about half, leading to opportunities being lost; prospective friends, clients and dates going uncontacted; and chances to increase connectedness being squandered.[4]

Another related reason that we feel uneasy about expressing vulnerability is that we have a tendency to fixate on what might go wrong. We worry that by admitting to a mistake, we could lose our job. Or that if we try to connect with someone or seek their help, they will reject or humiliate us, and that we will therefore suffer a loss of status and self-esteem. The terrible consequence of this pessimism is that it is precisely during periods of psychological distress – when we are most in need of help – that we are least likely to request it. For example, even though close to 90 percent of bullied schoolchildren in the US positively rate peer-support systems set up to help them, only around 8 percent of victims actually use them.[5] As a result, those victims who understandably find it hard to muster the courage to ask for help suffer needlessly. Ironically, this can mean that regulators and policy-makers responsible for resourcing these worthwhile programmes misinterpret their under-utilisation as a limited need for such services, and cut the funding as a result. It takes a lot of courage for someone to overcome the embarrassment of admitting their vulnerability and the heavy loss it can inflict on their status. Paradoxically, as was the case with Archana Patchirajan, the expression of vulnerability can actually be interpreted as a sign of openness and confidence.[6]

Perhaps that's one reason why an increasing number of management and business schools advocate that leaders should learn to be comfortable about expressing their weaknesses and vulnerabilities. When messengers do make themselves vulnerable by revealing insecurities or potential weaknesses to others, they typically end up having more enjoyable social interactions and form closer connections as a result. If you share your thoughts, experiences, feelings and traits, others will either detect similarities ('You're just like me') or gain a better insight into how you tick. Either way, they will come to understand you better and your relationship with them will benefit.

The former British prime minister, Theresa May, offers a good example of a high-profile leader who took a risk and successfully turned a weakness into a strength, albeit for a limited time. Widely perceived as cold, robotic and not particularly accomplished at connecting with voters on a personal level, May was ridiculed when she was talked into dancing with a group of schoolchildren on the first day of a trade mission to Africa in the summer of 2018. Not the most comfortable or natural of dancers, her performance was widely derided as 'wooden' and 'cringe-worthy'. Twitter users mocked her for 'doing the Maybot' and laughed that 'someone forgot to oil her'. So it came as a huge surprise when several months later she boogied onto the stage at the Conservative Party Conference to Abba's 'Dancing Queen'. It was a bold move that could have resulted in further humiliation and relentless mocking. And it certainly led to another wave of Maybot-memes rippling their way across the Internet. But overall the reaction to her self-deprecating, wooden dancing was remarkably positive. Even Björn Ulvaeus, the Abba front man who co-wrote the song, was encouraging. 'I think she was very brave in doing that. It's a lady with not a lot of rhythm in her ... I was kind of touched actually.'[7] By embracing her vulnerability, May was able to get in on the joke, rather than be the butt of it. She established a level of connectedness that, for a brief time at least, softened previously harsh attitudes directed at her. Her conference party speech, given moments after jiving her way to the podium, was lauded as one of her best. Even her staunchest critics seemed impressed. Katy Balls, *The Spectator*'s deputy political editor, claimed 'the prime minister delivered one of her best speeches since taking office', while a *Guardian* editor concluded it 'was the most ambitious, and probably most successful speech of May's premiership'.[8] The Maybot had raised her game – temporarily, admittedly – as a messenger. Not by changing what she said, but by making herself vulnerable.

The upsides of expressing vulnerability are not restricted to high-status business and political messengers like Archana Patchirajan and Theresa May. In court, defence attorneys will frequently present their client as vulnerable – someone who was let down by the system, suffered a lot in life and lacked the capacity to deal with the tough conditions they faced – in order to try and get the judge and jury onside and gain some leeway. Good lawyers know that it often pays to 'play the victim'.[9] Similarly, contestants in talent shows often find themselves at an advantage if they possess a 'vulnerability' or unfortunate 'back-story', because both serve to set them apart from other competitors. Some of the previous winners of the popular UK entertainment show *Britain's Got Talent* offer cases in point. It was widely reported during the 2017 series that when the eventual winner, pianist Tokio Myers, was ten years old he witnessed the stabbing of his school teacher – a harrowing event for anyone, let alone a child. In 2018 the comedian Lee Ridley, aka *Lost Voice Guy*, who was disabled and unable to speak from an early age, triumphed with his witty one-liners delivered via a voice-synthesiser. The point here is not that they didn't deserve to win, but that a willingness to expose their vulnerabilities – far from harming their chances – may well have improved them. The need for a vulnerable back-story in TV reality competitions has led some to criticise shows such as these. The noted psychologist Glenn Wilson even claimed, '[the contestants'] deficiencies and short-comings are as important as their talent'.[10]

Naturally, the expression of vulnerability doesn't always require or involve such dramatic self-disclosure. Simply showing a pre-paredness to talk openly about oneself can be powerful. Negotiations that start with a 'getting-to-know-you' phase create an opportunity for parties to reveal who they are, which can create a sense of connectedness and so a greater ultimate chance of agreement. Bargaining processes that commence with an exchange of personal information are less likely to end in deadlock and more likely to result in a good outcome – for both parties. The process of self-disclosure can also benefit negotiations closer to home, boosting feelings of love between couples. Even police interviews of witnesses, it has been shown, gain from a more personal approach in terms of the quantity and quality of information subsequently obtained. Connected witnesses, it seems, make for good witnesses.[11]

Of course too much disclosure can be a bad thing. What messengers share with others should be appropriate to the context, and to the existing closeness of the relationship. To do otherwise runs the risk of instilling feelings of discomfort and embarrassment. Inappropriate disclosures are likely to go unreciprocated, be viewed negatively and, rather than increase connectedness, are more likely to result in a response of 'Oh my God! T.M.I.' But, as we've already suggested, to go to the opposite extreme and mask vulnerability altogether is to lose out on all sorts of potential upsides. For Archana Patchirajan, a willingness to appear vulnerable won her loyalty and support from her team in her darkest hour of need. For Theresa May, it provided a few welcome weeks of reduced pressure from her public. For others, it can bring additional knowledge and insight that inform a better decision. It might win understanding or forgiveness from a colleague that enables a work relationship to move on. Or even trigger the beginning of a lifelong loving partnership.

A helping hand

The impulse to give help when it's requested is a powerful one. It is an automatic, emotional response that, like many of the other messenger effects we describe in this book, is formed early in life.*12 Not just in humans, but in animals too. Rats, for example, will help free a companion trapped in a cage and will often do so before helping themselves to chocolate chips, strategically placed by researchers, which the rats enjoy very much. Given that rescuer rats choose to help rather than head straight towards the delicious treats, and that in freeing their imprisoned friends they are allowing them to gorge on the cookies, too, the motivation to help is clearly altruistic.[13]

Help is even on hand when it is not explicitly asked for. In an experiment conducted by Molly Crockett and her colleagues at University College London, pairs of participants were hooked up to an electric-shock machine and asked to make a series of choices, trading off money against pain. Participants could choose to earn larger rewards in exchange for a greater number of shocks, or receive fewer shocks in exchange for reduced monetary compensation. But there was a catch. Although they always got to keep the money, the shock was sometimes delivered to them and sometimes to their (anonymous) partner. They therefore stood to gain if they were prepared for their partner to suffer in exchange. In the event, few were. Most participants opted to forgo the additional money on offer, if taking it meant inflicting pain on someone else.[14] Feelings of compassion and guilt are powerful motivators. Such drivers help to explain why people will often go to great lengths to prevent harm being inflicted to complete strangers, and why a messenger seen as vulnerable and possessing little in the way of status still has an effective route to get people to listen.

In fact the mere act of drawing attention to a vulnerable person's needs can be powerfully persuasive. One study, entitled 'It's Not All About Me', found that drawing medical teams' attention to

---

* To see (cute) videos of children's helping behaviours, go to YouTube and type in 'Toddler altruism'.

self-centred concerns was significantly less effective in persuading them to comply with infection-control measures than communicating the impact their actions might have on vulnerable others. Signs above soap- and gel-dispensers in hospitals that stated, 'Hand hygiene prevents you from catching diseases' had little impact on the likelihood of a medic sanitising their hands before examining patients. However, a sign that directed attention towards patient-centred concerns – 'Hand hygiene prevents patients from catching diseases' – increased soap and gel use on wards by 45 percent.[15]

Of course it could be argued that medical professionals, more than most, should be predisposed to help others, given the job they have chosen to do. But even when a natural motivation doesn't exist, help can still, thankfully, remain on offer. This was fascinatingly demonstrated by the Harvard economist Felix Oberholzer-Gee in an experiment that involved requesting help in an environment where stress-levels run high and other people are likely to be a source of annoyance and frustration – a busy train station. With their long queues, weary passengers and testy staff, train stations are not the first places one thinks of as being havens of peace and goodwill. Rather the opposite, in fact. If the saying 'Every man for himself' applies anywhere, it's to the average ticket-office at the average train station, and it's hard to imagine how a station could be a venue that brings out the best in people. Nevertheless, Oberholzer-Gee sought to identify the most important factors that would persuade people in a long ticket queue to help a fellow passenger by giving up their place in line. On the surface the answer – which must have delighted his inner-economist – should come as no surprise: it was money.

All, however, was not as it seemed. In his studies, Oberholzer-Gee arranged for a number of stooges to play the role of a pleading late-running traveller, who would offer money to passengers ahead of them in the line for tickets to let them jump in. Many were happy to comply. And the more the would-be queue-jumpers offered, the more strangers were persuaded to give up their place in the queue.

So far, so obvious: higher offers of cash led to a greater willingness to let someone push in front. But what Oberholzer-Gee discovered was that very few of the passengers approached actually took the money. It would seem that it wasn't the money that mattered, but what the money represented – desperation. And the more money that was offered, the greater that desperation was perceived to be. Most of the people approached didn't think, 'Wow, if you're willing to pay $10 to cut in line, then you must be really rich.' What they were actually thinking was, 'Wow, if you're willing to pay $10 to cut in line, then you must really need to cut in line.' In this context, money signalled need. And people responded to that need by offering a (free) helping hand.[16]

The obligation to help

There's a seeming contradiction here. The experiments just described suggest that we are inclined to help people in need. Yet everyday experience tells us this is not always the case, while Stanley Milgram's famous electric-shock studies, mentioned earlier (see p.65), suggest that many people are actually willing to inflict pain on the vulnerable. What prompts people to show compassion on some occasions, but indifference – or even worse – on other occasions?

In the light of the Milgram experiment, it's tempting to answer the question simply in terms of status: we will respond sympathetically to a vulnerable messenger, who is likely to be (at least temporarily) in a position of low status, unless a messenger of high status (an authority figure) tells us otherwise. But that's not the full story. Various factors influence the extent to which we respond to vulnerability.

An important one is physical setting – in particular the proximity of the person receiving the message to the person sending it. Milgram found that *every single participant* in one experiment was willing to administer a potentially lethal 450-volt shock *if they had not previously seen or heard the victim*. But when he altered the design, and had participants actually place the hand of the victim onto the electrode plate themselves, only 30 percent delivered the jolt of electricity. The greater the distance that exists between a vulnerable person and a potential helper, the easier it is to ignore them. Or, in the case of Milgram's experiments, electrocute them.[17]

The astute reader may be wondering why – if this is true – participants in Molly Crockett's study should have been unwilling to deliver shocks to an *anonymous* partner, despite a financial incentive to do so. There seem to be two considerations in play here. One is that people generally construe causing harm to another purely out of self-interest – in this case, for personal financial gain – as immoral.[18] The other is that, whereas those in the Milgram experiments were able to abdicate personal responsibility for their actions and see themselves as simply carrying out orders, those in Crockett's study felt a greater sense of agency over their decisions: the responsibility for another's pain fell entirely on their shoulders.

The Salvation Army Red Kettle Campaign, one of the best-known and largest street fund-raising campaigns in the United States, provides a colourful illustration of how a simple statement that activates feelings of personal responsibility can influence our responses to vulnerable messengers. In the weeks leading up to Christmas, jolly volunteers, dressed in distinctive red aprons and Santa hats, ring bells as they solicit donations from pedestrians. The funds collected help to provide food, toys and clothing to huge numbers of vulnerable people. No surprise, then, that every now and then a few passers-by choose to donate. What is interesting, though, is the difference in the amount collected, according to whether volunteers simply rang their bells or found a way of engaging more closely with shoppers. Ringing a bell as shoppers walked in and out of the store elicited a donation on average every three minutes. However, the addition of a simple verbal request – 'Merry Christmas, please give today' – increased the number of donors by 55 percent and the total amount donated by 69 percent.[19] A simple verbal cue designed to put passers-by in the hot-seat proved incredibly powerful.*

The experience of Sean O'Brien from Liverpool in north-west England powerfully demonstrates how strong a motivator compassion can be, when someone is directly confronted with an individual, identifiable victim. Sean came to prominence in 2015 after performing an (at best) average dad-dance late one night in a bar. Standing a short distance away, a group of guys spotted Sean and one of them, seeing an overweight man enjoying himself, took out a phone, snapped some pictures and posted them online to the social-media site 4chan with the line, 'Spotted this specimen trying to dance the other week. He stopped when he saw us laughing.' The final shot revealed Sean looking forlornly down at the floor, knowing that he had just been mocked by a bunch of strangers.

The post went viral, prompting scores to troll and mock Sean. But Cassandra Fairbanks, who lives in Los Angeles and is a political activist and journalist for The Gateway Pundit website, was horrified by the bullying. She therefore took to Twitter – the social-media site she claimed once helped her find her lost dog – and posted a picture of Sean, asking, 'Anyone know this man or who posted this? There's a huge group of ladies in LA who would like to do something special ... We would like to fly him to LA for a VIP dance party with

---

* The drawback of having collectors ask for money explicitly was that many people took steps to avoid them.

the coolest and most awesome ladies in LA, please help.' She then added #FindDancingMan to her tweet. The social-media response was extraordinary. Two days later, Sean – the fat-shamed 'Dancing Man' – got in touch.

From there, things snowballed. Countless kind-hearted souls, hearing about Sean's story, reacted with sympathy for him, and with outrage at those who had bullied him. Arrangements were made to fly Sean, first to New York, where he danced live on TV with the singer-songwriter Meghan Trainor at the Rockefeller Plaza, then to Los Angeles, where Fairbanks came through on her promise and threw him a lavish party. In addition to Fairbanks's 'huge group of ladies', LA's socialites and even a few celebrities popped in to say hello. Moby dropped by to DJ. After the party, Sean would be for-given for thinking that his few moments of fame were over. Not so. The next day he was invited to throw the first pitch at the LA Dodgers' game against San Diego. And while all this was going on, scores of celebrities came out to attack online humiliation and bullying. The campaign, sparked by Fairbanks's #FindDancingMan tweet, was so successful that $70,000 was pledged to an anti-bullying charity.[20]

Why did the plight of Sean O'Brien, the Dancing Man of Liver-pool, result in an outpouring of goodwill and donations to an anti-bullying charity, when online bullying so often goes un-remarked and unchallenged? The reason is that people typically feel a greater obligation to help clear, identifiable victims like 'Dancing Man' than larger, abstract groups. A crowd is anonymous. A single person is a fellow human being. Consequently, while we find it dif-ficult to be empathetic to groups of victims, we find it relatively easy to identify with individuals. The Soviet dictator Joseph Stalin famously said, 'The death of a single Russian soldier is a tragedy. A million deaths is a statistic.'[21]

The way we react to news coverage powerfully illustrates this fundamental point. General stories of human suffering tend not to make much of an impact. A story that focuses on an individual, by contrast, is much more likely to draw a reaction. Coverage by the Western media of Saudi Arabia, for example, has tended to be highly critical, not least of the government of that country's military involvement in Yemen, where many thousands have died in Saudi air strikes. But it was the murder of the Saudi journalist Jamal Khashoggi that caused far greater outrage and had the most impact on Western perceptions. The Khashoggi case is a classic example of the 'identifiable victim effect' at work: a single tragedy involving a single messenger moves us, yet we are relatively indifferent to one involving multiple messengers if there is no clearly identifiable central figure.[22]

So strong is this instinct that it even extends to individuals who are fictional. And, in the case of the central character of the 1995 film *Babe*, to individuals that are fictional and not even human. The central plot of *Babe* concerns a talking pig, who helps around the farm by sorting the chickens and herding the sheep. He's even entered into a herding competition, where his skills are pitted against those of trained sheepdogs. He runs away, however, when he learns the horrifying fact that humans eat pigs. Fortunately, all ends well, but that didn't stop the cinema-going public at the time being shocked by Babe's potential fate and reacting strongly to it. According to an article published in the *Vegetarian Times*, the US Department of Agriculture reported that in the wake of the film's release, sales of pork and pork-related canned foods, such as Spam, fell to a five-year low. A large number of cinema-goers – particularly young girls – became 'Babe Vegetarians'. Even the actor James Cromwell, who played the role of the farmer in the film, turned vegan.[23]

It's not hard to see why people would react more emotionally to a living pig than a packet of bacon in a supermarket refrigerator. Pigs are sophisticated creatures. Like dogs, piglets are able to learn their names after two or three weeks and will respond when called. They are naturally social animals, too. They live in groups, greet their friends when they see them, rub noses together and groom each other. Like humans, they know which members of their social group are aggressive and dominant and which are gentler in nature (quite literally, hard and soft piggy messenger effects). But, so far as Babe Vegetarians were concerned, Babe had the added advantages of having a human-like mind, an ability to speak English and so a capacity to share experiences, feelings, desires and intentions.

The fact that cinema audiences should react so strongly to the story of an anthropomorphised pig clearly has lessons for vegetarian campaigners. And indeed recent successful campaigns have very cleverly played on the notion of the 'identifiable victim'. The Veganuary campaign is a case in point. Crowdfunded by £30,000-worth of posters placed inside carriages on the London Underground, the campaign's central message was to urge people to try veganism during the month of January. And rather than follow so many previous vegetarian campaigns and make a case based on facts and statistics, it opted to make an emotional case based on feelings of connectedness. Cute animals were chosen as messengers and were

Veganuary campaign adverts placed inside tube carriages on the London Underground.

given human names. The vulnerable, individual messenger had an impact. The campaign was said to have encouraged nearly 200,000 people to try going vegan for (at least) a month.[24]

One could make the case that, in an increasingly divided world, there is much to gain from a society that encourages everyone to be a little more empathetic with each other. However, as the Yale psychologist Paul Bloom argues, the challenge in relying on empathetic responses is that empathy is innumerate. People don't find it easy to identify with a 'statistical' victim.[25] Or as the American economist Thomas Schelling, who would later win the Nobel Prize, argued in 1968:

> There is a distinction between an individual life and a statistical life. Let a six-year-old girl with brown hair need thousands of dollars for an operation that will prolong her life until Christmas, and the post office will be swamped with nickels and dimes to save her. But let it be reported that without a sales tax the hospital facilities of Massachusetts will deteriorate and cause a barely perceptible increase in preventable deaths – not many will drop a tear or reach for their check books.[26]

There are many situations where it can be hard, even impossible, to identify who is most vulnerable, because they are often diffused across a large population. So our empathy drives us to help the vulnerable messenger in the spotlight, and not necessarily the neediest. In fact, the empathy we feel towards an identifiable sufferer can lead to wholly immoral decisions in the noble pursuit of alleviating pain – for example, when people choose to help a single identifiable suffering child rather than eight anonymous suffering children. Another example might be a healthcare professional who, by virtue of a closer connection to an identifiable patient in pain, might believe it more acceptable to bump that individual up the treatment waiting list, ahead of other faceless patients who have been waiting longer.[27]

The fact that it is easier to ignore the suffering of many statistical lives than it is one identifiable victim has led some to worry that national leaders may fail to properly consider the human costs of their actions during warfare. Given the abstract nature of large numbers of unidentifiable citizens, it might be less troubling for, say, the President of the United States to fire an arsenal of nuclear weapons at an enemy country than worry about the suffering of one named victim of the attack. It is a concern that led the late Harvard law professor Robert Fisher to suggest a somewhat controversial change to the protocol for initiating a nuclear attack. Wherever the president goes, Fischer proposed, a young man should accompany him. To make him a little more identifiable, let us assume that his name is Robert, he is twenty years of age and is tall, with dark curly hair. Robert's role is to carry a briefcase containing, not the nuclear launch codes, but a large butcher's knife. The launch codes themselves are contained in a small capsule inserted into Robert's chest, close to his heart. Should the president ever order the firing of nuclear weapons, he would first need to remove the knife from Robert's briefcase and, with his own hands, stab him in the chest to access the blood-covered capsule containing the nuclear codes. In other words, before a leader launches an attack that will probably kill hundreds of thousands of unidentifiable victims, they should first have to kill a single identifiable victim in a concrete and visceral manner. When Fisher suggested this idea to contacts at the Pentagon, he reported varying levels of astonishment. One high-placed official responded, 'My God, that's terrible. Having to kill someone would distort the President's judgement. He might never push the button.'[28]

The limits of vulnerability

It would, of course, be wrong to infer that because we are more sympathetically disposed to the vulnerable messenger when they are clearly identifiable, we will therefore always attend to, listen and respond to their message. Most of us walk past a homeless person on the street without acknowledging them. Most of us watch a charity appeal that focuses on the plight of a single child, but don't donate. We don't always stop to help someone who is clearly in distress.

One way to understand this is to view our emotional response to the vulnerable not as a fixed entity, but rather as lying along a continuum. At one end – the positive – reside feelings of compassion and connection that spur people on to help. At the other end – the negative – lie emotions such as anger, disgust and contempt that prompt people to react with indifference or, worse, hostility. A single messenger may trigger either extreme, or both, or something in the middle. The dad-dancing Sean O'Brien, for example, was hit both by a wave of contempt and disgust and by one of compassion and connection, from two separate sources.

What determines where on the scale we stand comes down to context, as well as our own particular instincts. Sometimes it can actually be pleasurable to watch others fail, particularly if we feel some sense of direct rivalry with them.[29] For example, on 27 June 2018 the popular UK tabloid paper *The Sun* delighted in reporting the elimination of the German football team from the group stages of the 2018 FIFA World Cup finals held in Russia. 'This is the magical moment that all England fans have waited for since 1966,' the newspaper's sports correspondent gleefully reported, as it tapped into a popular feeling about the national team's famous rival.[30] Similarly, the group who mocked and humiliated Sean O'Brien online almost certainly experienced feelings of superiority and contempt, which shunted their response to him away from sympathy and towards sadism.

In other cases, people seem able to automatically regulate their empathy and, in doing so, blunt any positive emotional response they might otherwise have felt towards another's suffering. A failure to empathise makes it easier to violate moral rules and helping norms.

The implications might be that people actively undertake inhumane acts, as Sean O'Brien's tormentors did. Or they might simply walk on by and ignore the vulnerable messenger's requests for help.

It is an unhappy fact that it can be easy to ignore a vulnerable messenger's suffering simply by rationalising reasons not to help. Let's say a wealthy woman, Belinda, walks past a homeless man on her way to work. The grubbily dressed man is clearly hungry and in distress, and is holding up a sign requesting that people spare some change. Belinda could let her natural empathetic responses guide her decision-making and thus choose to stop and hand over a few coins. Or she could suppress those feelings with rational objections: that she can't give money to every homeless person; that the man may only spend the money on alcohol and drugs; that her donation won't solve the problem and might encourage the man to carry on begging; that it might make more sense to make a contribution to a homeless charity. Whether or not each of these objections is justified is beside the point. The point is that by issuing her with a licence not to empathise and connect, these objections allow her to feel okay about her decision.[31]

One cognitive strategy that individuals employ to inhibit an empathetic response to vulnerable groups is to dehumanise them. Recent research at Princeton University has shown that when people look at stigmatised individuals, such as the homeless and drug addicts, activity in the area of the brain that is involved in understanding others' minds is reduced: they are registered as being somehow less human. As a result, their moral worth is greatly reduced in the eyes of others who, instead of showing pity or compassion, experience indifference. Their feelings of connectedness plummet.[32]

Dehumanisation plays an important role in human behaviour and, in certain circumstances, is crucial to our own well-being, even survival. It would not be a good idea, for example, for soldiers to feel empathy for the enemy firing at them. Or for victims to experience immediate compassion for their attackers. Similarly, a 250-pound, broad-shouldered line-backer might not be such an effective oppon-ent if he shares the pain that he inflicts on an opposing team's player after he has pummelled them to the ground in a tackle. If we perceive a threat from someone else, dehumanising them enables us to take more effective defensive or aggressive action.[33]

On occasion, an element of dehumanisation offers us an import-ant psychological benefit, too. Unsympathetic though it may sound, there are emotional and material costs attached to being empathetic. People who spend a lot of time with depressed individuals are known to start feeling depressed themselves.[34] Especially if they are closely and socially connected. Empathy can be a double-edged sword. It's critical to the day-to-day interactions of social groups, but because it exacts an emotional price it can, in certain circumstances, prove counter-productive. Doctors and other healthcare workers who experience personal anguish when interacting with distressed patients are more likely to suffer from emotional exhaustion and feel less able to cope with the demands of the job.[35] By contrast, those who are able to take steps to avoid developing close feelings of con-nectedness to their patients (for example, by not thinking about their patient's uniquely human emotions, such as hope, pity and pessimism) report fewer symptoms of burnout.

This may well be beneficial, not just for the healthcare profession-als, but for their patients, too. Some studies have found that medics are more caring and diligent in their work when a photograph of their patient is attached to their notes.[36] But Dutch researchers Joris Lammers and Deiderik Stapel suggest that doctors who are able to ignore the human-based traits of their patients are more likely to recommend treatments that, although more painful, are ultimately more effective than less distressing alternatives.[37] This conundrum epitomises the conflict between the *status*-driven and *connectedness*-driven messengers. As a patient, do you prefer the doctor who you think will downplay your human side, but who may come up with a more successful, if more painful, form of treatment? Or do you prefer the connected medic, who empathises with you and as a result might deliver a more caring, but possibly less effective plan? We imagine most people want the upsides of both and the downsides of neither!

Dehumanisation is also shaped by the extent to which a vulnerable messenger is believed to be responsible for, or deserving of, the difficulty they happen to be facing. After all, if a vulnerable messenger is solely and entirely responsible for their situation, having behaved or acted in ways that almost guarantee downfall and subsequent suffering, then it would be inappropriate for people to feel too much sympathy. Punishment and pain are there to deter people from engaging in foolish, damaging and self-destructive acts. Little surprise, then, that the motivation to respond with emotion and caring falls off a cliff if it emerges that a vulnerable messenger's pain is deserved.

A neuroscientific study led by Kai Fehse provides a fascinating insight into the mental processes involved when an audience considers the deservedness or otherwise of victims.[38] Participants were asked to read one of two versions of an account of a road-traffic accident. Both stated that 'a man had died in a car accident on the highway …', but while one went on to say that he had been 'passing carelessly in a curve [sic]', the other read that he was 'a father of four children'. It should come as no surprise that those who thought the man had been careless judged that, because he had been responsible for his fate, he deserved little compassion. What is interesting, though, is that the neurological data collected by researchers suggested that on registering that the victim was culpable, the areas in the brain responsible for the initial compassionate response (the left insula, medial prefrontal cortex and anterior cingulate cortex) were then inhibited by another area of the brain (the dorsolateral prefrontal cortex). At the risk of being overly simplistic (neuropsychological studies are invariably complex), it would appear that our brains are rather accomplished at pinning blame and, when they do, they crowd out any impulse to connect and empathise with the person at fault.

One implication of this research is that humans may be naturally inclined to search for evidence that vulnerable people are to blame for their own suffering. Victims of rape provide a clear and haunting example of these processes in action. It is well documented that victims of sexual attacks often go unheeded and are sometimes apportioned an element of blame. 'What can she expect, walking alone at night?' 'Look at the provocative way she was dressed.' 'She had clearly been drinking and, who knows, maybe took something else, too?' 'She led him on, what did she expect?' Blaming victims in this way, thereby ignoring their message of distress and the need for consolation and redress, may make it easier for others to justify reduced empathy and enable them to avoid the distress of sharing in a victim's pain.[39] The brain, it seems, is essentially looking for a way to avoid the emotional expenditure involved in empathising with a vulnerable person's message of distress, and it does so by actively seeking reasons why it should not have to.

The dehumanisation of messengers can also occur when the material costs of empathy – as opposed to the psychological costs – become salient. A 2014 *Journal of Neuroscience* paper found that when participants were assigned the role of manager in a labour market and were asked to recruit and pay for certain employees, they were more likely to view those they had paid for in a dehumanised way than those they hadn't; indeed, once payment was involved, there was reduced neural activity in the areas of the brain associated with taking consideration of another's perspective and seeking to understand their thinking.[40] These findings have considerable implications for the world of work. If, as the study suggests, employers have a tendency to focus on their employees' economic attributes, they will come to treat them as commodities rather than as fellow humans. And if, for some reason, the employees stop delivering the goods, they may find the empathy that would otherwise support them to be lacking.

Staying connected

The plight of the vulnerable messenger can be a fraught one – especially for those who, for whatever reason, become dehumanised in the minds of those in a position to help them. But there are ways that a vulnerable messenger who doesn't automatically engage others' sympathy can nevertheless win over an audience.

One way, as we suggested in the introduction to Part Two, is to stress what we have in common with others – in other words, to build a sense of connectedness. It has been shown that onlookers are more predisposed to help vulnerable emergency victims if they feel they share something with them, such as nationality.[41] And just as an awareness of dissimilarities can result in hostility between groups, so relatively trivial points of similarity can have a powerful positive effect. When a group of English soccer fans, all Manchester United supporters, were asked to walk from one building to another, having just completed a questionnaire on the things they liked about their team, they witnessed a passing jogger trip over. The jogger was, in fact, a member of a research team based at Lancaster University and was feigning the injury. In one scenario he wore a plain white shirt; in another, a Manchester United football shirt; and in a third, the shirt of Manchester United's arch-rival, Liverpool. In 85 percent of cases, the supporters willingly stopped and provided assistance when the jogger was wearing a Manchester United shirt, but only 30 percent helped the same jogger when he was wearing the neutral or the rival's shirt. In each instance the message was the same: 'I've fallen over, please help.' What differed was people's connectedness to the vulnerable person in distress.

If this study demonstrates what most people already intuitively know – that highlighting rivalry and difference is a sure way to encourage hostility between groups – then a second study highlights what can be done about reducing it. In a follow-up study, the Manchester United fans were asked what they liked about being a football supporter, instead of what they liked about their particular team. When subsequently confronted with the injured jogger, these fans – who had considered what they liked about *football* and were therefore focused on shared, rather than opposing, aspects of their identity – were much more likely to stop and help a rival in need.[42]

Another way to increase a sense of connectedness is, of course, to reduce the countervailing power of dehumanisation. This can be achieved by inviting people to interact with others or, more simply, just to imagine what it might be like to belong to another group. Studies have shown that frequent and enjoyable interaction between different groups leads to increased trust, empathy and forgiveness, even when those involved are from disparate communities – for example, in Northern Ireland and rival regions in Italy.[43] Even asking fourth-grade schoolchildren to imagine what it would be like to interact with an immigrant child of similar age, or asking teenagers to read books about intercultural topics, have been shown to reduce dehumanisation. The result is an increased willingness to connect with unknown immigrant children, whom the 'in group' may previously have ignored or rejected.[44]

Encouraging people to focus on the human attributes of a vulnerable messenger can also lead to reduced dehumanisation. When researchers Lasana Harris and Susan Fiske showed study participants pictures of homeless people and drug addicts, the typical reaction was one of disgust. Moreover, brain scans of the participants showed less activity in the neural regions that are usually active when we are contemplating another person's mind. Put simply, the participants were dehumanising them. However, when the participants were asked, 'Does this person like carrots?' as they viewed the pictures, the neural data from the brain scans suggested these areas were now lighting up; the participants were humanising the same messengers whom they had previously regarded with disgust.[45] Engaging in a task that required people to assign a mind to a vulnerable messenger resulted in that messenger being seen as more human. This suggests that those acting as agents for vulnerable people, such as charities, would be advised not just to talk about the practical measures needed to help, but also to stress features of a shared humanity.

The expression of vulnerability can, then, increase a sense of connectedness towards a messenger because it has the power to evoke compassion, guilt or fellow feeling. It is these qualities that, individually or in combination, compel people to respond to charitable appeals and help those, like the 'dancing man' Sean O'Brien, who are suffering. Connectedness dissuades people, like the vegan actor from Babe, James Cromwell, from acting in their own self-interest when they know their actions will cause harm to another living being. It can lead employees to offer to take pay-cuts so that their boss can get a business back on its feet; help contestants gain support on talent shows; soften political rivals, making them more receptive to a prime minister's speech. It can even cause people to let others cut in front of them in a queue.

But vulnerability is not a one-way street. There is both a helper and a requester in this dance. And while this chapter has focused on the requesters, to whom we may or may not listen, the next chapter focuses on the helpers, to whom we are most likely to expose our vulnerabilities.

The trustworthy.

7

TRUSTWORTHINESS

Core Principles, Conflicts of Interest and
Those Who Are as Faithful as Their Options

IN THE SUMMER OF 1961, Stephen Ward, man about town and osteopath to the rich and famous, was at a weekend party at Cliveden House, the Berkshire ancestral home of Lord Astor. With him was Christine Keeler, a wannabe model and topless showgirl, who had earlier moved into his London home and pursued what, by all accounts, was a platonic relationship with him. Also at the party was John Profumo, Secretary of State for War. Profumo was immediately taken by Keeler – perhaps it was the sight of her swimming in the nude that captured his attention – and a brief sexual liaison followed. Profumo was unaware, however, that Keeler was seeing other men whom Stephen Ward had introduced to her, including Ivanov Yevgeny, an assistant naval attaché at the Russian embassy with alleged connections to the KGB. At the height of the Cold War, Britain's Secretary of State for War was having an affair with a nineteen-year-old topless dancer who also happened to be sleeping with a Russian spy!

Two years later, long after Profumo had ceased seeing Keeler, rumours about their liaison started to become public, given extra spice by suggestions of a Russian connection. Something clearly needed to be done to scotch the rumour-mongering and so, on the advice of the parliamentary Chief Whip, Profumo agreed to make a personal statement in the House of Commons to set the record straight. On the morning of 22 March 1963 he stood up in the House and announced, 'There was no impropriety whatever in my acquaintance with Miss Keeler.'[1]

That should have been that. As the late political journalist Wayland Young noted, members' personal statements are, by tradition, never questioned. They are occasions for the display of a special degree of trust. Profumo certainly believed this. After delivering his message of personal integrity he promptly rose, left the House of Commons and set off for Sandown Park for an afternoon of horse-racing in the company of the Queen Mother.

Unfortunately for Profumo, the police now began investigating Stephen Ward's business dealings and his connections to Russia. And in the course of their enquiries they learned from Christine Keeler that she had, indeed, had an affair with the Secretary of State for War. Officers also interviewed Keeler's flatmate, another would-be model named Mandy Rice-Davies, who was also well known to Ward. She corroborated Keeler's account. Soon the truth was out, and Profumo found himself with no alternative but to admit all to his wife and resign.

The fallout from the scandal was not merely a political and social disgrace for a Conservative minister. Ultimately it contributed to the downfall of a government. The opposition Labour Party alleged that the Conservative prime minister, Harold Macmillan, had kept details of an inquiry into Ward's dealings secret for political reasons. 'The Prime Minister was gambling on the issue never seeing the light of day.'[2] The newspapers, too, were relentlessly critical. It seemed, said one, 'that the prime minister is in an intolerable dilemma from which he can only escape by being proved either ludicrously naïve or incompetent or deceitful – or all three.'[3] A few months later, on the eve of the Conservative Party conference,

Macmillan fell on his sword, claiming ill-health. A year later the Tories were swept from power.

What ultimately destroyed Profumo was not his affair with Christine Keeler. It was the fact that he lied to the House of Commons. Similarly, Macmillan's position was undermined not because one of his ministers had misbehaved, but because his judgement of trustworthiness had been shown to be at fault. Trust is crucial to any human relationship. It influences how a messenger relates to others, how they are perceived and therefore how strong their personal relationship is. It also underlies every human transaction. In its absence, it is hard to have successful romantic relationships, build productive workplace collaborations or foster prosperous economic exchanges. The extent to which people trust others directly impacts on their ability to create benefits that, individually, either would find difficult to generate alone.[4]

As the Profumo case demonstrates, trust needs to exist as much between groups as between individuals. People need to trust their leaders. Nations need to trust each other. Confidence that another country won't renege on a trade agreement, or default on a commitment to address a global challenge such as climate change, is crucial to the continued success of any partnership. Only with trust, and the subsequent output of trust – cooperation – can individuals, groups, communities, societies and countries accomplish feats that would almost certainly languish, if left to individuals alone to achieve.

So what exactly is trust?

Trust can mean many things to many people. We trust Daniel because his incentives are aligned with our own. We trust Alex because she has proved loyal in the past. We trust Elle because she has a strong track record of honourable behaviour. We trust William because it is easy to check in on what he is doing. We trust Samantha because she honours contracts. At its core, trust reflects the expectations that we hold about another person's actions and intentions – it is a prediction of future good faith.

There are two broad forms of trust: *competence*-based trust and *integrity*-based trust.[5] Competence-based trust assumes confidence in a messenger's capabilities and is determined primarily by what is known about their past performance – the assumption being that this provides a good idea of how they will behave in the future. In a nod to the term assigned to cricket and rugby players who can be relied upon to catch the ball consistently, we call them a 'safe pair of hands'. Integrity-based trust, by contrast, is governed by the belief that a messenger will abide by virtuous social rules and norms, even if a temptation to violate them arises. It assumes adherence to a set of principles that most other people consider acceptable.

In the previous chapter we described how the vulnerable messenger has to take social risks in order to be heard. The messenger who relies on trust, by contrast, is asking others to take a gamble on them. And, as John Profumo discovered, if those others then find that they have been let down or betrayed, the consequences can be wide-reaching and even catastrophic.

The trust game

Trust is essential if social groups are to cooperate and thrive.[6] This basic truth is nicely demonstrated by the Trust Game – the rather uninspiringly named experimental paradigm established by behavioural scientists – in which one player has to decide how much money to send to a second player, knowing that whatever they send will be tripled, but not knowing for sure how much the other player will choose to send back. It's clear that the first player has to make a judgement as to the trustworthiness of the other participant, based perhaps on how persuasive that person is or – more usually – what they know or can glean about them – or no information whatsoever.[7] It is also clear that just as a lack of trust will cause one player to lose out, if each can trust the other, both will benefit.

The same principle applies in everyday life. When you do a colleague a favour, it's in the knowledge that they might return it in due course. Both parties gain. If you lend money to a friend, it's in the belief that they will pay you back as soon as they can. If they don't, your friendship will suffer and you won't lend to them again. If they do, your friendship is maintained and either of you might lend to the other in the future. Without trust, social transactions and relationships break down.

Our level of general trust is tempered by an *injunctive norm*,* which suggests that people should generally be prepared to trust others. To openly signal distrust to a stranger's face can be socially risky. So, for example, to look suspiciously at a taxi driver when getting into their cab after landing in an unfamiliar country late at night, while perhaps understandable, is unlikely to go down well. It will be viewed as insulting and might actually make you less safe. It has even been suggested that individuals who refuse to trust strangers are themselves regarded as less moral. Generally speaking, therefore, people feel that they ought to trust others, and others will generally approve morally of them if they do so.[8]

Surveys have shown that citizens of countries that typically answer towards the upper end of the trust scale – when asked, 'Generally speaking, would you say that most people can be trusted or would you say that you can't be too careful when dealing with people?' – find it easier to cooperate with those around them and are more likely to do volunteer work. They think more democratically. They also tend to rank higher in terms of subjective well-being.[9]

---

* 'Injunctive norms' describe what most people believe are the appropriate ways to think and act.

When citizens believe they can trust the people around them, it is easier for them to make alliances and work with others. Scandinavian nations fare best, with upwards of 60 percent, in recent World Values Surveys, reporting that people, in general, can be trusted. For South American countries, including Colombia, Brazil, Ecuador and Peru, this drops to just 10 percent.[10]

Such findings suggest that levels of trust are shaped by society in general, not just by personal interactions. People in societies with higher generalised trust cooperate with one another, and worry less about being exploited or betrayed, because they assume that those around them will be true to their word. By the same token, if people's faith is shaken by particular scandals or controversies – whether the Watergate scandal, the collapse of Enron, the circumstances leading to the invasion of Iraq in 2003 or the banking crisis of 2007–8 – their overall levels of trust will tend to decline.[11] That audiences with higher generalised trust and the societies to which they belong are more likely to cooperate highlights an important consequence for any messenger. Regardless of the messenger's status, connectedness or the actual content of the message, their success will often be influenced by how predisposed an audience is to believe that people are in general trustworthy. After a few scandals it is easy to see how people come to infer that everyone in business and politics must be corrupt, driven by the desire for gain and willing to bend all sorts of moral rules in order to get what they want. If trust is essential to the smooth working of society, it's also very easy to undermine it.

The way in which generalised trust can be lost in the wake of a scandal is well illustrated by the fallout from the revelation of golfer Tiger Woods's fall from grace in 2009. At the time, Woods's fame and the levels of acclaim accorded to him were such that in the eighteen months that followed his decision to endorse Nike golf balls, Nike's share of the market increased from 1.5 to 6.6 percent. Indeed it is reckoned that during Woods's ten-year endorsement of Nike, they sold close to an additional ten million golf balls. Given his association with the brand, it therefore comes as no surprise that when stories of his adultery emerged, Nike sales should have tanked. Less than a month later, two University of California economists estimated the shareholder cost of Wood's libido – not just to Nike, but also to other brands he was associated with – to be upwards of $5 billion.[12] But the impact of his disgrace went beyond his sponsors. Over the next few months other brands of golf balls experienced a fall in sales, too, even though they had no association whatsoever with Tiger Woods. This is not an isolated phenomenon. When scandals like this break, it is not just the company that sponsors the messenger that stands to lose. Entire industries can suffer.[13] This, after all, was what happened during the banking crisis of 2007–8: *several* banks were shown to have behaved foolishly or unethically, but the reputation of pretty much *all* banks suffered. When trust is lost, the shadow cast can loom very large indeed.

The trust matrix

What should govern where we decide to place our trust? Some see it simply as a form of social risk-taking – a bet, of sorts, that we place on our prediction of someone else's future behaviour, or, as many scholars would put it, a simple risk–reward calculation.[14] Trust in this context is governed by the sort of game theory that underlies the Trust Game. It involves only a few variables, although each can be complex and difficult to estimate. The first thing to do is estimate the potential gains and losses that could result from trusting or not trusting. Next we have to try to assess the other side's current trustworthiness, by calculating what they have to gain or to lose by being trustworthy – or not – in the situation that currently faces them. We then: 1) multiply the probability that they will reciprocate our trust by what we stand to gain from cooperation; 2) multiply the probability that they will betray our trust by what we stand to lose in this case; and 3) calculate the overall expected value of trusting and compare this to the expected value of not trusting.

	Other person reciprocates trust	Other person betrays trust
Trust	Gain×Probability of reciprocity	Loss×Probability of betrayal
Don't trust	Expected value if you choose not to trust	

The trust matrix: To decide whether to trust or not, you can calculate the expected values associated with each possible outcome.

One way to illustrate this is to consider one of the plot lines in George R. R. Martin's epic book and television series *Game of Thrones*. Imagine that you are Lord Eddard 'Ned' Stark, a man who is totally loyal to the king, Robert Baratheon, and who has been called to the capital to serve as the Hand of the king. You travel south to the capital to investigate an alleged murder, assisted by Lord Petyr Baelish – also known as Littlefinger – who is the Kingdom's Master of Coin (aka Treasurer / CFO), but whom you do not fully trust, since he once told your wife that he loved her.

As your investigation continues, you come to learn that the queen has cheated on the king, and that her children are not Robert Baratheon's, but were in fact conceived with her twin brother. That means that their future claim to the throne is compromised and that in fact the king's brother, Stannis Baratheon, is now the rightful heir.

216

Before you can reveal this information to the king, however, he is involved in a 'mysterious' hunting accident, leaving the queen's illegitimate firstborn son in charge of the Kingdom (once he comes of age) unless you act to restore justice. You hatch a plan to recruit the king's law-enforcement unit – the City Watch – to overpower the men guarding Queen Cersei and take her and her children into custody. But to do this, you will need to persuade Littlefinger to bribe the City Watch to take your word over the queen's. The dilemma you face is whether you can trust Littlefinger to perform this crucial act, or whether – given his previous untrustworthiness – he is likely to betray you.

What do you do? Let's look at the variables in your trust matrix. Here, first, are the possible outcomes of trusting Littlefinger:

1. Littlefinger could comply with your request, dutifully pay the City Watch and assist in the arrest of Queen Cersei and her children.
2. Littlefinger could betray you and take Queen Cersei's side.
3. Or something else, which is hard to predict, might happen.

Now let's think through the possible outcomes if you don't trust Littlefinger, which are:

1. You could bypass Littlefinger and try to convince the City Watch yourself.
2. You could flee, return north to your daughters and men and join forces with the rightful king, Stannis Baratheon.
3. You could swear fealty to Queen Cersei's oldest son, despite knowing the truth of his heritage.

Some of these options will be more attractive to you than others, and so you might attempt to place a value against each of them. What is clear, however, is that the potential costs and benefits of placing trust in Littlefinger are very high indeed. You therefore need to move on to stage two in the game theorist's trust matrix: estimate the likelihood of reciprocity.

Continuing with the *Game of Thrones* example, what is the probability that Littlefinger will act in good faith? And what are the chances that, rather than reciprocate your trust, he will betray you? To get closer to the answer you are going to need to consider what Littlefinger's trust matrix looks like, which will require a bit of mind-reading. What does Littlefinger want? What does he stand to gain (or lose) if he cooperates with you? And what could he gain (or lose) by betraying you?

The problem here is that it's not nearly as easy to assess someone else's incentives as it is your own. You don't know if Littlefinger is as committed to restoring the rightful heir to throne as you are, although given that Littlefinger has already advised you against this course of action, you suspect he isn't. You also don't know if Littlefinger is motivated to keep his word. Again, you suspect not. Littlefinger doesn't seem that bothered about lying, and you believe him to lack honour. You also know that Littlefinger has a lot to gain if he betrays you. If Queen Cersei and her son were to take power, they would owe Littlefinger a great debt of gratitude. And with you out of the picture, Littlefinger may even be able to win over your wife, his old love, and take her as his bride.

In fact, what Ned Stark ultimately does is driven by a number of miscalculations. He wrongly assumes that everyone values honour, integrity and law as much as he does. He wrongly assumes that Littlefinger will cooperate because it is the right thing to do, and in accordance with the laws of the land. He misjudges Littlefinger's own connectedness with him. The course of action he then takes ultimately leads to his death. He has paid the ultimate price for placing trust in an untrustworthy messenger.

'Mandy Rice-Davis Applies'

Various immediate factors – often a combination of factors – serve to make individuals more or less trustworthy in particular circumstances. Sex is a powerful motivator, as it is in so many aspects of human behaviour where arousal and desire have a pronounced effect on judgement and decision-making. People will risk unwanted pregnancy, place themselves in danger of contracting a sexually transmitted disease and even violate their own moral codes in order to attain sexual gratification.[15] Ambition is a strong motivator, too. Those who, during the bitter arguments over whether or not Britain should leave the European Union, felt the 'Leave' campaign's figurehead Boris Johnson to be dissembling and untrustworthy argued that he was more interested in pursuing his ambition to be prime minister than in doing what was right for the country: 'The only thing Boris is interested in is himself,' said a senior government source.[16]

A simple desire to avoid the embarrassment of having skeletons in the cupboard exposed can also cause people to be untrustworthy. John Profumo's dishonesty was prompted by the likelihood of personal humiliation and professional damage, if details of his affair emerged. During Stephen Ward's trial for living off immoral earnings, Keeler's flatmate Mandy Rice-Davies claimed that she had had an affair with Lord Astor, the owner of Cliveden House where the infamous party by the pool had taken place. Ward's defence lawyer scoffed at her, telling the court that Lord Astor had vigorously denied having an affair with her and, indeed, ever having met her. Rice-Davies's response, famously giggled as she stood in the witness box of Marylebone's Crown Court, would go down in history: 'Well, he would [say that], wouldn't he?'

So celebrated was her response that 'Mandy Rice-Davies Applies' (or M.R.D.A. for short) has become a useful litmus test of whether people in particular circumstances will lie to avoid immediate difficulties: it's the de facto response on Internet sites like Reddit (it

Mandy Rice-Davies (left) and Christine Keeler (right), key players in the infamous 1960s Profumo affair. The former's response in court to a denial about an alleged extra-marital affair, 'Well he would [say that], wouldn't he', is now commonly used by those who wish to draw attention to a messenger's motives when questioning their trustworthiness.

even warrants a place in the *Oxford Dictionary of Quotations*) for directing attention to the conflict between a messenger's proclaimed motivations and their actual incentives.[17]

The problem for others, of course, is spotting and assessing such conflicts in the first place. When people are aware of them, they are duly cautious. In Chapter 1 we mentioned how overt celebrity endorsements of products can backfire: consumers come to assume that because the celebrity is presumably being paid for providing glowing praise, the endorsement is therefore less credible. But as wily advertisers know, it is possible to mask self-interested motives: those who pay celebrities to *use* products, rather than openly endorse them, are markedly more successful.[18] Motives are not always clear-cut, and they can be concealed. As Littlefinger says: 'A man with no motive is a man no one suspects. You always keep your foes confused. If they don't know who you are or what you want, they can't know what you plan to do next.'

The challenges posed by the difficulties involved in reading people's motives help to explain why we are frequently driven to assess what someone is like, rather than seek to quantify how likely they are to be trustworthy in a particular situation. We could ask, 'What is the probability I can trust this person?' Many of us instead choose to ask the far simpler question, 'What are my general evaluations of their character?' The former would involve the weighing of evidence that is not always clear-cut. The latter allows us to make the sort of easy snap judgements that humans make every day.

And here, essentially, we look for one of three broad character types. The first is those we believe are not tempted to deceive or betray us. The second is those who we suspect might be tempted to do so, but who are likely to suffer internal conflicts, arising from their moral code or their feelings of loyalty and connectedness, which could well overcome their temptation to let us down. The third is what the stand-up comedian Chris Rock once described as those who are 'as faithful as their options'. He was referring to men who cheat on their partners (as he himself did), but the basic rule applies much more generally. People in the first and second categories may on occasion let us down. It's the third category, however, that comprises those most likely to betray our trust. Such people are devoid of integrity. They lack any internal motivation to remain loyal to their connections. They would probably sell their own grandmother if the price was right.

If the 'faithful as his options' messenger ranks as least trustworthy, which of the other two is the more reliable? The messenger who overcomes temptation? Or the one who was never tempted in the first place? It is easy to see why the un-tempted messenger would be viewed as more trustworthy. Pure of heart, they have no need to reject alternative options because no option is as good as their current one. The rub, of course, is that very little is known about how they would react, if confronted with a strong incentive to act disloyally. The Yale psychologists Christina Starmans and Paul Bloom find that people who experience internal conflict, and are able to overcome it, are often seen as possessing greater moral strength.[19] But it's not as straightforward as that. In relationships, for example, it has been shown that the most trustworthy men are not those who normally manage to overcome temptation, but those who never experienced it in the first place. Their connectedness to their partner has caused them automatically to disengage attention from attractive alternatives. As a result, they are almost 50 percent less likely to have sex outside marriage than those wandering-eye, tempted individuals.[20] The celebrity who resists the urge to sleep with a beautiful, flirty fan may be seen to have passed a moral test, but the very fact they had to resist the urge makes them ultimately less trustworthy.

Core principles and inconsistent characters

The fact that, rather than engage in elaborate game theory, we tend to make general assumptions about personality, when assessing someone's trustworthiness, has major implications for our interpretation of the factors that go to make one of our three categories of trustworthy messenger. In theory, we should be seeking information about others' external and internal incentives to cooperate, weigh them against our own, and then make a decision about whether or not to trust. In reality, because our judgements are being shaped by our overall impression of someone, we make our decisions in a far less sophisticated way. Viewing someone as truthful and regarding them as trustworthy are not the same thing. Truth is fact-based and requires a weighing of evidence and likelihood. Trust is relationship-based and relies on broader and vaguer assessments.

And, in some instances, being deemed to be trustworthy is more important than being regarded as truthful.

This apparent conundrum is well illustrated by popular attitudes towards Donald Trump. As messengers go, he surely falls into the 'faithful as his options' category. He has resisted calls to release information about his tax returns, despite every recent president before him having done so. He has been accused of having affairs (which he has denied); and of paying his personal attorney Michael Cohen to buy former *Playboy* model Karen McDougal's silence about his alleged relationship with her (an accusation he also denies). By mid-2019, according to fact-checkers at *The Washington Post*, he had made more than 9,000 false or misleading claims while president.[21]

Yet his core fan-base regards Trump as trustworthy.

There are, arguably, two reasons for this. The first is that he has not violated his core principles. He campaigned as someone who would ban Muslims from certain countries entering the US, would build a wall along the southern border, would cut taxes and free America from international climate-change agreements. Whether or not these were admirable undertakings is beside the point. The fact is that he delivered, or at least tried to deliver, on all these key promises.[22] He said he would introduce travel bans; he introduced at least three. He said he would build a physical barrier along the Mexican border; he declared a National Emergency in an attempt to do so. He said he would cut taxes; he did. He said he would seek to take the US out of the Paris climate-change agreement; again, he was true to his word.

Moreover, while Trump's opponents may have dismissed him as being as faithful as his options, his supporters regard these options as being aligned and in concert with their own principles and world-view. They like someone who claims to be an outsider, rather than a slick Washington politician. They admire his can-do attitude and his indifference to norms of conduct, cooperation, compromise and what they would term as political correctness. And while his opponents regard him as capricious and impulsive, Trump's fans cheer his 'shoot from the hip' attitude. They know what he stands for, and what he stands for is what they believe in.

Researchers have shown that individuals who conform to and follow certain group norms from the beginning earn themselves 'group credits'. These can be cashed in, to cover the cost of the occasional mistake. If a sufficient quantity is stored up, it might even cover a major policy shift or change of mind that represents a departure from what made that individual popular in the first place.[23] It should come as no surprise, therefore, that, according to a study by the psychologist Briony Swire-Thomson, even when Trump supporters learn that he has lied or supplied false information, their intention-to-vote remains largely unaffected.[24] Polls, including those by Gallup, report that while the number of US citizens who regard the president as 'honest and trustworthy' dropped by a staggering 10 percentage points from February to April 2018, his overall approval ratings faltered not one jot.[25] Those, by contrast, who fail to build up a bank of 'group credits' can find themselves very quickly out of favour. France's President Macron is a case in point. His lack of a political tribe – whether on the left or the right – which was initially seen as a demonstration of his prowess, swiftly became a problem as those on all sides crowded in to attack him. It's hard to build up group credits when group lines are blurred. At the time of his inauguration, Macron's approval ratings stood at 55 percent. Just one year later they had plunged to an all-time low of 35 percent.[26]

There's a second factor in play, too. We mentioned earlier that breaches of trust can lead to a general loss of faith in particular sectors, institutions and governments. But in those instances where someone is able to preserve a bond of trust, they can actually shift the dial on what is deemed acceptable behaviour. A recent PRRI/Brookings poll found that white evangelicals in the US – a strongly

Trump- and Republican-supporting demographic, as well as one of the most likely to believe that society should place a strong value on moral character – have substantially shifted their views on this issue. In 2011, 70 percent of white evangelicals believed that elected officials who commit immoral acts in their personal life should not be trusted to behave ethically and fulfil their duties in their public and professional life. By the time of the 2016 presidential election, this figure had fallen to just 30 percent.[27] It seems that the importance voters place on personal integrity is elastic and can be stretched according to the nature and popularity of the candidate. The Roman writer Publilius Syrus may have said that 'trust, like the soul, never returns once it is gone', but trust can be flexible. As Harvard researchers Max Bazerman and Francesca Gino have demonstrated, people's likelihood to criticise the unethical behaviour of others decreases gradually as the transgressions become increasingly normalised. Moreover, once criticism loses its voice, silence can easily be interpreted as assent, encouraging yet further unethical behaviour.[28]

The power of maintaining consistency with one's core principles is also nicely demonstrated by the contrasting political fates of Eliot Spitzer, the Harvard- and Princeton-educated former attorney-general and governor of New York State; and Keith Vaz, the long-serving British MP who formerly served as chairman of the Home Affairs Select Committee. Both were caught out in sex scandals: Spitzer in 2008, when he was wire-tapped making plans to meet a prostitute at his Washington hotel; Vaz in 2016, when he paid two male prostitutes cash in exchange for sexual services.[29] But whereas Spitzer felt compelled to resign, Vaz remained in post and was later appointed to the Justice Select Committee. Such very different outcomes to very similar cases inevitably invites the question: why?

Clearly, there may well have been some purely local factors at work here, but it's worth emphasising how much the two men had in common: both had high-profile jobs, both were married, both came from societies where a dim view has traditionally been taken of politicians who get involved with prostitutes, and both apologised very publicly. However, there was one clear difference between them: they had previously taken very different stances on the activity that got them into trouble. Spitzer, who had developed a knack for delivering snappy, media-friendly quotes such as 'I don't care about motivation. I care about credibility', had prosecuted a number of prostitution rings during his time as attorney-general. Vaz, by contrast, had openly advocated the decriminalisation of sex work and had publicly declared that men who pay for sex should not face prosecution. It could be argued that, as chair of the Home Affairs Select Committee, Vaz had opened himself up to accusations of a conflict of interest, as he had been chairing an inquiry into whether buyers of sexual services should face criminal sanctions. But the fact that he was consistent in his spoken attitudes about prostitution worked strongly in his favour. Spitzer was betrayed by his perceived hypocrisy.

The power of a consistent narrative applies equally when evidence of wrongdoing is rather more ambiguous. In one of their studies, psychologists Daniel Effron and Benoît Monin asked people to consider a fictitious case involving a manager, named Hutchinson, who had been accused of sexual harassment.[30] Hutchinson, it was stated, had invited a female colleague to dinner to discuss a possible promotion. According to the female colleague, he had then hinted that an intimate engagement with him would help secure the promotion. She had declined the invitation and Hutchinson had promoted someone else. According to Hutchinson himself, the dinner had been meant as nothing more than an occasion for an informal, but strictly professional interview, and the woman had misunderstood his intentions. He also revealed that he had invited other candidates to dinner and that, in the end, he promoted the person he thought was the strongest candidate.

Effron and Monin, however, introduced a subtle twist into this narrative. In one version, it was stated that Hutchinson had successfully reduced incidents of sexual harassment at his company by implementing anti-harassment policies. In the other, this piece of information was omitted.

When participants in the study were asked for their views, those who had read about Hutchinson's previous attempts to reduce sexual harassment in the company refused to believe that he was guilty. Quite simply, the narrative didn't fit with what they knew about his character. Those who were unaware of this additional fact, by contrast, proved far more likely to judge him guilty. In contrast to Spitzer, Hutchinson's prior efforts to tackle sexual exploitation worked in his favour: because the evidence was ambiguous, people looked for consistency between his excuse and his character, rather than the inconsistency between the allegations and his previous stance.

This helps to explain why cases of sexual misconduct – for instance – often take so long to surface. Larry Nassar, the 'Olympics doctor' who was the USA Gymnastics' osteopathic physician for some twenty years, is a case in point. So trusted was Larry that, even after allegations made against him by a former gymnast and a second anonymous accuser were publicised by the *Indianapolis Star*, hardly anyone – including many of the parents of the girls Nassar was abusing – believed that Larry could be guilty of sexual assault.[31] He had built up an enormous store of messenger credits with his colleagues and clients. He was trusted. Parents of girls training to be Olympians were told that he was the best in the business; and, indeed, he seemed to know exactly what was wrong when patients described their symptoms, and what they should do to help fix the injury. The girls he treated called it 'the magic of Larry'.

Not only was Nassar trusted for his competence, but people also trusted his integrity. He had established a reputation as someone who put others' needs before his own. 'No matter what time, what day, you call me and I will get her in for treatment,' he told the girls' parents. And he did. Whenever his friends faced a problem, Larry was there to help. He was the guy people trusted to help them shovel snow in the winter and take them to the hospital in a medical emergency. Moreover, he was able to hide his abuse under the guise of medical professionalism. Nassar performed unusual treatments, including a 'sacrotuberous-ligament release', which involved putting his fingers between his female client's legs and pressing near her vulva. It is a legitimate treatment that physical therapists may offer to help alleviate back and hip pain. It therefore introduced a degree of ambiguity into what he was up to. There was no doubt that he had been intimately touching young girls in sensitive areas. The question was whether his actions had been appropriate.

So when the first accusations were made, none of Larry's associates believed them. The allegations were wholly inconsistent with their view of the man. It was only once the police found Nassar's hard-drive, which contained graphic images of young children, that people finally started to listen. All his previous actions had established such a powerful impression of trustworthiness that it took incontrovertible evidence to shake others' assumptions and beliefs.

Building trust

Consistency goes to the heart of our perception of trustworthiness for the simple reason that it helps us predict how someone will behave in the future. Donald Trump is, of course, a strange example of consistency. In most circumstances it is demonstrated in a rather more straightforward way. Quite simply, we infer trustworthiness if we are party to repeated, consistent, positive interactions with someone else.[32]

It's something that Frank Flynn at Stanford Business School observed when he examined the effects of social exchange between 161 engineers who worked in a telecommunications firm.[33] Drawing on surveys and performance records, Flynn found that those workers who maintained equal and reciprocal exchanges with their co-workers were not only the most productive members of the organisation, but were considered the most trustworthy, too. And as the frequency of these reciprocal exchanges increased, so did a variety of tangible and intangible benefits: collaboration, performance and trust. Flynn suggests that colleagues who have proven trustworthy in the past are likely to be given more leeway in the future because they can be relied upon to act in good faith. More people will listen to them. More people are willing to help them.

Recommendations on online trading platforms and marketplaces work in precisely the same way. By confirming the quality of past interactions, they offer a message about likely future performance. Those who have looked at transactions on eBay (which claims that up to 60 percent of buyers leave feedback about sellers after a purchase) find that the benefits of good reviews are twofold.[34] The first is the obvious one: if someone reads a positive review on eBay, they are more likely themselves to place an order. The second shows that a good reputation increases the value of the seller in terms of what they can charge.

The study showed that an online retailer with twice as many positive ratings as a comparable rival could charge a 0.35 percent premium for a used mobile phone, 0.55 percent more for a new phone and 3.7 percent more for a DVD. These differentials may seem small but, of course, they are averaged across a vast range of sellers, from large corporations to one-man bands. What they serve to show is that when we are faced with essentially the same message from a number of messengers (Do you want to buy a phone?), we are not solely influenced by price: trustworthiness has a value, too (Does the retailer seem to be the real deal, or might they be passing off a stolen or counterfeit phone?). A large number of positive ratings thus has a monetary value. It's not surprising, therefore, that online reputation systems do seem by and large to work. They act as a powerful incentive for messengers to be true to their word.

It should also be pointed out that not all reviews are equal. A retailer with, say, six five-star reviews, two four-star reviews and two one-star reviews may average a pretty credible four stars overall, but the two one-star reviews are likely to loom larger in a potential client's mind, for the simple reason that negative ratings have a stronger impact than positive ones. Most of us will have experienced the ease with which we can dissuade ourselves from making an online purchase after reading a single bad review, even if it is followed by dozens of positive ones. It is a phenomenon that appears to confirm another long-held belief about trustworthiness. It can take an awfully long time to build a trustworthy relationship but, like a fragile vase, it can be easily destroyed in an instant by a single careless act.[35]

The same holds true in our personal relationships. The messenger who betrays another's trust can activate powerful negative emotions that create a deep rift from which the relationship may never recover. People exhibit 'betrayal aversion' – they place more weight on losses that result from being betrayed than from losses that occur purely by chance.[36] Injunctive norms may well lead people to feel obliged to trust others, even when it is not in their material interest to do so. But the fear of betrayal acts as a powerful force in the opposing direction. It serves to drive people to be suspicious and sceptical of others. It serves as an ever-present barrier to the creation of trust between strangers.[37]

Trusting the unknown

To form a view of a person's future trustworthiness by assessing their previous record assumes that the record is available to us.

When it comes to judging public figures, friends, work colleagues and online retailers, the chances are that it will be. But how does one gauge trustworthiness when we first meet someone? The answer is that we rely on very rough-and-ready signals.

A key one is simple contact. Decades of research have shown that the chances of getting a stranger to cooperate with you are vastly enhanced (in fact by as much as 40 percent) if you can open a channel of communication before you make your request or move.[38] From the moment we meet someone for the first time, we're looking for clues about them. Do they seem friendly or shady? Do they fit the representation we have in our mind of a person who honours their commitments? If we can garner some positive information straight away – whether or not we qualify or reject our initial view later – we're more likely to look favourably on whatever transaction follows. Most of the time, simply by engaging with someone, we feel connected: we experience a shared humanity. And if that communication takes place face-to-face, so much the better. It is estimated that the spoken word is more effective than the written word by a factor of 2–3.[39] Once we actually meet a stranger, they cease to be an abstract name and become a real person. There is much to be said for knowing when to ditch the email and instead pick up the phone.[40]

Face-to-face contact also enables the triggering of that fundamental human impulse to infer personality from appearance. The trustworthy messenger has a face, just as much as dominant and competent messengers do, and we form a judgement about it just as swiftly – often within milliseconds. According to psychologists who developed computational models of faces based on how trustworthy people rate them to be, it would seem that while the untrustworthy face bears an expression remarkably similar to anger, the trustworthy face looks happy.[41] This basic fact holds true even when the face being judged is 'expression neutral'. Some people have faces that in their resting state simply look a little happier than others. If you are

231

fortunate enough to have a natural expression that suggests happiness, you are likely to be perceived as more trustworthy. If you are unfortunate enough to have a natural expression that suggests anger, however slight, you will be regarded as less trustworthy.

It may seem rather bizarre that humans should make these kinds of links. After all, how happy a person naturally looks and their trustworthiness have absolutely nothing in common. But it would seem that what we are responding to is how approachable someone appears to be. If they look happy, we feel safe with them and so we trust them more. If they look angry, we are more cautious and so less trusting. In a Trust Game scenario, researchers have found that those given the role of the 'trustor' typically send more money to trustworthy-looking investors. And in the real world it's been shown that people who have more trustworthy faces are more likely to get loans funded on peer-to-peer lending sites, even though more relevant information about their credit history, debt-to-income ratio, income and employment status is readily available.[42]

If this seems alarmingly simplistic, it is. On the whole, people prefer cues that are easy to process. It's hard – near-impossible – to figure out what another person's true motives or intentions are. It's much easier, and requires much less effort, to make a quick assessment of them based on how they look.[43] After all, we use facial signals to infer others' states of mind every day of our lives. The fact that most of us are notoriously bad at picking up on cues as to whether someone else is telling the truth or not doesn't stop us from trying.[44] Nor does the fact that our hit rate for trustworthiness isn't much better. There may be, at best, only a weak link between who we judge as looking trustworthy and who actually is, but that doesn't stop us from making looks-based inferences.[45]

As we spend longer with other people, we start relying on other intuition-based cues to form trustworthiness judgements, including how we feel about them. Our emotional responses seem to be a more reliable guide than single-glance impressions made on the basis of facial appearance. This was fascinatingly demonstrated in a study that involved pairs of women, only recently introduced to each other, being shown harrowing film footage of the aftermath of the nuclear bombs dropped on Hiroshima and Nagasaki and then being asked to chat with one another. What one volunteer in each pair didn't know, though, was that the other had been told to 'behave in such a way that your partner does not know you are feeling any emotions at all'. Once the film had been run and the participants' discussion observed, two things became very apparent. The first was that the women asked to suppress their true feelings became hypertensive – that is, their blood pressure increased. The second was that their partners also experienced raised blood pressure: not from suppressing their emotions, but rather because they could intuitively tell that the woman with whom they were talking was hiding something. Their bodies reacted to the apparent lack of trust.[46]

It is a feeling that we have all experienced: a 'there's something off here' sensation when, as observers, we suspect that a messenger's words and emotional signals are somehow misaligned. And, as the women who talked to one another after watching the film of Hiroshima and Nagasaki found, it has physical and neurological manifestations. In another study, participants were positioned inside a PET (positron emission tomography) scanner, attached to a skin-conductance recorder, and shown video-clips of actors telling first-person accounts of either a sad or a neutral story, with facial expressions that were either congruent or incongruent with the story being told. What the researchers found was that when the participants witnessed a mismatch between the narrative and the emotional expression displayed by the actor, their skin-conductance response increased and there was greater activation in areas of the brain thought to be involved in processing social conflict. In other words, their brains and bodies were registering that 'there's something off here'.[47] And that sense that something isn't quite right, while it may not serve as an accurate lie-detector, seems generally to work well enough for people on a day-to-day basis.[48]

The upside of a downside

If our immediate judgement of someone's trustworthiness is influenced by how they look, then how they talk (as opposed to the meat of what they actually say) can also shape our views. For example, if someone draws our attention to a potential weakness in their argument before presenting its strengths, we are more likely to assume they are trustworthy. We are disarmed by the very fact that they haven't said, 'It's going to be so great', 'This is easily the best idea', 'Bigly in fact', 'No one has ever done it better.' And, just as with experts who win people's confidence by admitting uncertainty (see p.72), we assume they are more credible. Trial attorneys who admit to a weakness, before a rival attorney points to it, win more cases. Political campaigners who begin speeches by saying something positive about an opponent will often receive a boost in perceived trustworthiness. Advertisers who point out a small drawback in their product or service, before highlighting its strengths, can experience large increases in sales – an approach that is particularly successful when an audience is already aware of the weakness (and so the damage has been done anyway).[49] In a similar way, phrases such as 'I'm not going to lie to you ...' or 'I don't wish to complain, but ...' or 'I'll be honest ...' can be remarkably effective in boosting levels of trust. Such *'dispreferred markers'*, as they are known, are a way of introducing a note of doubt or negativity while emphasising the sincerity of the speaker and thus maintaining perceptions of their likeability and trustworthiness. Indeed, they can influence how others respond to their message. For example, negative reviews that contain such phrases do less damage to consumers' willingness to pay for the reviewed item than those that have not been softened.[50]

(Re)building trust

When a messenger's trustworthiness is called into question, various options are open to them. The first is a tactic frequently employed by Donald Trump, usually in response to allegations put forward by the mainstream media: outright denial. 'What you're seeing and what you're reading is not what's happening,' he often claims.[51] It is, however, a risky strategy. If conclusive evidence is then produced to prove that the person issuing the denial is lying, their fall will be all the steeper and the more damaging.

Then there is justification and excuse. According to sociologists Marvin Scott and Stanford Lyman, a justification is when an individual accepts responsibility for a negative outcome, but denies their actions were immoral – as, for example, when a soldier kills an enemy in battle. An excuse is when an individual accepts their actions were immoral, but denies responsibility for them – as when a soldier argues that in killing, say, a civilian, he was merely following orders.[52]

And, finally, there is apology. An apology is typically thought of as the appropriate, moral and mature action that a messenger should take, when responsible for a damaging act. It can mitigate negative reactions to a wrongdoing and help re-establish social connection and cooperation. So, for example, studies find that disgruntled customers are more willing to forgive the company that accepts direct responsibility for what has gone wrong and expresses regret, than the one that seeks to lay the blame elsewhere. Obviously, for the person or party issuing the apology there's a risk, since the very act of apologising is an acknowledgement or confirmation of guilt. Someone who offers a fulsome apology may find themselves simultaneously being admired for openness and criticised for what has happened.[53] Even so, an apology is a very powerful tool – provided, that is, three fundamental rules are followed. It needs to be made quickly. It needs to be made sincerely. And it needs to be made in a way that shows remorse and a commitment to change in the future.[54]

Speedy apologies help dispel uncertainty, anger and frustration, as anyone who has ever encountered deafening silence at an airport in meltdown will know. They do, however, have to be calibrated. If an airline quickly signals the delay, apologises and provides a sufficiently concrete reason – including, in the case of a mechanical breakdown, explaining what has gone wrong and what is being done to fix it – then the apology will generally be accepted. A pre-emptive catch-all apology won't cut it. That said, a quick 'placeholder' apology, when the facts are not yet fully known, is still vastly preferable to saying nothing: 'Folks, we are really sorry about the delay. At the moment we are not entirely clear what is causing it, but be assured that I am doing my utmost to find out, so we can get you on your way and avoid this happening in the future.'

Facebook's dismal performance in 2014 offers a case study in how not to offer a speedy apology. It was the year when the social-media giant manipulated the newsfeeds of close to 700,000 users for a week, as they sought to determine whether their users would write either more positive or more negative posts, according to whether they had previously been exposed to mostly positive or negative news. The results supported the concept of 'emotional contagion' and were duly published in a top-ranking scientific journal. However, what Facebook believed would be a boon to its understanding of customers quickly became a major public-relations burden. There was a public outcry when people discovered they had been manipulated on a social-media platform that they used multiple times daily and, up to that time, had largely trusted.

236

However, it was close to a week before Mark Zuckerberg – Facebook's CEO – got round to saying anything about the matter. And even then all he had to offer was a listless comment about 'poorly communicating' the study. To add insult to injury, the justification for Facebook's actions came via a carefully worded statement that pointed users to the fact that the then-9,000-word User Agreement they had signed afforded Facebook 'presumed consent'. Several months later another Facebook spokesperson issued another faceless statement saying, 'We were unprepared for the reaction', and 'There are things we should have done differently'. Conspicuously absent were the words 'sorry' or 'we apologise'.

It was perhaps fortunate for Facebook that the event was soon forgotten. The modern world moves on rapidly. Yet there were warning signs of public disquiet that, when it came to the use of personal data, should have served up a valuable lesson. Not to mention an additional lesson in 'how not to respond to a betrayal of trust'. But it wasn't just the world that forgot. Facebook did, too. Less than four years later, it cost them dearly.

In 2018 a whistle-blower named Christopher Wylie reported to the UK newspaper *The Observer* how Cambridge Analytica, a UK-based political consulting company – founded by conservative billionaire Robert Mercer and Donald Trump's key advisor, Steve Bannon – had harvested information from fifty million Facebook profiles.[55] Particularly wrenching to users was Wylie's account of how Facebook had allowed Cambridge Analytica to collect data not only from users who consented to take their survey, but also from friends and family connected to the survey-takers. From the initial couple of hundred thousand users who agreed for their data to be used for 'academic purposes', Cambridge Analytica was able to build a sophisticated model that mined data from millions of other Facebook users connected to them. The data was then allegedly sold to politicians Ted Cruz and Donald Trump in the US, and to Brexit campaigners in the UK, in an attempt to influence election and referendum outcomes.* 'We exploited Facebook to harvest millions of people's profiles. And built models to exploit what we knew about them and target their inner demons. That was the basis the entire company was built on,' Christopher Wylie told *The Observer*.[56]

Speedy apologies are sincere apologies. Yet it was not until five days after the news broke that Mark Zuckerberg finally addressed the public – influenced, seemingly, by the mounting evidence and public outrage, rather than remorse. 'We have a responsibility to protect your data, and if we can't then we don't deserve to serve you,' Zuckerberg wrote. 'I've been working to understand exactly what happened and how to make sure this doesn't happen again. The good news is that the most important actions to prevent this from happening again today we have already taken years ago. But we also made mistakes, there's more to do, and we need to step up and do it.'[†57]

Again, no apology. And little substantive explanation for Facebook's failure to protect its users' data, either. For a long time Facebook even refused to call it a 'data breach', instead choosing to recycle the 'presumed consent' argument, which they had relied upon so heavily four years previously. Facebook was eventually fined £500,000 – the maximum permitted penalty – for a lack of transparency and failing to protect users' information. 'Facebook has failed to provide the kind of protections they are required to

---

* The Trump campaign denied the allegation: https://www.theguardian.com/technology/2017/oct/26/cambridge-analytica-used-data-from-facebook-and-politico-to-help-trump

† The decision to release a written statement was interesting, too. Written statements can be disseminated quickly, but gains in speed come at a price. That cost is the loss of humanity. It is easier to strike the right tone through speech that includes cues such as tone and expression, which can signal sincerity. But speech is fraught with pitfalls, too, especially for the more uptight, wooden communicator – labels previously directed towards Zuckerberg.

under the Data Protection Act,' said Elizabeth Denham, the UK's information commissioner. Once again fortune favoured Facebook. Had the new European General Data Protection (GDPR) Act, implemented in April 2018, applied, the penalty could have been as much as 4 percent of Facebook's global turnover. About $1.9 billion. But even a momentous fine of that scale would have paled in significance to the damage done to their reputation. In July 2018 Facebook's share price fell by 18 percent. It represented a loss in value of some $119 billion.[58]

It was the worst day for any company in stock-market history.

In the aftermath of the trust scandal, it is interesting to note Facebook's huge investments in what can only be described as 'apology ads'. It is also interesting to note that a significant amount of this expenditure has been directed to the very media platforms that have suffered most as a result of the rise in social-media platforms: TV, print newspapers, magazines, billboards and advertising boards of buses and trains. From Atlanta to Amsterdam, London to LA, St Petersburg to Sydney, the message is that 'Facebook is changing.'

'From now on, Facebook will do more to keep you safe and protect your privacy,' the ads claim.

Well, they would say that, wouldn't they?

Can people change?

Maurice Schweitzer, a professor at the Wharton School of Business, together with Columbia University's Adam Galinsky and Harvard Business School's Alison Wood Brooks, claim that the most important feature of any effective apology is the demonstration of *a commitment to change*. 'An apology should create distance from the "old self",' they write, 'and establish a "new self" that will not engage in similar behaviour.'[59] Such a promise can be very powerful and persuasive. But can a leopard truly be trusted to change its spots?

A fascinating study conducted by Schweitzer and Wood Brooks suggests that much depends on the mindset of the recipients of an apology *before* it is issued and a promise to change is made. The two professors organised a Trust Game that involved participants handing money to an investor, in the hope of seeing positive returns. It soon emerged, however, that the investor was not to be trusted. No funds were returned at the end of the first round. Or at the end of the second round. Unsurprisingly, trust rapidly eroded. After the second round only 6 percent of participants were prepared to risk handing over their $9 endowment of cash again.

But after the third round they received a message from the investor: 'Sorry, I gave you a bad deal. I can change. I will return $9 from now on.' From then on, true to his word, the investor started returning substantial sums, and trust started to recover. What was interesting, though, was that it didn't recover equally across all participants. Before playing the Trust Game, one group of participants had been given an article to read that stated that a person's character is like a rock: it doesn't change. The other group had also been asked to read an article about human behaviour, but this one stated that a person's character is not fixed, but changes incrementally with each new decision and experience. In the final round of the game, only 38 percent of the participants who had read the 'character is like a rock' article invested. But 53 percent of those who had read that 'character can change' were willing to trust in a previously untrustworthy messenger.[60]

Can a leopard change its spots? Yes. But only if those they betrayed are willing to accept that spots can be changed. If the audience believes that character is fixed, they are unlikely to give them the chance.

Of course in the most extreme breakdowns of trust, a simple apology – even if accompanied by a clear commitment to change – simply will not do. All that is left is to rebuild trust in the way that humans build relationships: slowly and transparently.

One of the most heartening examples of this is the way in which Brazil and Argentina managed to effect a reconciliation in the late 1970s and 1980s, in a period marked by hostility over nuclear arms. The US National Intelligence Agency believed that if Argentina built a nuclear device, security relationships in the entire region would be forever damaged. It also speculated that Brazil might seek to achieve a nuclear-weapons capability of its own, to 'buttress its own security and restore a sense of national prestige'. The relationship between Brazil and Argentina was already poor. The nuclear element made it far worse.

Yet the leaders of both countries, Brazil's José Sarney and Argentina's Raúl Alfonsín, managed to turn the situation round. 'We established a trusting relationship between us,' Sarney said in 2015. 'What we see happening now with immense difficulty with Iran, we did here in South America without international mediation.' Slowly and carefully, the two countries took a series of small reassuring steps, leading to the eventual setting-up of a mutual nuclear-inspections programme that increased transparency and developed closer bilateral cooperation.[61]

At the same time, the two men worked to improve their personal relationship. When Alfonsín first met Sarney, he mentioned a wish to visit the Itaipú Dam, which had been at the centre of an international waters dispute for close to a decade. Sarney acquiesced. Alfonsín then reciprocated by inviting Sarney to visit Argentina's Pilcaniyeu nuclear facility. It was a gesture of trust on both men's part that ushered in a new spirit of reciprocity. As Francesca Granelli, a visiting fellow in the War Studies Department at King's College London, documents in her wonderful account of the crisis, both leaders undertook a personal commitment to lead transparent 'Confidence and Security Building Measures', including military-to-military contact, scientific and technical exchanges and the formation of a joint nuclear-policy committee. The fact that tensions between the two South American nations were so acute actually worked in their favour. Both felt vulnerable, were prepared to express their vulnerability and, by doing so, were able to create genuine and sustainable trust. A trust strong enough to withstand future stormy weather.

8

CHARISMA

Vision, Surgency and the Mystery of Magnetism

JOHN MARKS IS NINETY-FOUR YEARS OLD and has bags of charisma. Born the son of a Jewish publican, he colourfully recalls how, as a child, he would watch his father manage bars in the tough, hard-working, hard-drinking London suburbs while his mother, Rose, ran the family home. It was a noisy and welcoming place, filled with love: chock-full of people on the inside and livestock on the outside. Dogs, geese, chickens, rabbits and even the odd goat would roam a garden that was popular with the shabbily dressed, sometimes shoeless local kids, who would often be invited to share the family's supper. It was probably their best meal of the week.[1]

During the Second World War the young John Marks's education was interrupted as the city's children were gathered up and shipped off to the countryside, out of reach of the German bombing campaigns that were destroying great swathes of London. But in an early sign of his rebellious nature, Marks ran away from his countryside school, and fled back to London to be with his parents. Perhaps it was the love and caring of others that he frequently witnessed as a child that led to his decision to study medicine. He qualified – fittingly – on 5 July 1948, the same day that the UK's revolutionary new (and free) National Health Service was born.

And maybe it was this caring disposition, combined with a seem-ingly innate and healthy dose of defiance and rebellion, that would lead to his forty-year medical career becoming such an accom-plished, active and notable one.

Marks was a founder member of the Royal College of General Practitioners, played a major role in keeping abortion legal in the UK and campaigned for the wearing of car seatbelts – saving hun-dreds, maybe thousands, of lives in the process. He argued for respecting the privacy of AIDS sufferers at a time when the world's collective fear of HIV often resulted in panic and hysteria. In 1984 he became chairman of the British Medical Association (BMA), and subsequently butted heads with Prince Charles over his suggestion that BMA stood for 'bigoted, moribund and apathetic'. Were it not for his defiant government-opposing stance on health reform and the introduction of an internal market into the supply of healthcare, he would probably now be known as *Sir* John Marks.

He is also the grandfather of Joseph Marks.

When Marks junior told Marks senior about the book he was writing – a book about modern-day messengers – his grandfather was naturally both proud and interested. 'One of the chapters is about charisma, is it?' quizzed the charismatic nonagenarian. 'Well, that's pointless! It's easy to spot charisma. But impossible to define it.' And he's right. It is very difficult to put a finger on exactly what makes a messenger charismatic. When people talk about charisma, they typically use ambiguous, abstract terms that need defining themselves. 'Compelling attractiveness or charm that can inspire devotion in others,' reads one definition, leaving one to wonder what compelling attractiveness and compelling charm look like. As John Antonakis, a researcher of organisational behaviour at the University of Lausanne, argued as recently as 2016, charisma remains an 'ill-defined and ill-measured gift'.[2] That doesn't mean, though, that it doesn't exist. After all, charisma is, as John Marks says, easy to spot.

Most people would say of charisma what US Supreme Court Justice Potter Stewart once famously said of hard-core pornography, 'I know it when I see it!'[3] People tend to agree which messengers are charismatic and which are not. Indeed, people who rate themselves highly on charisma in personality surveys tend to be the ones that others regard as charismatic.[4] We know it when we see it.

Charisma is often linked, like a linguistically conjoined twin, with the word leadership. The same mystical qualities that create the perception of charisma are often the same characteristics that cause people to listen to, and follow, certain leaders. For that reason we also tend to associate the term with particular people, rather than analyse it as a quality in itself. When we say 'charismatic' we conjure up an image of Princess Diana, or Oprah Winfrey, or Barack Obama, or Mahatma Gandhi – even Adolf Hitler. Little surprise, then, that despite widespread public and academic interest in the concept, those who have researched it have confined their study almost exclusively to the domain of leadership. Indeed, one of the earliest formal examinations of charisma was undertaken by the German philosopher Max Weber, who spoke directly of its essential role in leadership:[5]

> The term 'charisma' will be applied to a certain quality of individual personality by virtue of which he is considered extraordinary and treated as endowed with supernatural, superhuman, or at least specifically exceptional powers or qualities. These are such as are not accessible to the ordinary person, but are regarded as of divine origin or as exemplary, and on the basis of them the individual concerned is treated as a 'leader'.

No wonder so many modern theories of leadership assign such great importance to charisma, and charismatic chief executives are so highly sought-after and well compensated. A meta-analysis of data spanning close to a quarter of a century has shown that charismatic leaders not only possess an ability to inspire their troops to ever higher levels of performance, but also simultaneously embed deeper levels of commitment in their psyche.[6] This is particularly so at times of crisis or great change. In Chapter 3 we described how dominant messengers often prove particularly effective during periods of conflict or uncertainty. Charismatic messengers thrive at such moments, too: their ability to galvanise others has a powerfully persuasive effect.[7] Weber hinted at this association, noting that charismatic messengers are often at the forefront of social and revolutionary change. During such periods, people want someone to unite behind – both for who they are and for what they represent.

There is an element of self-selection here. Those who possess certain trappings of charisma – for example, a desire to stand out from the crowd, a willingness to speak up in public, unconventional attitudes, and so on – are more likely to want, and put themselves forward for, leadership roles.[8] But to associate charisma only with leadership would be a mistake. Charisma is something many people have. We find it among our friends, family members and even strangers.

The elements of charisma

Charisma involves a constellation of characteristics: self-confidence; expressiveness; energy; optimism about the future; rhetorical ability; an ease with risk-taking; challenging the status quo; and creativity (to name but a few). But because any given charismatic individual will not possess these qualities in equal measure – and, indeed, may lack some of them altogether – it has proved astonishingly difficult for researchers to pinpoint and measure the key characteristics. There are nevertheless some telltale signs that often mark out who is more likely to be regarded as charismatic.

One of these is an ability to articulate a collective identity and vision. Martin Luther King, Jr espoused equality, compassion and love. Adolf Hitler channelled a country's anger. Churchill stood for a nation's resilience. Eva Perón was a flag-waver for the underdog. In other ways they were all very different from one another, but they were all able to tap into the collective identity of the group they were addressing – by reminding their listeners of a shared history, of a need for change, and by articulating an idealised vision of the future. Each, in their own way, possessed a talent for reducing complexity, sometimes to almost binary choices involving in-groups and out-groups, the included and the excluded or the heroes and the villains. In so doing, they evoked a sense of connectedness amongst their followers, who developed an affiliation not just with each other, but also with a collective goal, which they were inspired to put ahead of their own self-interest. They became transformed. The charismatic messenger who led them was regarded as transformative.[9]

Such an ability also enabled them to elicit a sense of awe in those who encountered them. Awe, like charisma, sounds rather vague, but is a recognised state of mind that, according to researchers, diminishes individual ego and enhances a desire to connect. It can therefore alter people's ethical behaviour. Psychologist Paul Piff found that, after being asked to recall a time when they experienced awe, or standing in a grove of towering trees, participants in his studies were not only more likely to feel a diminishing sense of self, but also a greater willingness to engage in prosocial acts.[10] Awe, in other words, prompts people to view themselves as part of a larger entity. They may even reward the charismatic leader with cult or hero-like status, regardless of whether that leader goes on to live up to their expectations.

There are various ways in which charismatic leaders successfully articulate their view of a future, idealised world. One particularly powerful one is their use of metaphor – according to Aristotle, an essential weapon in anyone's rhetorical armoury. Metaphors are a potent tool because they are immediate and often intensely visual. They invoke symbolic meanings and trigger emotional reactions, without actually changing the meaning of what is being communicated. Think, for example, of Bill Clinton's 1993 inaugural address and its use of a seasonal metaphor to direct the attention of the American people to new beginnings: 'you, my fellow Americans, have forced the spring. Now we must do the work the season demands'.[11] Or of that key phrase in John F. Kennedy's speech promoting the 1960s space race: 'This nation has tossed its cap over the wall of space ...'[12] A metaphor doesn't need to be particularly original. It simply needs to be immediate and emotional, hence the impact of British parliamentarian Enoch Powell's 'Rivers of Blood' speech in 1968, which warned against mass immigration by lifting a line directly from Virgil's epic poem, the *Aeneid*: 'As I look ahead, I am filled with foreboding; like the Roman, I seem to see "the River Tiber foaming with much blood".'[13]

There is statistical evidence for a link between the use of metaphors and perceived charisma. Jeffery Scott Mio, a professor of psychology at California State Polytechnic University, has closely studied the use of this particular figure of speech by past US presidents, and found that those who score highly on Simonton's Charisma ratings* also deployed large numbers of metaphors in their inaugural speeches.[14] For example, John F. Kennedy, Franklin D. Roosevelt, Lyndon Johnson and Ronald Reagan (who all score above the seventy-fifth percentile of charismatic US presidents) used an average of twenty metaphors in their first-term inaugural speeches. By contrast, Grover Cleveland, Rutherford B. Hayes, James

---

* Dean Simonton, a professor of Psychology at UC-Davis, considered US presidents from five key vantage points: namely, their interpersonal, charismatic, deliberative, creative and neurotic styles.

Monroe and William Taft (who score below the twenty-fifth percentile) deployed, on average, a mere three. Scott Mio also notes that those presidents who scored low on Simonton's Charisma Scale were most likely to lose a re-election campaign and serve just one term. Franklin Delano Roosevelt has the highest Simonton's charisma score of all presidents. In his inaugural address, which lasted only three minutes and thirty-eight seconds, he used twenty-one metaphors (that's one every ten seconds). He won four terms in office.

If metaphors trigger immediate, often emotional responses, so do stories and anecdotes. Stories have an added advantage: they can help form a personal bond between speaker and listener, by triggering thoughts of shared experience, background and struggles. While campaigning to become Mayor of London, Sadiq Khan would make much of the fact that he was one of eight children born to Pakistani immigrants. 'My dad was a bus driver and my mum was a seamstress,' he would declare at hustings.[15] It was a successful strategy. Companies, too, spin stories that amount to personal mythologies, such as Apple's story of how Steve Jobs and Steve Wozniak dropped out of college to build early prototypes in Jobs's parents' garage in Los Altos, California. Such back-stories allow an audience, whether consumers or voters, to identify with a messenger's characteristics.

As for the type of back-story that people respond to best, that depends on whether they are seeking status or connectedness. When primed to feel compassion and connectedness, people are more likely to prefer a person or, say, a business with an underdog story: the politician who has raised themselves up by their boot straps; the little independent coffee shop that is struggling to compete with the mammoth conglomerate next door. However, when people feel proud, a preference for a high-status person or a brand with a leading, well-known or prestigious back-story is activated. Those who are accustomed to feeling inferior to richer, more dominant, competent and physically attractive messengers are especially likely to root for the underdog with a good back-story. Those with status are more likely to prefer the top-dog.[16]

Surgency

Another quality often associated with charisma is surgency: a temperament typically characterised by a positive outlook, high energy and a strong desire for rewarding experiences. People with surgency are seen as optimistic, sociable and approachable. Most psychologists attest to the idea that personality can be described along five major dimensions: conscientiousness; agreeableness; neuroticism; openness; and extraversion; and it is the last of these traits, extraversion, to which surgency is most closely linked.[17]

Surgency and emotional expression are inextricably intertwined. Charismatic messengers tend to be more emotionally expressive than others, and are able to successfully engage their audiences at an emotional level, whether positively (Martin Luther King) or negatively (Hitler). When surgency is connected with positive emotion, it makes others more likely both to pay attention and to cooperate and, because the emotion is infectious, it spreads from person to person.[18] Put simply, the more expressive the messenger, the more likely their audience is to 'catch' their enthusiasm.

The psychologist William Doherty has developed an Emotional Contagion Scale to measure people's propensity to catch emotions from others.[19] Those, he argues, who are most susceptible to emotional contagion are skilled at reading emotional expressions; they pay close attention; and they see themselves as interrelated rather than independent from others. These are precisely the qualities that surgency appeals to. Mimicry, which also features high on Doherty's Emotional Contagion Scale, is another key feature of surgency. And it's perhaps partly for this reason that body language is so important to the charismatic messenger, too. Genuine smiling, increased eye contact, animated gestures – all these amplify the charismatic person's message, in much the same way that a skilled use of spices creates a fine curry.[20]

This was compellingly demonstrated in a series of remarkable studies that took footage of people delivering speeches, removed the soundtracks and transformed the speakers themselves into animated stick-figures. Volunteers were asked to watch the resulting videos (free now, of course, from verbal cues and facial expressions) and rate the stick-people on specific personality traits, which included trustworthiness, dominance and competence, as well as psychology's big-five personality traits: conscientiousness; agreeableness; neuroticism; openness; and extraversion. A clear pattern emerged. Those animated characters judged to possess energy, enthusiasm and expressiveness (aka surgency) employed many more hand-movements overall, punctuated with only fleeting moments of stillness.

Not just that: after simply looking at the stick-people's physical movements, volunteers' personality ratings were also predictive of the amount of applause the original speech had received – their (correct) assumption being that those who employed energetic and expressive body language, and therefore who appeared surgent, were more likely to have received acclaim.[21] It seems that hand-movements act as a 'second language' of sorts. They form a dialect that reveals cues and traits to an audience, enabling them to make decisions about a messenger's surgency. These hand-gestures are literally communicating the messenger's underlying emotions and send signals of how they genuinely feel about an issue or situation. They are crucial to the messenger's chances of securing an audience's attention, their willingness to listen and, ultimately, their preparedness to take action.

If the stick-people experiment seems a little theoretical, evidence from online TED Talks confirms the general pattern. Take, by way of example, a couple of talks on leadership. One, given by Fields Wicker-Miurin, a former strategy director at the London Stock Exchange, who now heads the international social enterprise Leaders' Quest, tells the stories of three remarkable leaders – a local chief of an Amazonian tribe, the head of an Indian NGO, and the curator of a local museum from south-west China. It is a good talk. Clear. Well-evidenced. Character-rich. It convincingly shows that we can learn important lessons about leadership from people and places that have traditionally been missing from the typical business-school MBA syllabus, with its models and fancy graphs.[22]

The second TED Talk is by author and organisational consultant Simon Sinek. He, too, talks about leaders – both individuals and organisations – and how they inspire actions in others. Like Wicker-Miurin's talk, Sinek's talk is a good one. Clear. Well-evidenced. It evokes characters, too, like Martin Luther King and the Wright Brothers.[23]

However, where the two talks diverge is in the way they have been received. At the time of writing, Wicker-Miurin's talk has been viewed online just over a million times. Sinek's talk has been viewed more than forty-three million times. How does one eighteen-minute talk about leadership so convincingly thump another eighteen-minute talk on the same topic? Of course many factors may be in play, but it's hard to avoid the conclusion that Sinek's greater use of hand-gestures plays an important part in the contin-uing popularity of his talk.

The author and body-language trainer Vanessa Van Edwards has analysed hundreds of TED Talks with the goal of figuring out why some talks become wildly popular and others sink without trace – even when the talks concern broadly similar subjects and are made up of messages that are comparable in terms of content and attractiveness.[24] And it was Van Edwards who designed a study that goes some way to explaining why Simon Sinek's talk on leadership attracted forty times more viewers than Fields Wicker-Miurin's. Employing a crowd-sourced team of online researchers and asking them to analyse the verbal and non-verbal patterns displayed by a range of TED Talks, Van Edwards was able to identify an intriguing pattern. The most successful talks on TED.com are made by presenters who use almost twice as many hand-gestures as their less successful peers: an average of 465 compared to 272, in a typical eighteen-minute TED Talk. The more speakers talk with their hands, the more they are viewed as warm and energetic. The number of gestures predicts viewers' ratings of the speaker's charisma. Less animated, more stilted speakers are more likely to be seen as cold and analytical.

Of course life is never quite that straightforward: one can always have too much of a good thing. During the 2016 presidential primaries, Republican governor John Kasich was ridiculed for his combative and all-too-frequent 'ninja hand-gestures'. On one memorable occasion, during a debate on foreign policy, Kasich accompanied his fly-swatting hand-gestures with a rallying cry that the United States should 'punch the Russians in the nose'.[25] Confrontational? Certainly. But charismatic? Almost certainly not.

Thinking fast, and flow

When researchers place charisma under the metaphorical microscope, in an attempt to identify its central ingredients, there is an inevitable tendency to seek a link with intelligence. Understandably so. We associate charisma with leadership. We assume that leaders are intelligent. Ergo, charismatic people are intelligent people.

In fact research has shown that there is very little, if any, correlation between a messenger's charisma and their general intelligence.[26] It takes no more than a moment's reflection to come up with a list of individuals who possess only average levels of intelligence, yet are bursting with charismatic ability; and an even greater number of incredibly smart people who lack it entirely. It may seem superficially plausible that a clever person should know how to convey their message in a charismatic manner – one that enables their audience to better connect with what they are saying – but those who are charismatic possess an intuitive ability, much like those who are good at kicking a football, rather than one produced via rational and deliberative thought.

Take Albert Einstein. The father of modern theoretical physics would surely make everyone's 'most intelligent' list. Yet he wasn't a great public communicator. Or even an average one. Indeed, his lectures were a byword for boredom. When he taught a class on thermodynamics at the University of Bern, shortly after publishing his famous $E=mc^2$ equation, only a handful of students attended. And they were all his close friends. The following term his university decided to cancel the class completely. Einstein's application to join the faculty at the Swiss Federal Institute of Technology would have failed, had it not been for the intervention of a friend who assured the president of the institute that, despite not being 'the finest of talkers', Einstein was nevertheless intellectually worthy of the post. '[His] lectures tended to be regarded as disorganized,' wrote his biographer, Walter Isaacson, who notes that Einstein was never the most inspiring of teachers.

Einstein is not the only brilliant man to have been a poor communicator. As the Wharton organisational psychologist Adam Grant astutely points out, 'Although it's often said that those who can't do teach, the reality is that the best doers are often the worst teachers.'[27] Ironically, the best, most charismatic teachers are often not the professors who achieved fame through scholarly research, but junior academics who know how to communicate.[28] Grant's view is that 'it's not just what they know; it's about how recently and easily they learned it, and how clearly and enthusiastically they communicate it'.

That doesn't mean, though, that there are no features associated with intelligence that are also linked to charisma. One mental gift that many charismatic people frequently have is the ability to process information quickly and fluidly: they think fast and so are able to make immediate judgements about situations and calibrate their behaviour accordingly. Such quick thinking precludes the agonised indecisiveness from which much cleverer people often suffer. It can also equip the charismatic person with a repertoire of responses, often in the form of quick-witted comments, creatively expressed ideas and funny one-liners, which leave the less furnished amongst us looking on enviously, thinking, 'I wish I had thought of that.' Mental speed facilitates skilful social functioning. The result: quick thinkers are smooth talkers.[29]

A slower, more reflective messenger may be in possession of far more wisdom than the quick-witted charmer. The charmer may be found out, if they're put on the spot by a tricky question from a knowledgeable audience. As, for example, when asked to explain Einstein's theory of relativity.

Charisma's hard and soft sides

The large array of characteristics that have been shown to underlie charisma, and the tendency to define it by outcomes, have made it hard to create a clear theoretical framework that explains what exactly it is. Or, at least, that was the case until recently. The work of Dr Konstantin Tskhay, however, has suggested an underlying pattern. Tskhay's research points to charisma being composed of a pair of factors that happen to mirror two messenger effects outlined in this book: the hard effect of dominance and the soft-messenger effect of warmth.[30] Charismatic messengers, according to Tskhay, are able to assert themselves, lead a group and have presence in a room (dominance), but are also simultaneously able to get along with people, make them feel comfortable and convey positive regard (warmth). Essentially, the charismatic messenger is dominant enough to attract attention and make themselves heard, but not so much as to be perceived as aggressive or domineering. Rather than rule by coercion, charismatic people rule by charm. Tskhay's questionnaire, designed to measure charisma via assessments of dominance and warmth, is highly predictive of whether or not the messenger will be viewed as charismatic and persuasive. When, for example, audiences listened to a messenger making either strong or weak arguments in favour of supporting wind-power rather than other sources of electricity (gas or oil, for instance), those who scored higher on Tskhay's General Charisma Inventory Scale were more persuasive, regardless of the message itself or the strength of the rationale that supported it. Bottom line: even though listeners were trying to focus on the strength of the arguments being made, they were more persuaded by those who expressed them charismatically.

Of course, not all charismatic figures in history have exhibited warmth. Hitler, for one, comes to mind. But that doesn't disprove Tskhay's fundamental insight into the blend of qualities that are required. Hitler may have lacked warmth, as it is typically understood, but he was able to project a sense of connectedness effectively. Laurence Rees's documentary *The Dark Charisma of Adolf Hitler* featured an interview with Jutta Ruediger, who described how when she looked at Hitler she suddenly felt a connection with him: 'I myself had the feeling that here was a man who did not think about himself and his own advantage,' she said, 'but solely about the good of the German people.' Or as Hans Frank, who heard Hitler speak in a Beer

Hall in 1920, put it: 'he uttered what was in the consciousness of all those present'. And according to Emil Klein, who heard Hitler speak in the 1920s, 'The man gave off such a charisma that people believed whatever he said.'

Dominance and warmth are normally viewed as mutually contradictory. It's assumed that the person who is competitive and confrontational cannot also be warm, kind and caring. By the same token, someone who is warm can all too easily be assumed to be a pushover. But the charismatic person is able to balance these two qualities: they are generally able to avoid the aggression and anger that are traits of a dominant messenger, or at least channel them towards an 'out-group', and through a strong sense of individual connection. When hard- and soft-messenger effects are aligned in this way, they are a powerful weapon.

Can you learn to be charismatic?

Charisma, much like intelligence, is a gift. In the same way that an ability to solve complex maths problems doesn't come naturally to the majority of us, so an aptitude to communicate in an emotionally laden, energetic and engaging way is something that only a lucky minority possess. But that doesn't mean we can't all learn a few tricks from the charismatic messenger. We can work on the way we address groups of people, employing appropriate metaphors, using non-verbal cues such as hand-gestures and suitable facial expressions, and seeking to tap into shared emotions and a sense of community. John Antonakis, who has played such a leading role in mobilising the scientific community to agree on a workable definition of charisma,*

---

* Antonakis defines charisma as 'values-based, symbolic, and emotion-laden leader signaling'.

has also pioneered the scientific study of charisma training and found that such skills can indeed be developed.[31]

Recall the study we cited at the very beginning of this book, which found that teachers who display signs of dominance and warmth – the yin-and-yang of charisma – make a better impression on their students and receive better evaluations (see p.13–14). Recall, too, how those students subsequently rated them as better teachers.[32] Imagine what might have happened if Einstein had been able to take John Antonakis's charisma training before he started teaching his thermodynamics classes. Instead of the class being cancelled, might more students have turned up to his future lectures? And had that enthusiasm been ignited and passed down from teacher to teacher, university to university, school to school, would more of today's children – when asked, 'What do you want to be in the future?' – answer 'scientist' rather than what they answered in the UK survey: rich; famous; or rich and famous?

As we head to the Conclusion of this book, it is worth taking a moment to reflect on the journey so far. Part One explored society's hard messengers: those who possess status formed by socio-economic position, competence, dominance and physical attractiveness. In Part Two we explored the soft messengers who exemplify the connectedness-driven characteristics of perceived warmth, vulnerability, trustworthiness and charisma. It is our contention that almost every facet of our lives – the values we hold, the choices we make, the politics we follow, what we believe as truth, what we dismiss as fake or irrelevant, our attitudes, the groups we join and the ones we reject – is influenced not only by the content of messages sent, but also by the messengers delivering them. Messengers are fundamental to the very fabric of society and our place within it; they wield incredible power, not just over what we think and believe, but ultimately over *who we are* and *who we become*. So which of these messenger features have the most power over us? Which serve as the most important inputs, when deciding who to listen to and believe? How might various messenger effects interact with each other? And what can we do to become more aware of, and understand, the potential implications of these potent effects?

This is the area to which we will now turn our attention.

CONCLUSION

Listening ... Believing ... Becoming

In 1981 the British government's Home Office issued a pamphlet entitled *Civil Defence: Why We Need It*, which sought to justify the need to prepare for a possible nuclear attack. When the topic was then discussed in Parliament, one minister asked who would be best placed to relay important information to the public, were the worst to happen.

Two names were put forward: Kevin Keegan and Ian Botham.[1]

To be clear, neither Keegan nor Botham was an expert on civil defence. Neither had received any training in what to do in the immediate aftermath of an attack, or in how to cope with the civil dislocation and unrest that would follow. And they had not been told how to disseminate messages that might calm nerves and reduce uncertainty. In short, they were very definitely not the answer to the question 'Who is most qualified to deliver important messages in the event of a nuclear war?' Local government officials, police officers and leaders of community groups would have been far more suitable for that role.

But Keegan and Botham hadn't been nominated because they were experts. Their names had been put forward because they possessed a certain kind of status. The former was, arguably at the time, the UK's best-known soccer player. The latter, earlier that year, had more or less single-handedly battered the Australians into submission in the Ashes Test cricket tournament.

Deploying someone who possesses status in one domain to deliver a message in another, which they know little to nothing about, is hardly an uncommon tactic. US presidential hopefuls do it all the time. In the 1920s Warren Harding successfully requisitioned the support of such Hollywood stars as Al Jolson and Mary Pickford in his bid to win the White House. In the early 1960s John F. Kennedy famously commandeered Dean Martin and his 'Rat Pack' buddies. In 2007 Oprah Winfrey endorsed Barack Obama during an interview on CNN's *Larry King Live* – winning him an estimated 1,015,559 additional votes, according to one pair of US economists.[2]

A fascinating recent instance of a political endorsement by a celebrity was singer Taylor Swift's decision, during the 2018 US midterm elections, to promote a pair of Democratic candidates to her 110 million followers on Instagram. 'I will be voting for Phil Bredesen for Senate and Jim Cooper for House of Representatives,' she wrote. 'Please, please educate yourself on the candidates running in your state and vote based on who most closely represents your values. For a lot of us, we may never find a candidate or party with whom we agree 100% on every issue, but we have to vote anyway.' Swift had never previously revealed her political leanings. Indeed, some had criticised her for not using her influence to push for Hillary Clinton's election as president in 2016. Swift's decision to weigh in on the 2018 mid-term elections therefore divided opinion. Many were delighted. Others disapproved, arguing that she should 'stick to matters of country music, not country policy'.

Did Taylor Swift's Instagram post influence the outcomes of the mid-term elections? On one level, the answer would appear to be a fairly stark 'No'. After all, only one of her preferred candidates ended up winning. 'Taylor Swift couldn't sway a Tennessee election' and 'Taylor Swift endorsement falls flat' were the inevitable newspaper headlines that followed.[3]

But a closer look reveals that the true picture is rather more nuanced and complex.

One key point to bear in mind is that, according to a CBS poll released the day before Swift's post, Phil Bredesen – Swift's preferred candidate – was eight points behind his Republican opponent, Marsha Blackburn.[4] Swift was not making an intervention in a tight race. Tennessee was a staunchly Republican state that had voted for that party's candidates in the previous four presidential elections (60 percent voted for Donald Trump in 2016). It was unlikely that Republican voters were going to change their views overnight just because a pop star suggested they should. If anything, the reverse probably proved true. Swift's tirade against their preferred candidates galvanised voters on the right, turning them against her, rather than against those at whom she was aiming her attack.[5] After she revealed her position, Republican voters no longer felt a connectedness to her and instead began to view her with disdain: in their eyes, her messenger status had changed from 'beloved home-grown star' to 'Hollywood liberal elitist'.

But others do seem to have listened to Swift. Those (many of them millennials) who revered the pop star, and felt closer to her than to any particular political party, suddenly started getting off their apolitical backsides and registered to vote. Vote.org – a non-partisan group that works to increase voter turnout – reported that 212,871 new voters registered on the site within forty-eight hours of Swift's post. That's close to the number who registered in the whole of the preceding month. More than half of them (131,161) were between the ages of eighteen and twenty-nine. In the previous four mid-term elections, only 20 percent of eligible citizens in that age group had voted. Yet according to the *New York Post*, the number of eighteen-to twenty-nine-year-olds submitting early votes for the mid-terms in the wake of Swift's post jumped by a whopping 663 percent, compared with those who did so in 2014.[6] Bredesen may have lost, but who knows what those additional voters – drawn from a group often said to be disillusioned with, and disengaged from, the current political system – might do in the future? These former non-voters may become politically transformed, simply because they responded to a heartfelt message from a high-status messenger to whom they felt connected.

Taylor Swift's political intervention shows how complex messenger effects can be. But it also demonstrates that just because they're complex, that doesn't mean they can't also be astonishingly powerful. Sometimes in ways that we wouldn't intuitively expect. Imagine a contestant, Jane, in the hot-seat on *Who Wants to Be a Millionaire?* – the TV game-show where contenders are asked increasingly difficult trivia-questions, for a chance to win snowballing amounts of money. Things are going well until she is asked a question that, should she answer it correctly, will win her a handsome prize. The problem is that the question – about an old 1950s movie she has never heard of – completely baffles her. Acutely aware that it's too risky to make a guess, she decides to deploy one of the 'lifelines' the game allows and phone a friend for advice. But which friend? Jane recalls having chatted about cinema with a couple of friends – one of whom knew much more than the other – but her memory of their film knowledge is imperfect. It also happens to be the case that one of these two friends shares Jane's political views, while the other very much doesn't. But that's not what Jane is thinking about now. She's thinking about which friend is more likely to get a movie trivia-question right.

This *Who Wants to Be a Millionaire?* scenario shares many features with a study one of us conducted with Eloise Copland, Eleanor Loh, Cass Sunstein and Tali Sharot, which we first referred to at the beginning of Part Two (see p.148). Our results suggest that Jane will end up ringing the friend who shares her political views, even if she has witnessed evidence suggesting that this friend knows less about movie trivia than the one who disagrees with her politically.[7] Objectively, she knows that political agreement has absolutely nothing to do with cinematic knowledge. But she's not being objective. She's making a classic human error: believing that different skills and attributes – rather than being independent of one another – are inextricably connected. And that just because her friend is similar to her in one domain, she is also likely to be competent in an entirely unrelated one. In essence, Jane is listening to the siren voice of the messenger.

So powerful is this voice that it can be a looming presence in our minds, frequently leading us to make connections that are, to all intents and purposes, illogical: Kevin Keegan is a great soccer player and was captain of the national team, so we can trust him in the event of nuclear annihilation. Taylor Swift is a great pop singer, therefore we should follow her political advice. The results of our study suggest that if Tennessee Republicans had been asked, 'How intelligent is Taylor Swift?' on 9 October, the day after she penned the Instagram post, they would have rated her much lower than they would have done just two days before. The behaviourist Edward Thorndike dubbed this phenomenon the *Halo Effect*.[8] In the course of his studies, many of which were conducted in large corporations, he discovered how often people would assume that a strength or weakness in one area was matched by a similar strength or weakness in another. Managers asked to rate employees on two different characteristics – for example, 'leadership' and 'intelligence', or 'dependability' and 'decisiveness' – had a tendency to allow their rating of one characteristic to guide their feelings on a second, often unrelated, one. Employees deemed to be strong leaders would, more often than not, also be rated as intelligent. Those thought to be indecisive would tend to be assumed to be wanting in other areas as well. Few employees were deemed to be intelligent but indecisive, or dependable but unintelligent. Essentially, there were two groups: good employees and bad ones. It seems that people don't just judge a book by its cover; they go on to judge the entire library. Once an audience perceives a messenger to be in possession of one messenger effect – often via nothing more than a single signal of their fame, warmth, competence, charisma or attractiveness – then a powerful 'halo effect' influences how that messenger is evaluated on other traits.

Such assumptions play out at an inter-personal level, too. If you meet someone at a conference and discover that you are both friends with someone you regard as kind, you may well assume that the person you have just encountered is kind, too.[9] By the same token, if that person is friends with someone you're not keen on, you may well take an instant dislike to them, too. These principles are, of course, also at work in the associations we make between people and objects, as the world of advertising shows very clearly. We'll view a T-shirt favourably if it's worn by someone we like or whom we perceive to possess status. Or, as was the case with Nike poster-boys Tiger Woods and Lance Armstrong, we may turn against things we previously liked, simply because the messenger who promoted them has fallen from favour.[10]

It's not hard to see the implications associated with falling into the trap of this messenger bias. If we are more prepared to listen to a celebrity than an expert, to purchase something simply because of its association with an attractive person, or to respond positively to a political viewpoint simply because it's made by a friend, then it is scarcely surprising that we live in a world awash with 'fake news', conspiracy theories and poor advice. These messenger traits, and the signals that alert us to their presence, have a worrying consequence. Tough though it can be to admit, we risk listening to the wrong messengers. Of course our tendency is to assume that *we* have immunity to these effects. We tell ourselves that it is other people who are susceptible to the dubious messages of ill-informed messengers who simply possess prominence or connections. That we possess a resistance to enable us to neutralise such forces. That we won't be fooled by the attractive messenger wearing the prestigious logo, or fall into the trap of preferring a like-minded amateur to a dissimilar, but much smarter, expert. Neither will we succumb to the charismatic politicians whose policies promise so much, but deliver so little. We believe we're the students described in Chapter 1, who sneered at the idea that they wouldn't sound a horn at an immobile car simply because it was a high-status one.

The evidence, of course, suggests otherwise.

So what can be done? Two ideas come to mind.

First, it should pay to be truthful and trustworthy. Disinformation is insidious. A 2018 study, for example, which analysed more than 125,000 news stories circulated on Twitter that had been categorised as either fact or fiction, using six independent fact-checking bodies, showed that 'fake news' is more virulent than real news, and that false stories spread faster, deeper and more disparately across audiences than true ones.[11] Phoney or exaggerated stories – especially about terrorism, science, finance and urban legends – are particularly likely to be disseminated and are generally regarded as more 'novel' and 'sharable' than real news. Bots, counter to many people's beliefs, are just as likely to spread facts as fiction. Not so humans. The sad truth is that people produce 'fake news', and people are most likely to propagate it.

This depressing finding suggests that consideration should be given to programmes and policies that make it possible for heightened levels of trustworthiness in society's most important message platforms to carry some kind of reward.

News-labelling tools that signal the reliability of news items and articles, rather like traffic-light systems on food packaging, might help. So too would the use of algorithms on popular social-media and news platforms that preferentially display content from sources that its users rate as trustworthy. Another recent study finds evidence to support such an idea. Using news from sixty sources – including mainstream media outlets such as CNN, NPR, BBC and Fox News, as well as more partisan websites like Breitbart and now8news.com – the study found, perhaps surprisingly, that readers are quite good at distinguishing between low- and high-quality sources. As good, in fact, as eight fact-checkers employed to independently assess trustworthiness.[12] This suggests that the ability to discern between truth and fact is as much a function of laziness as it is of ideology, partly because there is just too much information being broadcast.[13] Therefore, trust-labels and algorithms could be combined with policies that incentivise media platforms to publish honest facts and credible stories. One idea worth investigating is the potential to offer tax breaks or incentives (maybe in the form of reduced corporate taxes) to those news organisations and social-media outfits independently judged to occupy heightened positions of trust. To be clear, we are not suggesting that shareholders and executives be allowed to keep the extra cash. Rather, it should be distributed equally among all staff, so that everyone has skin in the game. Both in terms of practising and policing trustworthiness.

Policing trustworthiness through taxation and other policies is a complicated business, so a second, and perhaps easier place to start, is with ourselves. A better understanding of how our minds respond to these potent messenger traits may lead to us becoming more aware of the pitfalls that await us. Consequently, it might be useful for people to learn earlier, rather than later in life precisely how their brains operate. At the age of sixteen, students in most countries take exams in subjects such as maths, English and the sciences. Psychology rarely features. Indeed, while just over 40 percent of students in countries including America and the UK study geography for at least two years by the age of sixteen, only 2 percent study psychology.[14] Should we infer that geography is more useful and popular? Perhaps not. When entering further and higher education, psychology degrees appear more popular than geography degrees and increasingly feature as compulsory modules in other undergraduate and postgraduate degree programmes, such as economics, marketing, communication and politics.[15] Regardless, it is a fact that most people leave school without an education in basic psychology, or what kind of messenger signals they are most likely to respond to.

Arguably, society's most important messengers are not just its teachers, but also its parents. They have an important role to play by encouraging conversations and discussions at home about the questions and issues that we face daily. How do we decide who we should believe? Are we too swayed by charisma, confidence and looks? These, after all, are issues that face us all and are not going to go away. We hope this book provides some of the answers. We also hope that it points the way to some practical lessons to be learned from both hard and soft, effective messengers.

One messenger to rule them all?

One question we've been asked a number of times in the course of our research is whether there is one messenger trait, out of the eight we have identified, that is particularly powerful – that trumps all the others. A recent meta-analysis, which integrated the results of multiple studies examining the impact of celebrity endorsements in advertisements, suggests that there might be. Trustworthiness.[16] This same quality was included in a trio of traits (expertise and similarity were the others) in an influential UK Government report.[17] It also scores highly in another set of large-scale studies that sought to establish which traits people around the world most value (those surveyed ranged from individuals in remote communities in Japan, Ecuador and Mauritius, to those living in major cities in the UK, the US and Australia). In the advertising survey, competence came second and attractiveness third. In the valued-traits survey, competence again featured prominently, with warmth towards the top of the list.[18]

The obvious caveat here is that people were responding to very specific questions: one to do with advertising, and one to do with character traits. And even then, while trustworthiness and competence scored highly in both surveys, a gulf clearly exists between the understandable choice of attractiveness in the advertising survey and the equally understandable choice of warmth in the global one. This fact alone should be sufficient to demonstrate the dangers in assuming that some messenger effects are automatically stronger than others. Rather, what it shows is that while a perception of trustworthiness is clearly key in a wide range of situations, the effectiveness of all the various messenger effects that we have discussed is very much down to the specific contexts and circumstances at hand.

The seemingly binary choice of hard and soft is a case in point. As a rule, hard messengers are more likely to have an impact on audiences looking to gain something tangible from them: resources or information, or a leader to follow. Soft messengers appeal more to those interested in less tangible benefits: a sense of a personal bond or loyalty, or mutual respect. Interestingly, the hard-messenger effect of attractiveness can be powerful in what otherwise appear to be soft-messenger scenarios, just as the soft-messenger effect of charisma plays out well in hard-messenger situations. And any effect will become more important when those around show a general lack of it.[19] The skilled messenger, therefore, needs not only to be able to signal their possession of various traits, but also be alive to the specific situations where one is more likely to carry sway than another.

Take hierarchies, for example – or, more specifically, those at the top of them. Hard messengers tend to do well at attaining positions in, and rising through, organisational hierarchies.[20] This is especially so in times of uncertainty or conflict, when the perception of external threats is such that people respond well to traits such as dominance.

But this doesn't mean that leadership requires continuous expressions of status. The results of a recent study examining supervisor–subordinate dynamics in the Taiwanese military showed that those who behave in a dominant-authoritarian manner towards their subordinates are less likely to attain a good performance from them, and consequently end up being more dissatisfied with their employees than leaders who, while assertive, are also compassionate.[21] Indeed, those leaders perceived by others to possess status are precisely the ones most likely to benefit from adopting a softer approach by demonstrating warmth, trustworthiness and their own vulnerabilities.

This last point chimes with a well-known phenomenon in psychology – the *pratfall effect* – which describes how a temporary loss in status can make a messenger appear more human, and therefore likely to receive more favourable evaluations.[22] The effect was first demonstrated in the 1960s by the social psychologist Elliot Aronson, who showed that if an intelligent and competent messenger is witnessed making a blunder – for the purposes of Aronson's study, this involved spilling a cup of coffee on themselves – observers rated them as no less competent than before, but as much more likeable. By contrast, people witnessing a less competent messenger making the same mistake typically regarded their blunder as further evidence that they were, indeed, incompetent – and viewed them as less likeable, too. For the high-status messenger, a small flaw added yin to their yang: it made them appear a rounder, more complete person.

There are other highly complex and context-relevant features of human society that cut across messenger effects. Notable among these are ones to do with gender and culture.

Gender

Stereotypically, men are society's hard messengers: they have therefore traditionally been regarded as more authoritative than women, and so better suited for positions of leadership and power. Conversely, women have been viewed as soft messengers: caring, consensual, emotionally sensitive – even vulnerable (think damsel in distress).[23] As a result, they have been – and continue to be – at a severe disadvantage in those situations where hard-messenger effects are most in play. Others may not listen to them or will place too little value on their advice and ideas. They may also be passed over for promotion or election to public office.

The situation tends to be even worse for women with children. Research has shown that professional women with children are much more likely to be questioned about their ability to juggle their professional duties with their parental ones than men in the same position. Their proficiency is also likely to be doubted. In one study, people were first asked to rate the profiles of a range of management consultants in terms of their perceived competence and warmth, and then to say who they would prefer to see working on a project. By and large, parents were rated as being warmer than those consultants who didn't have children. But women suffered a double-whammy. If they were childless, they were viewed as competent but colder. If they had children, they were assumed to be warm but less competent. For men with children, there was no such trade-off. In fact it was all gain: their competence rating stayed the same, but their warmth rating received a boost.[24]

It's because men have traditionally been awarded higher status that in the 1970s advertisers assumed they would be better placed to sell things: up to 70 percent of adverts run in that decade featured a male as the central figure. And although we may think that we now live in more enlightened times, the fact remains that a 2017 meta-analysis of forty-six studies found that male celebrities remain the most effective messengers when it comes to endorsing products, brands or political candidates. Their perceived power, expertise and confidence weigh heavily with their audience.[25]

There is, of course, one hard-messenger trait that society in general, and advertisers in particular, associate more with women than with men: attractiveness. It's a quality that is capitalised on to grab attention, arousing sexual interest in men and aspiration in other women ('I want to look like her and have what she's got'). Consequently, while virtually naked men are uncommon in adverts, near-naked women are ubiquitous.[26]

The attractiveness cue can lead to unwanted behaviour on the part of the viewer: evidence shows that after looking at adverts that sexually objectify women, men are more likely to focus on their physical appearance and care less about their human-centric qualities in real life.[27] Such adverts can also create social expectations among women, with those who perceive themselves as less attractive seeing themselves as less worthy.[28] Some have sought to buck this trend. In 2004, Dove – a personal-care brand of body moisturisers, hair-care products, shower gels and antiperspirants – challenged consumers to re-evaluate female beauty by using regular women (as opposed to professional models) of varying shapes and sizes as brand advocates. Although the campaign did not win universal approval, it certainly incited dialogue about the expectations and pressures that advertisers are placing on women. Somewhat depressingly, it appears that females' responses to such ads may depend on how men react to them. A recent study found that women who were shown pictures of

US size 8–10 female models (rather than the standard size 2) experienced increased levels of self-esteem and satisfaction only if they had been told that the pictures had been picked out by *men* as being attractive. Those who were shown the pictures but did not receive this information, or who were told that other women found the average-sized female models attractive, experienced no such boost.[29]

If the attractiveness cue has caused problems for women, the dominance cue that is so associated with men has historically caused problems for the whole of society. Many have argued – admittedly not without being challenged – that the last half-century or so has been the most peaceful of humankind's tenure on the planet.[30] As a result, it's tempting to infer that dominant messengers perhaps don't possess the same levels of power and influence they once enjoyed, and that in our increasingly connected world, softer messages will often hold greater sway. And it has been claimed by some that, 'If women ruled the world, there would be fewer conflicts and wars.' This may be true, but we offer a different perspective. Given that society's harder messengers – especially those who are dominant and authoritarian – typically thrive in situations of crisis, threat and competitive conflict, an alternative conclusion may be more apt.

If there were less conflict and fewer wars, then women, who are stereotyped as warmer and more empathetic than men, would probably rule the world.

Culture

In interdependent cultures – where group cohesiveness is valued more than individual contribution – *soft*-messenger traits like warmth and trustworthiness are more highly prized. In independent cultures, *hard* traits appear a more effective route to a messenger's success. This is true both at the organisational and the societal level.[31] Latin American countries, which are typically thought of as more collectivistic, are more likely to favour *soft*-messenger traits, such as warmth and generosity, whereas individualistic countries like North America place greater value on *hard* traits, such as dominance and socio-economic position. People from collectivistic cultures are also less likely to adopt self-promoting and self-enhancing strategies than those from individualistic ones.[32] For example, studies find that Chinese children are likely to display modesty after performing a good deed. Canadian children, by contrast, are much more inclined to boast if they are deemed to have behaved well.[33]

In the political sphere, the messenger traits likely to predict electoral success also differ from culture to culture. In the US, a politician who is regarded as dominant is also likely to be regarded as competent and will gain votes accordingly. In Japan, by contrast, politicians viewed as warm are more likely to be regarded as competent and may well receive the most votes. Indeed, the Japanese culture generally places great emphasis on ideals of modesty, humility and self-improvement.[34]

What, then, is one to make of the numerous cases of wholly collectivistic cultures voting into office wholly dominant hard leaders such as Xi Jinping of China and Nicolás Maduro of Venezuela? Here something else is clearly going on. The extent to which a country is led by a leader who possesses mainly hard- or soft-messenger traits is also affected by that culture's Power Distance Index – a term coined by Dutch social psychologist Geert Hofstede to describe how much citizens expect, and are willing to accept, an unequal distribution of power within a culture.[35] Countries with a high Power Distance Index culture-score (China scores eighty, Venezuela eighty-one) accept that power is unevenly distributed and therefore power becomes centralised to fewer leaders. In lower Power Distance cultures (the US scores forty, the UK thirty-five and Finland thirty-one) citizens are more independent and demand leaders who have a much more balanced array of messenger traits: hard on the occasions when it's needed but, in the main, likeable and connected.

Listening … believing … becoming

Messengers represents the fruits of our investigation into more than sixty years' worth of research exploring the traits of communicators to whom people are most inclined to listen. It is a body of research that is as rich as it is broad, spanning every walk of life, from the workplace to politics to the home, and forms of communication that range from everyday conversation to the media and the online world. The eight messenger effects we have discussed – four of them 'status-driven' hard effects, and the other four 'connectedness-driven' soft effects – underpin every aspect of daily social interaction. And they help to explain three key processes. Who we listen to. What we believe. And who we become.

Listening

Each of these eight messenger cues has an attention-capturing quality that is automatic and unthinking. However, the latest research suggests that those perceived as powerful and dominant, who can potentially have the greatest impact on our welfare, are attended to more quickly than softer types.[36] Similarly, attractive individuals also draw attention particularly easily and quickly, due to the evolutionary and social value of this messenger characteristic.[37] Of course just because a person commands attention, this doesn't guarantee that any ideas, opinions or requests then expressed are accepted or complied with. But it does mean they won't fall on deaf ears. The very fact that they are receiving attention and being listened to means they are more likely to be given consideration.

Believing

If people are drawn in by these eight messenger cues, the way they respond is shaped by the assumptions they simultaneously make about those delivering them. Potentially life-saving advice sounds more convincing when delivered by someone who has all the appearance of being an expert. Instructions issued during a fire drill appear more credible when hollered by an individual with a dominant-sounding voice. Encouragement and empathy seem more genuine when delivered by a messenger who is perceived as warm. People may be prompted to listen by any messenger effect, but their preparedness to believe what they hear is influenced by the extent to which the nature of the messenger and the nature of their message mesh.

Becoming

As listeners become more attentive and receptive, a third factor comes into play. Not only do they potentially start to believe a messenger, but that belief can begin to shape how they then behave and who they become. A shy teenager might be prompted by an aggressively dominant friend to take drugs or join a gang; or they might be persuaded by a charismatic classmate to stick to the straight and narrow. An adult's choice of career or partner might be shaped by the influence of one particularly powerful messenger. So too might their decision to vaccinate their child or not, impacting not only on their child's health outcomes, but also on those of many others around them. An apolitical person may be turned into a serial voter by a celebrity. In some cases it might even be the celebrity who is voted for, leading to the possibility of an entire country's future becoming shaped not necessarily by a proficient messenger, but simply by one who is prominent and dominant.

Our fundamental personalities may be genetically coded and remain relatively stable over time, but just about everything else in our lives is fair game to the messengers in society that we listen to.

ACKNOWLEDGEMENTS

There are a large number of people to whom we are not only indebted for their role in this book, but whom we also have the remarkable good fortune to call friends, colleagues, collaborators and loved ones.

Topping the list are Lindsay Martin and Lauren Porter.

Lindsay has experienced life as an author's better half with good grace, understanding and humour. Her unyielding support and love are impossible to value, but it should be known that they absolutely are valued.

Lauren, similarly, has put up with countless retellings of the book's key themes and anecdotes, always with a smile. She is an incredible companion, bringing light and good cheer into just about every situation she encounters.

To Sarah Tobitt, Catherine Scott, Araminta Naylor, Bobette Gordon, Eily VanderMeer, Cara Tracy, Greg Neidert, Karen Gonsalkorale, Chris Kelly, Bastien Blain and Filip Gęsiarz – who have not only been willing advocates for this project, but loyal colleagues – our heartfelt thanks go to each of you.

We have also been incredibly lucky to benefit from the individual and collective insights of a group of researchers, peers and professional colleagues, who reviewed and provided welcome and instructive feedback on early and later drafts of the book. Our thanks go to Alex Chesterfield, Alex Jones, Alice Soriano, Antoine Ferrere, Christian Hunt, Dil Sidhu, Eric Levy, Francesca Granelli, Helen Mankin, Ian Burbidge, Julian Seaward, Justin Jackson, Lauren Gordon, Marielle Villamaux, Marius Vollberg, Matt Battersby,

Nasrin Hafezparast, Neil Mullarkey, Nick Pope, Nicole Brigandi, Paul Adams, Paul Dolan, Rob Blackie, Rob Metcalfe, Robert Cialdini, Rupert Dunbar-Rees and Suzanne Hill.

Special thanks to Eloise Copland, whose keen eye and attention to detail have proved so valuable in ensuring that we got our facts straight and our claims credibly aligned with the published evidence. And to Tali Sharot, whose academic mentoring helped immeasurably in shaping how we thought about and conveyed the research discussed in this book.

Our thanks and appreciation go to John Mahaney and his team at Public Affairs in New York, who have proved themselves a dedicated and attentive editorial and publishing team. John's wise advice and guidance in streamlining the work, bringing to prominence its most essential components and readying it for a US readership are especially appreciated.

Jim Levine and the team at Levine Greenburg Rostan have, once again, proven themselves indispensable, providing timely advice, wise counsel, patient diplomacy, good grace and welcome support. Our thanks and appreciation also go to Isabelle Ralphs, Elle Gibbons, Keith Edson Anderson, Alex Myers, Karen Beattie, Josie Unwin and Miguel Cervantes.

Finally, to Nigel Wilcockson, at Penguin Random House. Nigel is the reason this book exists, and to him we owe a great debt of gratitude. Not only did he see the potential in an idea that we had merely scribbled down on a single page, but he also possessed the vision and drive to turn that idea into what you hold in your hands today. He epitomises what a successful messenger in the world of publishing looks like – competent, trustworthy, warm and immensely likeable. We thank him accordingly.

Stephen Martin and Joseph Marks
London, 2019

REFERENCES

Introduction

1   The story of Cassandra comes from the *Agamemnon* of Aeschylus.
2   Buffett, W. (2000), 'Letter to the Shareholders of Berkshire Hathaway Inc.', p.14. Available at: http://www.berkshirehathaway.com/letters/2000pdf.pdf; Dukcevich, D. (2002), 'Buffett's Doomsday Scenario'. Available at: https://www.forbes.com/2002/05/06/0506buffett.html#3b3635e046a5
3   Lewis, M. (2011), *The Big Short: Inside the doomsday machine*, New York, NY: W.W. Norton.
4   Schkade, D. A. & Kahneman, D. (1998), 'Does living in California make people happy? A focusing illusion in judgments of life satisfaction', *Psychological Science*, 9(5), 340–6.
5   Meindl, J. R., Ehrlich, S. B. & Dukerich, J. M. (1985), 'The romance of leadership', *Administrative Science Quarterly*, 30(1), 78–102.
6   John, L. K., Blunden, H., & Liu, H. (2019), 'Shooting the messenger', *Journal of Experimental Psychology: General*, 148(4), 644.
7   http://news.bbc.co.uk/local/bradford/hi/people_and_places/arts_and_culture/newsid_8931000/8931369.stm
8   Ambady, N. & Rosenthal, R. (1992), 'Thin slices of expressive behavior as predictors of interpersonal consequences: A meta-analysis', *Psychological Bulletin*, 111(2), 256–74. See also Rule, N. O. & Sutherland, S. L. (2017), 'Social categorization from faces: Evidence from obvious and ambiguous groups', *Current Directions in Psychological Science*, 26, 231–6; Tskhay, K. O. & Rule, N. O. (2013), 'Accuracy in categorizing perceptually ambiguous groups: A review and meta-analysis', *Personality and Social Psychology Review*, 17(1), 72–86.
9   Ambady, N. & Rosenthal, R. (1993), 'Half a minute: Predicting teacher evaluations from thin slices of nonverbal behavior and physical attractiveness', *Journal of Personality and Social Psychology*, 64(3), 431–41.

10 Todorov, A., Pakrashi, M. & Oosterhof, N. N. (2009), 'Evaluating faces on trust-worthiness after minimal time exposure', *Social Cognition*, *27*(6), 813–33; Willis, J. & Todorov, A. (2006), 'First impressions: Making up your mind after 100ms exposure to a face', *Psychological Science, 17*(7), 592–8.

11 Jones, E. E. & Pittman, T. S. (1982), 'Toward a general theory of strategic self-presentation', in J. Suls (ed.), *Psychological Perspectives on the Self*, Hillsdale, NJ: Erlbaum, Vol. 1, pp.231–62.

Part One: Hard Messengers

1 Gangadharbatla, H. & Valafar, M. (2017), 'Propagation of user-generated content online', *International Journal of Internet Marketing and Advertising, 11*(3), 218–32.

2 https://www.washingtonpost.com/news/the-fix/wp/2017/08/15/obamas-response-to-charlottesville-violence-is-one-of-the-most-popular-in-twitters-history/?utm_term=.4d300c2e83aa

3 Kraus, M. W., Park, J. W. & Tan, J. J. (2017), 'Signs of social class: The experience of economic inequality in everyday life', *Perspectives on Psychological Science, 12*(3), 422–35.

Chapter 1: Socio-Economic Position

1 Dubner, S. J. (22 July 2015), *Aziz Ansari Needs Another Toothbrush* [Audio podcast]. Retrieved from: http://freakonomics.com/podcast/aziz-ansari-needs-another-toothbrush-a-new-freakonomics-radio-episode/

2 Chan, E. & Sengupta, J. (2010), 'Insincere flattery actually works: A dual attitudes perspective', *Journal of Marketing Research, 47*(1), 122–33; Fogg, B. J. & Nass, C. (1997), 'Silicon sycophants: The effects of computers that flatter', *International Journal of Human-Computer Studies, 46*(5), 551–61.

3 Gordon, R. A. (1996), 'Impact of ingratiation on judgments and evaluations: A meta-analytic investigation', *Journal of Personality and Social Psychology, 71*, 54–70.

4 https://eu.desertsun.com/story/life/entertainment/movies/film-festival/2016/12/30/want-red-carpet-autograph-try-these-tricks/95963304/; there are also

websites that provide autograph-letter templates. Again, the principle of compliment before request is clearly evident: https://www.wikihow.com/Write-an-Autograph-Request-Letter

5   The two UK-based surveys investigating the career aspirations of ten-year-olds: https://www.taylorherring.com/blog/index.php/tag/traditional-careers/ and http://www.telegraph.co.uk/news/newstopics/howaboutthat/11014591/One-in-five-children-just-want-to-be-rich-when-they-grow-up.html

6   Berger, J., Cohen, B. P. & Zelditch, M. (1972), 'Status characteristics and social interaction', *American Sociological Review*, 37(3), 241–55.

7   Doob, A. N. & Gross, A. E. (1968), 'Status of frustrator as an inhibitor of horn-honking responses', *The Journal of Social Psychology*, 76(2), 213–18.

8   Guéguen, N., Meineri, S., Martin, A. & Charron, C. (2014), 'Car status as an inhibitor of passing responses to a low-speed frustrator', *Transportation Research Part F: Traffic Psychology and Behaviour*, 22, 245–8.

9   Veblen, T. (2007), *The Theory of the Leisure Class: An economic study of institutions*, New York, NY: Oxford University Press (original work published 1899).

10   Nelissen, R. M. & Meijers, M. H. (2011), 'Social benefits of luxury brands as costly signals of wealth and status', *Evolution and Human Behavior*, 32(5), 343–55.

11   Zahavi, A. (1975), 'Mate selection – a selection for a handicap', *Journal of Theoretical Biology*, 53(1), 205–14.

12   Van Kempen, L. (2004), 'Are the poor willing to pay a premium for designer labels? A field experiment in Bolivia', *Oxford Developmental Studies*, 32(2), 205–24.

13   Bushman, B. J. (1993), 'What's in a name? The moderating role of public self-consciousness on the relation between brand label and brand preference', *Journal of Applied Psychology*, 78(5), 857–61.

14   Ward, M. K. & Dahl, D. W. (2014), 'Should the devil sell Prada? Retail rejection increases aspiring consumers' desire for the brand', *Journal of Consumer Research*, 41(3), 590–609.

15   Scott, M. L., Mende, M. & Bolton, L. E. (2013), 'Judging the book by its cover? How consumers decode conspicuous consumption cues in buyer–seller relationships', *Journal of Marketing Research*, 50(3), 334–47.

16   Solnick, S. J. & Hemenway, D. (2005), 'Are positional concerns stronger in some domains than in others?', *The American Economic Review*, 95(2), 147–51.

17   Lafargue, P. (1883). *The Right to be Lazy*. Translated by Charles Kerr. Available at: https://www.marxists.org/archive/lafargue/1883/lazy/

18 Kraus, M. W., Park, J. W. & Tan, J. J. (2017), 'Signs of social class: The experience of economic inequality in everyday life', *Perspectives on Psychological Science, 12*(3), 422–35.

19 Becker, J. C., Kraus, M. W. & Rheinschmidt-Same, M. (2017), 'Cultural expressions of social class and their implications for group-related beliefs and behaviors', *Journal of Social Issues, 73*, 158–74.

20 Bjornsdottir, R. T. & Rule, N. O. (2017), 'The visibility of social class from facial cues', *Journal of Personality and Social Psychology, 113*(4), 530–46.

21 Blease, C. R. (2015), 'Too many "friends," too few "likes"? Evolutionary psychology and "Facebook depression"', *Review of General Psychology, 19*(1), 1–13; Kross, E., Verduyn, P., Demiralp, E., Park, J., Lee, D. S., Lin, N., Shablack, H., Jonides, J. & Ybarra, O. (2013), 'Facebook use predicts declines in subjective well-being in young adults', *PloS one, 8*(8), e69841.

22 Kraus, M. W. & Keltner, D. (2009), 'Signs of socioeconomic status: A thin-slicing approach', *Psychological Science, 20*(1), 99–106.

23 Berger, J., Rosenholtz, S. J. & Zelditch, M. (1980), 'Status organizing processes', *Annual Review of Sociology, 6*, 479–508.

24 Anderson, C., Hildreth, J. A. D. & Howland, L. (2015), 'Is the desire for status a fundamental human motive? A review of the empirical literature', *Psychological Bulletin, 141*(3), 574–601; Sidanius, J. & Pratto, F. (2001), *Social Dominance: An intergroup theory of social hierarchy and oppression*, New York, NY: Cambridge University Press.

25 Van Vugt, M., Hogan, R. & Kaiser, R. B. (2008), 'Leadership, followership, and evolution: Some lessons from the past', *American Psychologist, 63*(3), 182–96.

26 Lerner, M. J. (1980), *The Belief in a Just World: A fundamental delusion*, New York, NY: Plenum Press.

27 Furnham, A. F. (1983), 'Attributions for affluence', *Personality and Individual Differences, 4*(1), 31–40.

28 Sloane, S., Baillargeon, R. & Premack, D. (2012), 'Do infants have a sense of fairness?', *Psychological Science, 23*(2), 196–204.

29 Jonason, P. K., Li, N. P. & Madson, L. (2012), 'It is not all about the Benjamins: Understanding preferences for mates with resources', *Personality and Individual Differences, 52*(3), 306–10.

30 Van de Ven, N., Zeelenberg, M. & Pieters, R. (2009), 'Leveling up and down: The experiences of benign and malicious envy', *Emotion, 9*(3), 419–29.

31 Lefkowitz, M., Blake, R. R. & Mouton, J. S. (1955), 'Status factors in pedestrian violation of traffic signals', *Journal of Abnormal and Social Psychology, 51*(3), 704–6.

32 Maner, J. K., DeWall, C. N. & Gailliot, M. T. (2008), 'Selective attention to signs of success: Social dominance and early stage interpersonal perception', *Personality and Social Psychology Bulletin*, 34(4), 488–501.

33 https://www.scmp.com/news/hong-kong/health-environment/article/2132545/experts-denounce-canto-pop-stars-claim-harmful-flu

34 Knoll, J. & Matthes, J. (2017), 'The effectiveness of celebrity endorsements: A meta-analysis', *Journal of the Academy of Marketing Science*, 45(1), 55–75.

35 http://fashion.telegraph.co.uk/news-features/TMG8749219/Lacoste-asks-Norway-police-to-ban-Anders-Behring-Breivik-wearing-their-clothes.html

36 https://www.cbsnews.com/news/kanye-im-the-voice-of-this-generation/

37 https://www.wmagazine.com/story/kanye-west-on-kim-kardashian-and-his-new-album-yeezus

38 https://www.nytimes.com/2013/06/16/arts/music/kanye-west-talks-about-his-career-and-album-yeezus.html

39 Campbell, W. K., Rudich, E. A. & Sedikides, C. (2002), 'Narcissism, self-esteem, and the positivity of self-views: Two portraits of self-love', *Personality and Social Psychology Bulletin*, 28(3), 358–68; Campbell, W. K., Brunell, A. B. & Finkel, E. J. (2006), 'Narcissism, interpersonal self-regulation, and romantic relationships: An agency model approach', in K. D. Vohs & E. J. Finkel (eds), *Self and Relationships: Connecting intrapersonal and interpersonal processes*, New York, NY: Guilford Press, pp.57–83.

Chapter 2: Competence

1 Davis, N. M. & Cohen, M. R. (1981), *Medication Errors: Causes and prevention*, Michigan, MI: George F. Stickley.

2 Cialdini, R. B. (2009), *Influence: The Psychology of Persuasion*, New York, NY: HarperCollins.

3 Henrich, J. & Gil-White, F. J. (2001), 'The evolution of prestige: Freely conferred deference as a mechanism for enhancing the benefits of cultural transmission', *Evolution and Human Behavior*, 22(3), 165–96.

4 Engelmann, J. B., Capra, C. M., Noussair, C. & Berns, G. S. (2009), 'Expert financial advice neurobiologically "offloads" financial decision-making under risk', *PLoS one*, 4, e4957.

5 Milgram, S. (1974), *Obedience to Authority*, London: Tavistock Publications.

6 Mangum, S., Garrison, C., Lind, C., Thackeray, R. & Wyatt, M. (1991), 'Perceptions of nurses' uniforms', *Journal of Nursing Scholarship*, 23(2), 127–30;

Raven, B. H. (1999), 'Kurt Lewin address: Influence, power, religion, and the mechanisms of social control', *Journal of Social Issues, 55*(1), 161–86.

7 Leary, M. R., Jongman-Sereno, K. P. & Diebels, K. J. (2014), 'The pursuit of status: A self-presentational perspective on the quest for social value', in J. T. Cheng, J. L. Tracy & C. Anderson (eds.), *The Psychology of Social Status*, New York, NY: Springer, pp.159–78.

8 Ekman, P. (2007), *Emotions Revealed: Recognizing faces and feelings to improve communication and emotional life*, New York, NY: Henry Holt and Company.

9 Rule, N. O. & Ambady, N. (2008), 'The face of success: Inferences from chief executive officers' appearance predict company profits', *Psychological Science, 19*(2), 109–11.

10 Rule, N. O. & Ambady, N. (2009), 'She's got the look: Inferences from female chief executive officers' faces predict their success', *Sex Roles, 61*(9–10), 644–52.

11 Ballew, C. C. & Todorov, A. (2007), 'Predicting political elections from rapid and unreflective face judgments', *Proceedings of the National Academy of Sciences, 104*(46), 17948–53.

12 Antonakis, J. & Dalgas, O. (2009), 'Predicting elections: Child's play!', *Science, 323*(5918), 1183.

13 Pulford, B. D., Colman, A. M., Buabang, E. K. & Krockow, E. M. (2018), 'The persuasive power of knowledge: Testing the confidence heuristic', *Journal of Experimental Psychology: General, 147*(10), 1431–44.

14 Anderson, C., Brion, S., Moore, D. A. & Kennedy, J. A. (2012), 'A Status-enhancement account of overconfidence', *Journal of Personality and Social Psychology, 103*(4), 718–35.

15 Bayarri, M. J. & DeGroot, M. H. (1989), 'Optimal reporting of predictions', *Journal of the American Statistical Association, 84*(405), 214–22; Hertz, U., Palminteri, S., Brunetti, S., Olesen, C., Frith, C. D. & Bahrami, B. (2017), 'Neural computations underpinning the strategic management of influence in advice giving', *Nature Communications, 8*(1), 2191.

16 Karmarkar, U. R. & Tormala, Z. L. (2010), 'Believe me, I have no idea what I'm talking about: The effects of source certainty on consumer involvement and persuasion', *Journal of Consumer Research, 36*(6), 1033–49.

17 Sezer, O., Gino, F. & Norton, M. I. (2018), 'Humblebragging: A distinct – and ineffective – self-presentation strategy', *Journal of Personality and Social Psychology, 114*(1), 52–74.

18 Godfrey, D. K., Jones, E. E. & Lord, C. G. (1986), 'Self-promotion is not ingrati-ating', *Journal of Personality and Social Psychology*, *50*(1), 106–15.

19 Lewis, M. (2011), *The Big Short: Inside the doomsday machine*, New York, NY: W.W. Norton.

20 Pfeffer, J., Fong, C. T., Cialdini, R. B. & Portnoy, R. R. (2006), 'Overcoming the self-promotion dilemma: Interpersonal attraction and extra help as a conse-quence of who sings one's praises', *Personality and Social Psychology Bulletin*, *32*(10), 1362–74.

21 Wright, L. A. (2016), *On Behalf of the President: Presidential Spouses and White House Communications Strategy Today*, Connecticut, CT: Praeger.

22 Tormala, Z. L., Jia, J. S. & Norton, M. I. (2012), 'The preference for potential', *Journal of Personality and Social Psychology*, *103*(4), 567–83.

23 https://www.theguardian.com/technology/2017/apr/10/tesla-most-valuable-car-company-gm-stock-price

24 https://www.nytimes.com/video/us/politics/100000004564751/obama-says-trump-unfit-to-serve-as-president.html

Chapter 3: Dominance

1 https://www.vox.com/policy-and-politics/2016/9/27/13017666/presidential-debate-trump-clinton-sexism-interruptions

2 Cheng, J. T., Tracy, J. L., Foulsham, T., Kingstone, A. & Henrich, J. (2013), 'Two ways to the top: Evidence that dominance and prestige are distinct yet viable avenues to social rank and influence', *Journal of Personality and Social Psychology*, *104*(1), 103–25.

3 Henrich, J. & Gil-White, F. J. (2001), 'The evolution of prestige: Freely conferred deference as a mechanism for enhancing the benefits of cultural transmission', *Evolution and Human Behavior*, *22*(3), 165–96.

4 Altemeyer, R. (2006), *The Authoritarians*. Available at: https://theauthoritarians.org/Downloads/TheAuthoritarians.pdf

5 Halevy, N., Chou, E. Y., Cohen, T. R. & Livingston, R. W. (2012), 'Status confer-ral in intergroup social dilemmas: Behavioral antecedents and consequences of prestige and dominance', *Journal of Personality and Social Psychology*, *102*(2), 351–66.

6 Sidanius, J. & Pratto, F. (2004), *Social Dominance: An Intergroup Theory of Social Hierarchy and Oppression*, Cambridge, UK: Cambridge University Press.

7   Fiske, S. T. (2010), 'Interpersonal stratification: Status, power, and subordina-
    tion', in S. T. Fiske, D. T. Gilbert & G. Lindzey (eds), *Handbook of Social
    Psychology*, Hoboken, NJ: John Wiley & Sons, pp.941–82; Henrich, J. & Gil-
    White, F. J. (2001), 'The evolution of prestige: Freely conferred deference as a
    mechanism for enhancing the benefits of cultural transmission', *Evolution and
    Human Behavior*, 22(3), 165–96.

8   Deaner, R. O., Khera, A. V. & Platt, M. L. (2005), 'Monkeys pay per view:
    Adaptive valuation of social images by rhesus macaques', *Current Biology*, 15(6),
    543–8. See also Shepherd, S. V., Deaner, R. O. & Platt, M. L. (2006), 'Social
    status gates social attention in monkeys', *Current Biology*, 16(4), R119–R120.

9   Hare, B., Call, J. & Tomasello, M. (2001), 'Do chimpanzees know what con-
    specifics know?', *Animal Behaviour*, 61(1), 139–51.

10 Mascaro, O. & Csibra, G. (2014), 'Human infants' learning of social structures:
    The case of dominance hierarchy', *Psychological Science*, 25(1), 250–5.

11 Gazes, R. P., Hampton, R. R. & Lourenco, S. F. (2017), 'Transitive inference of
    social dominance by human infants', *Developmental science*, 20(2), e12367.

12 Enright, E. A., Gweon, H. & Sommerville, J. A. (2017), '"To the victor go the
    spoils": Infants expect resources to align with dominance structures',
    Cognition, 164, 8–21.

13 Vacharkulksemsuk, T., Reit, E., Khambatta, P., Eastwick, P. W., Finkel, E. J. &
    Carney, D. R. (2016), 'Dominant, open nonverbal displays are attractive at zero-
    acquaintance', *Proceedings of the National Academy of Sciences*, 113(15),
    4009–14.

14 https://www.huffingtonpost.com/2013/05/12/worl-photo-caption-contest-
    shirtless-putin_n_3263512.html

15 Tiedens, L. Z. & Fragale, A. R. (2003), 'Power moves: complementarity in domi-
    nant and submissive nonverbal behavior', *Journal of Personality and Social
    Psychology*, 84(3), 558–68; Hall, J. A., Coats, E. J. & LeBeau, L. S. (2005),
    'Nonverbal behavior and the vertical dimension of social relations: a meta-
    analysis', *Psychological Bulletin*, 131(6), 898–924.

16 Mauldin, B. & Novak, R. (1966), *Lyndon B. Johnson: The Exercise of Power*, New
    York, NY: New American Library.

17 Mast, M. S. & Hall, J. A. (2004), 'Who is the boss and who is not? Accuracy of
    judging status', *Journal of Nonverbal Behavior*, 28(3), 145–65.

18 Charafeddine, R., Mercier, H., Clément, F., Kaufmann, L., Berchtold, A.,
    Reboul, A. & Van der Henst, J. B. (2015), 'How preschoolers use cues of domi-
    nance to make sense of their social environment', *Journal of Cognition and
    Development*, 16(4), 587–607.

19 Lewis, C. S. (1952), *Mere Christianity*, New York, NY: Macmillan.

20 Shariff, A. F., Tracy, J. L. & Markusoff, J. L. (2012), '(Implicitly) judging a book by its cover: The power of pride and shame expressions in shaping judgments of social status', *Personality and Social Psychology Bulletin*, *38*(9), 1178–93.

21 Tracy, J. L. & Matsumoto, D. (2008), 'The spontaneous expression of pride and shame: Evidence for biologically innate nonverbal displays', *Proceedings of the National Academy of Sciences*, *105*(33), 11655–60.

22 Tracy, J. L. & Robins, R. W. (2007), 'The prototypical pride expression: development of a nonverbal behavior coding system', *Emotion*, *7*(4), 789–801.

23 Shariff, A. F. & Tracy, J. L. (2009), 'Knowing who's boss: Implicit perceptions of status from the nonverbal expression of pride', *Emotion*, *9*(5), 631–9.

24 Tracy, J. L., Shariff, A. F., Zhao, W. & Henrich, J. (2013), 'Cross-cultural evidence that the nonverbal expression of pride is an automatic status signal', *Journal of Experimental Psychology: General*, *142*(1), 163–80.

25 Tracy, J. L., Cheng, J. T., Robins, R. W. & Trzesniewski, K. H. (2009), 'Authentic and hubristic pride: The affective core of self-esteem and narcissism', *Self and Identity*, *8*(2), 196–213.

26 Martin, J. D., Abercrombie, H. C., Gilboa-Schechtman, E. & Niedenthal, P. M. (2018), 'Functionally distinct smiles elicit different physiological responses in an evaluative context', *Scientific Reports*, *8*(1), 3558.

27 Sell, A., Cosmides, L., Tooby, J., Sznycer, D., Von Rueden, C. & Gurven, M. (2009), 'Human adaptations for the visual assessment of strength and fighting ability from the body and face', *Proceedings of the Royal Society of London B: Biological Sciences*, *276*(1656), 575–84.

28 Carré, J. M. & McCormick, C. M. (2008), 'In your face: facial metrics predict aggressive behaviour in the laboratory and in varsity and professional hockey players', *Proceedings of the Royal Society B: Biological Sciences*, *275*(1651), 2651–6.

29 Zilioli, S., Sell, A. N., Stirrat, M., Jagore, J., Vickerman, W. & Watson, N. V. (2015), 'Face of a fighter: Bizygomatic width as a cue of formidability', *Aggressive Behavior*, *41*(4), 322–30.

30 Haselhuhn, M. P., Wong, E. M., Ormiston, M. E., Inesi, M. E. & Galinsky, A. D. (2014), 'Negotiating face-to-face: Men's facial structure predicts negotiation performance', *The Leadership Quarterly*, *25*(5), 835–45.

31 The image is available under the terms of a Creative Commons Attribution Licence and was published in Kramer, R. S., Jones, A. L. & Ward, R. (2012), 'A lack of sexual dimorphism in width-to-height ratio in white European faces using 2D photographs, 3D scans, and anthropometry', *PloS one*, *7*(8), e42705.

293

32 Cogsdill, E. J., Todorov, A. T., Spelke, E. S. & Banaji, M. R. (2014), 'Inferring character from faces: A developmental stud', *Psychological Science, 25*(5), 1132–9.

33 Little, A. C. & Roberts, S. C. (2012), 'Evolution, appearance, and occupational success', *Evolutionary Psychology, 10*(5), 782–801.

34 Stulp, G., Buunk, A. P., Verhulst, S. & Pollet, T. V. (2015), 'Human height is positively related to interpersonal dominance in dyadic interactions', *PLoS One, 10(2)*, e0117860.

35 Thomsen, L., Frankenhuis, W. E., Ingold-Smith, M. & Carey, S. (2011), 'Big and mighty: Preverbal infants mentally represent social dominance', *Science, 331* (6016), 477–80.

36 Lukaszewski, A. W., Simmons, Z. L., Anderson, C. & Roney, J. R. (2016), 'The role of physical formidability in human social status allocation', *Journal of Personality and Social Psychology, 110*(3), 385–406.

37 Judge, T. A. & Cable, D. M. (2004), 'The effect of physical height on workplace success and income: Preliminary test of a theoretical model', *Journal of Applied Psychology, 89*(3), 428–41.

38 Klofstad, C. A., Nowicki, S. & Anderson, R. C. (2016), 'How voice pitch influences our choice of leaders', *American Scientist, 104*(5), 282–7.

39 Tigue, C. C., Borak, D. J., O'Connor, J. J., Schandl, C. & Feinberg, D. R. (2012), 'Voice pitch influences voting behavior', *Evolution and Human Behavior, 33*(3), 210–16.

40 Klofstad, C. A., Anderson, R. C. & Nowicki, S. (2015), 'Perceptions of competence, strength, and age influence voters to select leaders with lower-pitched voices', *PloS one, 10*(8), e0133779.

41 Laustsen, L., Petersen, M. B. & Klofstad, C. A. (2015), 'Vote choice, ideology, and social dominance orientation influence preferences for lower pitched voices in political candidates', *Evolutionary Psychology, 13*(3), 1–13.

42 Banai, I. P., Banai, B. & Bovan, K. (2017), 'Vocal characteristics of presidential candidates can predict the outcome of actual elections', *Evolution and Human Behavior, 38*(3), 309–14.

43 Kipnis, D., Castell, J., Gergen, M. & Mauch, D. (1976), 'Metamorphic effects of power', *Journal of Applied Psychology, 61*(2), 127–35.

44 Bickman, L. (1974), 'The Social Power of a Uniform', *Journal of Applied Social Psychology, 4*(4), 47–61.

45 Brief, A. P., Dukerich, J. M. & Doran, L. I. (1991), 'Resolving ethical dilemmas in management: Experimental investigations of values, accountability, and choice', *Journal of Applied Social Psychology, 21*(5), 380–96.

46 https://www.nytimes.com/2007/05/10/business/11drug-web.html

47 https://www.moneymarketing.co.uk/im-like-a-whores-drawers-what-rbs-traders-said-over-libor/

48 Braver, S. L., Linder, D. E., Corwin, T. T. & Cialdini, R. B. (1977), 'Some conditions that affect admissions of attitude change', *Journal of Experimental Social Psychology*, 13(6), 565–76.

49 Schwartz, D., Dodge, K. A., Pettit, G. S. & Bates, J. E. (1997), 'The early socialization of aggressive victims of bullying', *Child Development*, 68(4), 665–75.

50 Rodkin, P. C., Farmer, T. W., Pearl, R. & Acker, R. V. (2006), 'They're cool: Social status and peer group supports for aggressive boys and girls', *Social Development*, 15(2), 175–204; Juvonen, J. & Graham, S. (2014), 'Bullying in schools: The power of bullies and the plight of victims', *Annual Review of Psychology*, 65(1), 159–85.

51 Salmivalli, C. (2010), 'Bullying and the peer group: A review', *Aggression and Violent Behavior*, 15(2), 112–20.

52 Van Ryzin, M. & Pellegrini, A. D. (2013), 'Socially competent and incompetent aggressors in middle school: The non-linear relation between bullying and dominance in middle school', *British Journal of Educational Psychology Monograph Series II*(9), 123–38.

53 Laustsen, L. & Petersen, M. B. (2015), 'Does a competent leader make a good friend? Conflict, ideology and the psychologies of friendship and followership', *Evolution and Human Behavior*, 36(4), 286–93.

54 Safra, L., Algan, Y., Tecu, T., Grèzes, J., Baumard, N. & Chevallier, C. (2017), 'Childhood harshness predicts long-lasting leader preferences', *Evolution and Human Behavior*, 38(5), 645–51.

55 Muehlheusser, G., Schneemann, S., Sliwka, D. & Wallmeier, N. (2016), 'The contribution of managers to organizational success: Evidence from German soccer', *Journal of Sports Economics*, 19(6), 786–819. See also Peter, L. J. & Hull, R. (1969), *The Peter Principle*, Oxford, UK: Morrow.

56 Faber, D. (2008), *Munich: The 1938 Appeasement Crisis*, New York, NY: Simon & Schuster.

57 Laustsen, L. & Petersen, M. B. (2016), 'Winning faces vary by ideology: How nonverbal source cues influence election and communication success in politics', *Political Communication*, 33(2), 188–211.

58 Laustsen, L. & Petersen, M. B. (2017), 'Perceived conflict and leader dominance: Individual and contextual factors behind preferences for dominant leaders', *Political Psychology*, 38(6), 1083–1101.

59 Nevicka, B., De Hoogh, A. H., Van Vianen, A. E. & Ten Velden, F. S. (2013), 'Uncertainty enhances the preference for narcissistic leaders', *European Journal of Social Psychology*, *43*(5), 370–80.

60 Ingersoll, Ralph (1940), *Report on England, November 1940*, New York, NY: Simon and Schuster.

61 Price, M. E. & Van Vugt, M. (2015), 'The service-for-prestige theory of leader–follower relations: A review of the evolutionary psychology and anthropology literatures', in R. Arvey & S. Colarelli (eds), *Biological Foundations of Organizational Behaviour*, Chicago: Chicago University Press, pp.169–201.

62 Zebrowitz, L. A. & Montepare, J. M. (2005), 'Appearance DOES matter', *Science*, *308*(5728), 1565–6.

63 Bagchi, R. & Cheema, A. (2012), 'The effect of red background color on willingness-to-pay: The moderating role of selling mechanism', *Journal of Consumer Research*, *39*(5), 947–60.

64 Hill, R. A. & Barton, R. A. (2005), 'Psychology: red enhances human performance in contests', *Nature*, *435*(7040), 293.

65 Kramer, R. S. (2016), 'The red power (less) tie: Perceptions of political leaders wearing red', *Evolutionary Psychology*, *14*(2), 1–8.

66 Galbarczyk, A. & Ziomkiewicz, A. (2017), 'Tattooed men: Healthy bad boys and good-looking competitors', *Personality and Individual Differences*, *106*, 122–5.

Chapter 4: Attractiveness

1 https://www.mirror.co.uk/news/world-news/actress-demands-pay-less-tax-9233636

2 Bertrand, M., Karlan, D., Mullainathan, S., Shafir, E. & Zinman, J. (2010), 'What's advertising content worth? Evidence from a consumer credit marketing field experiment', *The Quarterly Journal of Economics*, *125*(968), 263–306.

3 Maestripieri, D., Henry, A. & Nickels, N. (2017), 'Explaining financial and prosocial biases in favor of attractive people: Interdisciplinary perspectives from economics, social psychology, and evolutionary psychology', *Behavioral and Brain Sciences*, *40*, e19.

4 Langlois, J. H., Kalakanis, L., Rubenstein, A. J., Larson, A., Hallam, M. & Smoot, M. (2000), 'Maxims or myths of beauty? A meta-analytic and theoretical review', *Psychological Bulletin*, *126*(3), 390–423.

5   Langlois, J. H., Roggman, L. A., Casey, R. J., Ritter, J. M., Rieser-Danner, L. A. & Jenkins, V. Y. (1987), 'Infant preferences for attractive faces: Rudiments of a stereotype', *Developmental Psychology, 23*(3), 363–9.

6   Langlois, J. H., Roggman, L. A. & Rieser-Danner, L. A. (1990), 'Infants' differential social responses to attractive and unattractive faces', *Developmental Psychology, 26*(1), 153–9.

7   Langlois, J. H., Ritter, J. M., Casey, R. J. & Sawin, D. B. (1995), 'Infant attractiveness predicts maternal behaviors and attitudes', *Developmental Psychology, 31*(3), 464–72.

8   The fake (Heineken) version can be found here: https://www.snopes.com/fact-check/heineken-beer-ad-babies/ The original was published in *Life* magazine: Pepsico (12 September 1955). 'Nothing does it like Seven-up!' [Advertisement], *Life, 39*(11), 100.

9   Langlois, J. H. & Roggman, L. A. (1990), 'Attractive faces are only average', *Psychological Science, 1*(2), 115–21; Langlois, J. H., Roggman, L. A. & Musselman, L. (1994), 'What is average and what is not average about attractive faces?', *Psychological Science, 5*(4), 214–20.

10 Rhodes, G. (2006), 'The evolutionary psychology of facial beauty', *Annual Review of Psychology, 57*(1), 199–226; Little, A. C. (2014), 'Facial attractiveness', *Wiley Interdisciplinary Reviews: Cognitive Science, 5*(6), 621–34.

11 Burley, N. (1983), 'The meaning of assortative mating', *Ethology and Sociobiology, 4*(4), 191–203.

12 Laeng, B., Vermeer, O. & Sulutvedt, U. (2013), 'Is beauty in the face of the beholder?', *PLoS One, 8*(7), e68395.

13 Sadalla, E. K., Kenrick, D. T. & Vershure, B. (1987), 'Dominance and heterosexual attraction', *Journal of Personality and Social Psychology, 52*(4), 730–8. See also, Snyder, J. K., Kirkpatrick, L. A. & Barrett, H. C. (2008), 'The dominance dilemma: Do women really prefer dominant mates?', *Personal relationships, 15*(4), 425–44; Said, C. P. & Todorov, A. (2011), 'A statistical model of facial attractiveness', *Psychological Science, 22*(9), 1183–90.

14 Bruch, E., Feinberg, F. & Lee, K. Y. (2016), 'Extracting multistage screening rules from online dating activity data', *Proceedings of the National Academy of Sciences, 113*(38), 10530–5. See also http://www.dailymail.co.uk/femail/article-2524568/Size-matters-online-dating-Short-men-taller-counterparts.html

15 Pollet, T. V., Pratt, S. E., Edwards, G. & Stulp, G. (2013), 'The Golden Years: Men From The Forbes 400 Have Much Younger Wives When Remarrying

Than the General US Population', *Letters on Evolutionary Behavioral Science*, 4(1), 5–8.

16 Toma, C. L. & Hancock, J. T. (2010), 'Looks and lies: The role of physical attractiveness in online dating self-presentation and deception', *Communication Research*, 37(3), 335–51.

17 https://www.today.com/news/do-high-heels-empower-or-oppress-women-wbna32970817; see also Morris, P. H., White, J., Morrison, E. R. & Fisher, K. (2013), 'High heels as supernormal stimuli: How wearing high heels affects judgements of female attractiveness', *Evolution and Human Behavior*, 34(3), 176–81.

18 Epstein, J., Klinkenberg, W. D., Scandell, D. J., Faulkner, K. & Claus, R. E. (2007), 'Perceived physical attractiveness, sexual history, and sexual intentions: An internet study', *Sex Roles*, 56(2), 23–31.

19 Dion, K. K. (1974), 'Children's physical attractiveness and sex as determinants of adult punitiveness', *Developmental Psychology*, 10(5), 772–8; Dion, K. K. & Berscheid, E. (1974), 'Physical attractiveness and peer perception among children', *Sociometry*, 37(1), 1–12.

20 Maestripieri, D., Henry, A. & Nickels, N. (2017), 'Explaining financial and prosocial biases in favor of attractive people: Interdisciplinary perspectives from economics, social psychology, and evolutionary psychology', *Behavioral and Brain Sciences*, 40, e19.

21 Hamermesh, D. S. (2011), *Beauty Pays: Why attractive people are more successful*, Princeton, NJ: Princeton University Press.

22 Hamermesh, D. S. & Abrevaya, J. (2013), 'Beauty is the promise of happiness?', *European Economic Review*, 64, 351–68.

23 Rhode, D. L. (2010), *The Beauty Bias: The injustice of appearance in life and law*, New York, NY: Oxford University Press.

24 Busetta, G., Fiorillo, F. & Visalli, E. (2013), 'Searching for a job is a beauty contest', *Munich Personal RePEc Archive*, Paper No. 49825.

25 The Argentinian and Israeli studies, respectively: Bóo, F. L., Rossi, M. A. & Urzúa, S. S. (2013), 'The labor market return to an attractive face: Evidence from a field experiment', *Economics Letters*, 118(1), 170–2; Ruffle, B. J. & Shtudiner, Z. E. (2014), 'Are good-looking people more employable?', *Management Science*, 61(8), 1760–76.

26 Hosoda, M., Stone-Romero, E. F. & Coats, G. (2003), 'The effects of physical attractiveness on job-related outcomes: A meta-analysis of experimental studies', *Personnel Psychology*, 56(2), 431–62.

27 Berggren, N., Jordahl, H. & Poutvaara, P. (2010), 'The looks of a winner: Beauty and electoral success', *Journal of Public Economics*, *94*(2), 8–15.

28 Mazzella, R. & Feingold, A. (1994), 'The effects of physical attractiveness, race, socioeconomic status, and gender of defendants and victims on judgments of mock jurors: A meta-analysis', *Journal of Applied Social Psychology*, *24*(3), 1315–38.

29 Jacob, C., Guéguen, N., Boulbry, G. & Ardiccioni, R. (2010), 'Waitresses' facial cosmetics and tipping: A field experiment', *International Journal of Hospitality Management*, *29*(1), 188–90.

30 Guéguen, N. (2010), 'Color and women hitchhikers' attractiveness: Gentlemen drivers prefer red', *Color Research & Application*, *37*(1), 76–8; Guéguen, N. & Jacob, C. (2014), 'Clothing color and tipping: Gentlemen patrons give more tips to waitresses with red clothes', *Journal of Hospitality & Tourism Research*, *38*(2), 275–80.

31 Beall, A. T. & Tracy, J. L. (2013), 'Women are more likely to wear red or pink at peak fertility', *Psychological Science*, *24*(9), 1837–41.

32 Kayser, D. N., Agthe, M. & Maner, J. K. (2016), 'Strategic sexual signals: Women's display versus avoidance of the color red depends on the attractiveness of an anticipated interaction partner', *PloS one*, *11*(3), e0148501.

33 Ahearne, M., Gruen, T. W. & Jarvis, C. B. (1999), 'If looks could sell: Moderation and mediation of the attractiveness effect on salesperson performance', *International Journal of Research in Marketing*, *16*(4), 269–84.

34 https://www.independent.ie/world-news/shoppers-think-smiles-are-sexual-26168792.html

35 https://www.npr.org/2008/10/09/95520570/dolly-partons-jolene-still-haunts-singers

36 Maner, J. K., Gailliot, M. T., Rouby, D. A. & Miller, S. L. (2007), 'Can't take my eyes off you: Attentional adhesion to mates and rivals', *Journal of Personality and Social Psychology*, *93*(3), 389–401.

37 Leenaars, L. S., Dane, A. V. & Marini, Z. A. (2008), 'Evolutionary perspective on indirect victimization in adolescence: The role of attractiveness, dating and sexual behavior', *Aggressive Behavior*, *34*(4), 404–15. See also Vaillancourt, T. & Sharma, A. (2011), 'Intolerance of sexy peers: Intrasexual competition among women', *Aggressive Behavior*, *37*(6), 569–77.

38 https://www.psychologytoday.com/gb/blog/out-the-ooze/201804/why-pretty-girls-may-be-especially-vulnerable-bullying

39 http://www.dailymail.co.uk/femail/article-2124246/Samantha-Brick-downsides-looking-pretty-Why-women-hate-beautiful.html

40 Oreffice, S. & Quintana-Domeque, C. (2016), 'Beauty, body size and wages: Evidence from a unique data set', *Economics & Human Biology*, *22*, 24–34. See also Elmore, W., Vonnahame, E. M., Thompson, L., Filion, D. & Lundgren, J. D. (2015), 'Evaluating political candidates: Does weight matter?', *Translational Issues in Psychological Science*, *1*(3), 287–97.

41 Whipple, T. (2018), *X and Why: The rules of attraction: Why gender still matters*, London: Short Books Ltd.

42 Buss, D. M. (1989), 'Sex differences in human mate preferences: Evolutionary hypotheses tested in 37 cultures', *Behavioral and Brain Sciences*, *12*(1), 1–14; Li, N. P., Bailey, J. M., Kenrick, D. T. & Linsenmeier, J. A. (2002), 'The necessities and luxuries of mate preferences: Testing the tradeoffs', *Journal of Personality and Social Psychology*, *82*(6), 947–55; McClintock, E. A. (2011), 'Handsome wants as handsome does: Physical attractiveness and gender differences in revealed sexual preferences', *Biodemography and Social Biology*, *57*(2), 221–57.

43 Trivers, R. L. (1972), 'Parental investment and sexual selection', in B. Campbell (ed.), *Sexual selection and the descent of man*, Chicago, IL: Aldine, pp.136–79.

44 Baumeister, R. F., Catanese, K. R. & Vohs, K. D. (2001), 'Is there a gender difference in strength of sex drive? Theoretical views, conceptual distinctions, and a review of relevant evidence', *Personality and Social Psychology Review*, *5*(3), 242–73.

45 Downey, G. J. (2002), *Telegraph Messenger Boys: Labor, Communication and Technology, 1850–1950*, New York, NY: Routledge.

Part Two: Soft Messengers

1   Smith, D. (2016), *Rasputin: Faith, Power, and the Twilight of the Romanovs*, New York, NY: Farrar, Straus and Giroux.

2   Baumeister, R. F. & Leary, M. R. (1995), 'The Need to Belong: Desire for Interpersonal Attachments as a Fundamental Human Motivation', *Psychological Bulletin*, *117*, 497–529.

3   Powdthavee, N. (2008), 'Putting a price tag on friends, relatives, and neighbours: Using surveys of life satisfaction to value social relationships', *The Journal of Socio-Economics*, *37*(4), 1459–80; Helliwell, J. F. & Putnam, R. D. (2004), 'The social context of well-being', *Philosophical Transactions of the Royal Society B: Biological Sciences*, *359*(1449), 1435–46.

4   Cacioppo, J. T., Hawkley, L. C., Ernst, J. M., Burleson, M., Berntson, G. G., Nouriani, B. & Spiegel, D. (2006), 'Loneliness within a nomological net: An

evolutionary perspective', *Journal of Research in Personality*, *40*(6), 1054–85; Lauder, W., Mummery, K., Jones, M. & Caperchione, C. (2006), 'A comparison of health behaviours in lonely and non-lonely populations', *Psychology, Health & Medicine*, *11*(2), 233–45.

5 Stenseng, F., Belsky, J., Skalicka, V. & Wichstrøm, L. (2014), 'Preschool social exclusion, aggression, and cooperation: A longitudinal evaluation of the need-to-belong and the social-reconnection hypotheses', *Personality and Social Psychology Bulletin*, *40*(12), 1637–47; Ren, D., Wesselmann, E. D. & Williams, K. D. (2018), 'Hurt people hurt people: ostracism and aggression', *Current Opinion in Psychology*, *19*, 34–8.

6 Leary, M. R., Kowalski, R. M., Smith, L. & Phillips, S. (2003), 'Teasing, rejection, and violence: Case studies of the school shootings', *Aggressive Behavior: Official Journal of the International Society for Research on Aggression*, *29*(3), 202–14; Sommer, F., Leuschner, V. & Scheithauer, H. (2014), 'Bullying, romantic rejection, and conflicts with teachers: The crucial role of social dynamics in the development of school shootings – A systematic review', *International Journal of Developmental Science*, *8*(1–2), 3–24.

7 Finch, J. F. & Cialdini, R. B. (1989), 'Another indirect tactic of (self-)image management: Boosting', *Personality and Social Psychology Bulletin*, *15*(2), 222–32.

8 Cialdini, R. B. (2001), *Influence: Science and Practice*, New York, NY: Harper Collins; McPherson, M., Smith-Lovin, L. & Cook, J. M. (2001), 'Birds of a feather: Homophily in social networks', *Annual Review of Sociology*, *27*, 415–44.

9 Del Vicario, M., Bessi, A., Zollo, F., Petroni, F., Scala, A., Caldarelli, G., Stanley, H. E. & Quattrociocchi, W. (2016), 'The spreading of misinformation online', *Proceedings of the National Academy of Sciences*, *113*(3), 554–9; Sunstein, C. R. (2017), *#Republic: Divided democracy in the age of social media*, Princeton, NJ: Princeton University Press.

10 Marks, J., Copland, E., Loh, E., Sunstein, C. R. & Sharot, T. (2019), 'Epistemic spillovers: Learning others' political views reduces the ability to assess and use their expertise in nonpolitical domains', *Cognition*, *188*, 74–84.

11 https://www.marketingweek.com/2016/01/12/sport-englands-this-girl-can-campaign-inspires-2-8-million-women-to-get-active/

12 Department for International Development (2009), 'Getting braids not AIDS: How hairdressers are helping to tackle HIV in Zimbabwe': https://reliefweb.int/report/zimbabwe/getting-braids-not-aids-how-hairdressers-are-helping-tackle-hiv-zimbabwe

Chapter 5: Warmth

1   https://www.nytimes.com/1985/12/19/business/how-texaco-lost-court-fight.html

2   http://articles.latimes.com/1986-01-19/business/fi-1168_1_ordinary-people

3   Cuddy, A. J., Fiske, S. T. & Glick, P. (2008), 'Warmth and competence as universal dimensions of social perception: The stereotype content model and the BIAS map', *Advances in Experimental Social Psychology*, 40, 61–149.

4   Carnegie, D. (1936), *How to Win Friends and Influence People*, New York, NY: Simon & Schuster.

5   Gottman, J. M. & Levenson, R. W. (2000), 'The timing of divorce: Predicting when a couple will divorce over a 14-year period', *Journal of Marriage and Family*, 62(3), 737–45; Gottman, J. (1995), *Why Marriages Succeed or Fail: And how to make yours last*, New York, NY: Simon & Schuster.

6   Hamlin, J. K., Wynn, K. & Bloom, P. (2007), 'Social evaluation by preverbal infants', *Nature*, 450(7169), 557–9; Van de Vondervoort, J. W. & Hamlin, J. K. (2018), 'The early emergence of sociomoral evaluation: infants prefer prosocial others', *Current Opinion in Psychology*, 20, 77–81.

7   Brown, P. & Levinson, S. C. (1987), *Politeness: Some universals in language usage*, New York, NY: Cambridge University Press; Pinker, S. (2007), *The Stuff of Thought: Language as a window into human nature*, New York, NY: Viking.

8   Pinker, S. (2007), *The Stuff of Thought: Language as a window into human nature*, New York, NY: Viking.

9   Zerubavel, N., Hoffman, M. A., Reich, A., Ochsner, K. N. & Bearman, P. (2018), 'Neural precursors of future liking and affective reciprocity', *Proceedings of the National Academy of Sciences*, 115(17), 4375–80.

10 Francis, D., Diorio, J., Liu, D. & Meaney, M. J. (1999), 'Nongenomic transmission across generations of maternal behavior and stress responses in the rat', *Science*, 286(5442), 1155–8.

11 Luecken, L. J. & Lemery, K. S. (2004), 'Early caregiving and physiological stress responses', *Clinical Psychology Review*, 24(2), 171–91.

12 Rogers, C. R. (1957), 'The necessary and sufficient conditions of therapeutic personality change', *Journal of Consulting Psychology*, 21(2), 97–103; Rogers, C.R., Gendlin, E. T., Kiesler, D. & Truax, C. (1967), *The Therapeutic Relationship and Its Impact: A study of psychotherapy with schizophrenics*, Oxford, UK.

13 Ambady, N., LaPlante, D., Nguyen, T., Rosenthal, R., Chaumeton, N. & Levinson, W. (2002), 'Surgeons' tone of voice: A clue to malpractice history', *Surgery*, 132(1), 5–9.

14 Alison, L. J., Alison, E., Noone, G., Elntib, S., Waring, S. & Christiansen, P. (2014), 'The efficacy of rapport-based techniques for minimizing counter-interrogation tactics amongst a field sample of terrorists', *Psychology, Public Policy, and Law, 20*(4), 421–30.

15 Seiter, J. S. & Dutson, E. (2007), 'The Effect of Compliments on Tipping Behavior in Hairstyling Salons', *Journal of Applied Social Psychology, 37*(9), 1999–2007; Seiter, J. S. (2007), 'Ingratiation and gratuity: The effect of complimenting customers on tipping behavior in restaurants', *Journal of Applied Social Psychology, 37*(3), 478–85; Grant, N. K., Fabrigar, L. R. & Lim, H. (2010), 'Exploring the efficacy of compliments as a tactic for securing compliance', *Basic and Applied Social Psychology, 32*(3), 226–33.

16 Laustsen, L. & Bor, A. (2017), 'The relative weight of character traits in political candidate evaluations: Warmth is more important than competence, leadership and integrity', *Electoral Studies, 49*, 96–107.

17 Chozick, A. (2018), *Chasing Hillary: Ten Years, Two Presidential Campaigns, and One Intact Glass Ceiling*, New York, NY: HarperCollins.

18 Laustsen, L. (2017), 'Choosing the right candidate: Observational and experimental evidence that conservatives and liberals prefer powerful and warm candidate personalities, respectively', *Political Behavior, 39*(4), 883–908.

19 https://www.seattletimes.com/business/in-person-costco-president-craig-jelinek-keeps-a-low-profile/

20 Roberts, J. A. & David, M. E. (2017), 'Put down your phone and listen to me: How boss phubbing undermines the psychological conditions necessary for employee engagement', *Computers in Human Behavior, 75*, 206–17.

21 Ashford, S. J., Wellman, N., Sully de Luque, M., De Stobbeleir, K. E. & Wollan, M. (2018), 'Two roads to effectiveness: CEO feedback seeking, vision articulation, and firm performance', *Journal of Organizational Behavior, 39*(1), 82–95.

22 Newcombe, M. J. & Ashkanasy, N. M. (2002), 'The role of affect and affective congruence in perceptions of leaders: An experimental study', *The Leadership Quarterly, 13*(5), 601–14.

23 Van Kleef, G. A., De Dreu, C. K. & Manstead, A. S. (2010), 'An interpersonal approach to emotion in social decision making: The emotions as social information model', in *Advances in Experimental Social Psychology*, Oxford, UK: Academic Press, Vol. 42, pp.45–96.

24 Ariely, D. (2016), *Payoff: The Hidden Logic That Shapes Our Motivations*, London: Simon and Schuster.

25 Grant, A. M. & Gino, F. (2010), 'A little thanks goes a long way: Explaining why gratitude expressions motivate prosocial behavior', *Journal of Personality and Social Psychology*, *98*(6), 946–55.

26 https://www.govinfo.gov/content/pkg/PPP-1995-book2/pdf/PPP-1995-book2-doc-pg1264-3.pdf

27 Brooks, A. W., Dai, H. & Schweitzer, M. E. (2014), 'I'm sorry about the rain! Superfluous apologies demonstrate empathic concern and increase trust', *Social Psychological and Personality Science*, *5*(4), 467–74.

28 Official apology transcript: https://www.australia.gov.au/about-australia/our-country/our-people/apology-to-australias-indigenous-peoples; Kevin Rudd has the highest career-peak approval rating: https://www.theaustralian.com.au/national-affairs/newspoll

29 Cialdini, R. B. & de Nicholas, M. E. (1989), 'Self-presentation by association', *Journal of personality and social psychology*, *57*(4), 626–31.

30 Weidman, A. C., Cheng, J. T. & Tracy, J. L. (2018), 'The psychological structure of humility', *Journal of Personality and Social Psychology*, *114*(1), 153–78.

31 Van Kleef, G. A., De Dreu, C. K. W. & Manstead, A. S. R. (2006), 'Supplication and appeasement in conflict and negotiation: The interpersonal effects of disappointment, worry, guilt, and regret', *Journal of Personality and Social Psychology*, *91*(1), 124–42.

32 Marks, J., Czech, P. & Sharot, T. (in prep), 'Observing others give & take: A computational account of bystanders' feelings and actions'. See also Klein, N. & Epley, N. (2014), 'The topography of generosity: Asymmetric evaluations of prosocial actions', *Journal of Experimental Psychology: General*, *143*(6), 2366–79.

33 Minson, J. A. & Monin, B. (2012), 'Do-gooder derogation: Disparaging morally motivated minorities to defuse anticipated reproach', *Social Psychological and Personality Science*, *3*(2), 200–7.

34 Kraus, M. W. & Keltner, D. (2009), 'Signs of socioeconomic status: A thin-slicing approach', *Psychological Science*, *20*(1), 99–106.

35 Zebrowitz, L. A. & Montepare, J. M. (2005), 'Appearance DOES matter', *Science*, *308*(5728), 1565–6.

36 Todorov, A., Mandisodza, A. N., Goren, A. & Hall, C. C. (2005), 'Inferences of competence from faces predict election outcomes', *Science*, *308*(5728), 1623–6.

37 Keating, C. F., Randall, D. & Kendrick, T. (1999), 'Presidential physiognomies: Altered images, altered perceptions', *Political Psychology*, *20*(3), 593–610.

38 Zebrowitz, L. A., Kendall-Tackett, K. & Fafel, J. (1991), 'The influence of children's facial maturity on parental expectations and punishments', *Journal of Experimental Child Psychology*, *52*(2), 221–38.

39 Zebrowitz, L. A. & McDonald, S. M. (1991), 'The impact of litigants' baby-facedness and attractiveness on adjudications in small claims courts', *Law and Human Behavior*, *15*(6), 603–23.

40 Perrett, D. (2010), *In Your Face: The new science of human attraction*, New York, NY: Palgrave Macmillan.

41 Willer, R. (2009), 'Groups reward individual sacrifice: The status solution to the collective action problem', *American Sociological Review*, *74*(1), 23–43.

42 Restivo, M. & Van De Rijt, A. (2012), 'Experimental study of informal rewards in peer production', *PloS one*, *7*, e34358.

43 Hardy, C. L. & Van Vugt, M. (2006), 'Nice guys finish first: The competitive altruism hypothesis', *Personality and Social Psychology Bulletin*, *32*(10), 1402–13.

44 Yoeli, E., Hoffman, M., Rand, D. G. & Nowak, M. A. (2013), 'Powering up with indirect reciprocity in a large-scale field experiment', *Proceedings of the National Academy of Sciences*, *110*(2), 10424–9.

45 https://www.nytimes.com/2007/07/04/business/04hybrid.html

46 Griskevicius, V., Tybur, J. M. & Van den Bergh, B. (2010), 'Going green to be seen: Status, reputation, and conspicuous conservation', *Journal of Personality and Social Psychology*, *98*(3), 392–404.

Chapter 6: Vulnerability

1 https://hbr.org/2014/12/what-bosses-gain-by-being-vulnerable

2 Clausen, T., Christensen, K. B. & Nielsen, K. (2015), 'Does Group-Level Commitment Predict Employee Well-Being?', *Journal of Occupational and Environmental Medicine*, *57*(11), 1141–6.

3 Brown, B. (2015), *Daring Greatly: How the courage to be vulnerable transforms the way we live, love, parent, and lead*, London: Penguin.

4 Bohns, V. K. & Flynn, F. J. (2010), '"Why didn't you just ask?" Underestimating the discomfort of help-seeking', *Journal of Experimental Social Psychology*, *46*(2), 402–9. See also DePaulo, B. M. & Fisher, J. D. (1980), 'The costs of asking for help', *Basic and Applied Social Psychology*, *1*(1), 23–35.

5 Ibid.; and ibid.

6 Bruk, A., Scholl, S. G. & Bless, H. (2018), 'Beautiful mess effect: Self–other differences in evaluation of showing vulnerability', *Journal of Personality and Social Psychology*, 115(2), 192–205.

7 https://www.metro.news/theresa-mays-a-super-trouper-says-abbas-bjorn-ulvaeus/1325504/

8 https://www.theguardian.com/commentisfree/2018/oct/03/theresa-may-conference-speech-verdict-conservative-birmingham

9 Gray, K. & Wegner, D. M. (2011), 'To escape blame, don't be a hero – Be a victim', *Journal of Experimental Social Psychology*, 47(2), 516–19.

10 http://news.bbc.co.uk/1/hi/entertainment/8077075.stm

11 Collins, N. L. & Miller, L. C. (1994), 'Self-disclosure and liking: A meta-analytic review', *Psychological Bulletin*, 116(3), 457–75; Moore, D. A., Kurtzberg, T. R., Thompson, L. L. & Morris, M. W. (1999), 'Long and short routes to success in electronically mediated negotiations: Group affiliations and good vibrations', *Organizational Behavior and Human Decision Processes*, 77(1), 22–43; Vallano, J. P. & Compo, N. S. (2011), 'A comfortable witness is a good witness: Rapport-building and susceptibility to misinformation in an investigative mock-crime interview', *Applied Cognitive Psychology*, 25(6), 960–70; Stokoe, E. (2009), '"I've got a girlfriend": Police officers doing "self-disclosure" in their interrogations of suspects', *Narrative Inquiry*, 19(1), 154–82.

12 Davidov, M., Zahn-Waxler, C., Roth-Hanania, R. & Knafo, A. (2013), 'Concern for others in the first year of life: Theory, evidence, and avenues for research', *Child Development Perspectives*, 7(2), 126–31.

13 Bartal, I. B. A., Decety, J. & Mason, P. (2011), 'Empathy and pro-social behavior in rats', *Science*, 334(6061), 1427–30.

14 Crockett, M. J., Kurth-Nelson, Z., Siegel, J. Z., Dayan, P. & Dolan, R. J. (2014), 'Harm to others outweighs harm to self in moral decision making', *Proceedings of the National Academy of Sciences*, 111(48), 17320–5.

15 Grant, A. M. & Hofmann, D. A. (2011), 'It's Not All About Me: Motivating hand hygiene among health care professionals by focusing on patients', *Psychological Science*, 22(12), 1494–9.

16 Oberholzer-Gee, F. (2006), 'A market for time fairness and efficiency in waiting lines', *Kyklos*, 59(3), 427–40.

17 Milgram, S. (1974), *Obedience to Authority*, London: Tavistock.

18 Rosas, A. & Koenigs, M. (2014), 'Beyond "utilitarianism": Maximizing the clinical impact of moral judgment research', *Social Neuroscience*, 9(6), 661–7.

19 Andreoni, J., Rao, J. M. & Trachtman, H. (2017), 'Avoiding the ask: A field experiment on altruism, empathy, and charitable giving', *Journal of Political Economy, 125*(3), 625–53.

20 https://www.today.com/popculture/dancing-man-today-show-defies-bullies-dances-meghan-trainor-t22501

21 Jenni, K. & Loewenstein, G. (1997), 'Explaining the identifiable victim effect', *Journal of Risk and Uncertainty, 14*(3), 235–57.

22 For more information about identifiable victim effects, see: Lee, S. & Feeley, T. H. (2016), 'The identifiable victim effect: A meta-analytic review', *Social Influence, 11*(3), 199–215.

23 Nobis, N. (2009), 'The "Babe" vegetarians: bioethics, animal minds and moral methodology', in S. Shapshay (ed.), *Bioethics at the movies*, Baltimore, MD: Johns Hopkins University Press. See also https://www.newstatesman.com/culture/film/2016/08/babe-bfg-how-children-s-stories-promote-vegetarianism

24 https://www.veganfoodandliving.com/veganuary-launches-crowdfunding-campaign-to-place-vegan-adverts-on-the-london-underground/

25 Bloom, P. (2017), *Against Empathy: The case for rational compassion*, London: Penguin.

26 Schelling, T. C. (1968), 'The Life You Save May Be Your Own', in S. Chase (ed.), *Problems in Public Expenditure Analysis*, Washington, DC: The Brookings Institute.

27 Bloom, P. (2017), 'Empathy and its discontents', *Trends in Cognitive Sciences, 21*(1), 24–31.

28 Fisher, R. (1981), 'Preventing nuclear war', *Bulletin of the Atomic Scientists, 37*(3), 11–17.

29 Cikara, M. & Fiske, S. T. (2012), 'Stereotypes and schadenfreude: Affective and physiological markers of pleasure at outgroup misfortunes', *Social Psychological and Personality Science, 3*(1), 63–71.

30 https://www.thesun.co.uk/world-cup-2018/6641079/world-cup-2018-germany/

31 Kay, A. C. & Jost, J. T. (2003), 'Complementary justice: effects of "poor but happy" and "poor but honest" stereotype exemplars on system justification and implicit activation of the justice motive', *Journal of personality and social psychology, 85*(5), 823–37; Zaki, J. (2014), 'Empathy: a motivated account', *Psychological Bulletin, 140*(6), 1608–47.

32 Harris, L. T. & Fiske, S. T. (2006), 'Dehumanizing the lowest of the low: Neuroimaging responses to extreme out-groups', *Psychological Science, 17*(10), 847–53.

33 Haslam, N. & Loughnan, S. (2014), 'Dehumanization and infrahumanization', *Annual Review of Psychology*, *65*, 399–423.

34 Strack, S. & Coyne, J. C. (1983), 'Social confirmation of dysphoria: Shared and private reactions to depression', *Journal of Personality and Social Psychology*, *44*(4), 798–806.

35 Vaes, J. & Muratore, M. (2013), 'Defensive dehumanization in the medical practice: A cross-sectional study from a health care worker's perspective', *British Journal of Social Psychology*, *52*(1), 180–90.

36 http://www.nytimes.com/2009/04/07/health/07pati.html

37 Lammers, J. & Stapel, D. A. (2011), 'Power increases dehumanization', *Group Processes & Intergroup Relations*, *14*(1), 113–26.

38 Fehse, K., Silveira, S., Elvers, K. & Blautzik, J. (2015), 'Compassion, guilt and innocence: an fMRI study of responses to victims who are responsible for their fate', *Social Neuroscience*, *10*(3), 243–52.

39 Lerner, M. J. & Goldberg, J. H. (1999), 'When do decent people blame victims? The differing effects of the explicit/rational and implicit/experiential cognitive systems', in S. Chaiken & Y. Trope (eds), *Dual-process Theories in Social Psychology*, New York, NY: Guilford Press, pp.627–40; Harber, K. D., Podolski, P. & Williams, C. H. (2015), 'Emotional disclosure and victim blaming', *Emotion*, *15*(5), 603–14.

40 Harris, L. T., Lee, V. K., Capestany, B. H. & Cohen, A. O. (2014), 'Assigning economic value to people results in dehumanization brain response', *Journal of Neuroscience, Psychology, and Economics*, *7*(3), 151–63.

41 Kogut, T. & Ritov, I. (2007), '"One of us": Outstanding willingness to help save a single identified compatriot', *Organizational Behavior and Human Decision Processes*, *104*(2), 150–7.

42 Levine, M., Prosser, A., Evans, D. & Reicher, S. (2005), 'Identity and emergency intervention: How social group membership and inclusiveness of group boundaries shape helping behavior', *Personality and Social Psychology Bulletin*, *31*(4), 443–53.

43 Tam, T., Hewstone, M., Cairns, E., Tausch, N., Maio, G. & Kenworthy, J. (2007), 'The impact of intergroup emotions on forgiveness in Northern Ireland', *Group Processes & Intergroup Relations*, *10*(1), 119–36; Capozza, D., Falvo, R., Favara, I. & Trifiletti, E. (2013), 'The relationship between direct and indirect cross-group friendships and outgroup humanization: Emotional and cognitive mediators', *Testing, Psychometrics, Methodology in Applied Psychology*, *20*(4), 383–97.

44 Vezzali, L., Capozza, D., Stathi, S. & Giovannini, D. (2012), 'Increasing outgroup trust, reducing infrahumanization, and enhancing future contact intentions via imagined intergroup contact', *Journal of Experimental Social Psychology*, *48*(1),

437–40; Vezzali, L., Stathi, S. & Giovannini, D. (2012), 'Indirect contact through book reading: Improving adolescents' attitudes and behavioral intentions toward immigrants', *Psychology in the Schools*, *49*(2), 148–62.

45 Harris, L. T. & Fiske, S. T. (2007), 'Social groups that elicit disgust are differentially processed in mPFC', *Social Cognitive and Affective Neuroscience*, *2*(1), 45–51.

Chapter 7: Trustworthiness

1 http://news.bbc.co.uk/onthisday/hi/dates/stories/march/22/newsid_4271000/4271221.stm

2 https://api.parliament.uk/historic-hansard/commons/1963/jun/17/security-mr-profumos-resignation

3 http://archive.spectator.co.uk/article/14th-june-1963/4/political-commentary

4 Simpson, B. & Willer, R. (2015), 'Beyond altruism: Sociological foundations of cooperation and prosocial behavior', *Annual Review of Sociology*, *41*, 43–63.

5 Kim, P. H., Dirks, K. T., Cooper, C. D. & Ferrin, D. L. (2006), 'When more blame is better than less: The implications of internal vs. external attributions for the repair of trust after a competence- vs. integrity-based trust violation,' *Organizational Behavior and Human Decision Processes*, *99*(1), 49–65.

6 Tov, W. & Diener, E. (2008), 'The well-being of nations: Linking together trust, cooperation, and democracy', in Sullivan, B.A., Snyder, M. & Sullivan, J.L. (eds), *Cooperation: The political psychology of effective human interaction*, Malden, MA: Blackwell, pp.323–42.

7 Berg, J., Dickhaut, J. & McCabe, K. (1995), 'Trust, reciprocity, and social history', *Games and Economic Behavior*, *10*(1), 122–42; Camerer, C. & Weigelt, K. (1998), 'Experimental tests of a sequential equilibrium reputation model', *Econometrica*, *56*(1), 1–36. See also Rezlescu, C., Duchaine, B., Olivola, C. Y. & Chater, N. (2012), 'Unfakeable facial configurations affect strategic choices in trust games with or without information about past behavior', *PloS one*, *7*, e34293.

8 Pillutla, M. M., Malhotra, D. & Murnighan, J. K. (2003), 'Attributions of trust and the calculus of reciprocity', *Journal of Experimental Social Psychology*, *39*(5), 448–55; Krueger, J. I., Massey, A. L. & DiDonato, T. E. (2008), 'A matter of trust: From social preferences to the strategic adherence to social norms', *Negotiation and Conflict Management Research*, *1*(1), 31–52.

9 Tov, W. & Diener, E. (2008), 'The well-being of nations: Linking together trust, cooperation, and democracy', in Sullivan, B.A., Snyder, M. and Sullivan, J.L.

(eds), *Cooperation: The political psychology of effective human interaction*, Malden, MA: Blackwell, pp.323–42.

10 World Values Survey 6 (2014). Available at: http://www.worldvaluessurvey.org/wvs.jsp; see also: https://www.bi.team/blogs/social-trust-is-one-of-the-most-important-measures-that-most-people-have-never-heard-of-and-its-moving/

11 Bachmann, R. & Inkpen, A. C. (2011), 'Understanding institutional-based trust building processes in inter-organizational relationships', *Organization Studies, 32*(2), 281–301; Granelli, F. (2017), 'Trust and Revolution: A History', *Unpublished doctoral dissertation*. See also Putnam, R. D. (1995), 'Bowling alone: America's declining social capital', *Journal of Democracy, 6*(1), 65–78.

12 Chung, K. Y., Derdenger, T. P. & Srinivasan, K. (2013), 'Economic value of celebrity endorsements: Tiger Woods' impact on sales of Nike golf balls', *Marketing Science, 32*(2), 271–93; Knittel, C. R. & Stango, V. (2013), 'Celebrity endorsements, firm value, and reputation risk: Evidence from the Tiger Woods scandal', *Management Science, 60*(1), 21–37. Or see: https://gsm.ucdavis.edu/news-release/tiger-woods-scandal-cost-shareholders-12-billion

13 Dahlen, M. & Lange, F. (2006), 'A disaster is contagious: How a brand in crisis affects other brands', *Journal of Advertising Research, 46*(4), 388–97; Carrillat, F. A., d'Astous, A. & Christianis, H. (2014), 'Guilty by association: The perils of celebrity endorsement for endorsed brands and their direct competitors', *Psychology & Marketing, 31*(11), 1024–39.

14 Rousseau, D. M., Sitkin, S. B., Burt, R. S. & Camerer, C. (1998), 'Not so different after all: A cross-discipline view of trust', *Academy of Management Review, 23*(3), 393–404; Mayer, R. C., Davis, J. H. & Schoorman, F. D. (1995), 'An integrative model of organizational trust', *Academy of Management Review, 20*(3), 709–34; Thielmann, I. & Hilbig, B. E. (2015), 'Trust: An integrative review from a person–situation perspective', *Review of General Psychology, 19*(3), 249–77.

15 Ariely, D. & Loewenstein, G. (2006), 'The heat of the moment: The effect of sexual arousal on sexual decision making', *Journal of Behavioral Decision Making, 19*(2), 87–98.

16 https://www.independent.co.uk/news/uk/politics/boris-johnson-put-his-political-ambition-to-lead-the-tory-party-ahead-of-uk-interests-says-david-a6890016.html

17 For more details about the lives of Christine Keeler and Mandy Rice-Davies (the Profumo affair), see (Christine Keeler): https://www.independent.co.uk/news/uk/politics/christine-keeler-profumo-affair-secretary-war-stephen-ward-prostitute-affair-soviet-attache-cold-war-a8095576.html; (Mandy Rice-Davies):

https://www.telegraph.co.uk/news/obituaries/11303169/Mandy-Rice-Davies-obituary.html

18 Knoll, J. & Matthes, J. (2017), 'The effectiveness of celebrity endorsements: a meta-analysis', *Journal of the Academy of Marketing Science, 45*(1), 55–75.

19 Starmans, C. & Bloom, P. (2016), 'When the spirit is willing, but the flesh is weak: Developmental differences in judgments about inner moral conflict', *Psychological Science, 27*(11), 1498–1506.

20 McNulty, J. K., Meltzer, A. L., Makhanova, A. & Maner, J. K. (2018), 'Attentional and evaluative biases help people maintain relationships by avoiding infidelity', *Journal of Personality and Social Psychology, 115*(1), 76–95.

21 https://www.washingtonpost.com/politics/2019/04/01/president-trump-has-made-false-or-misleading-claims-over-days/; (*Playboy* model scandal): https://www.theguardian.com/us-news/2018/jul/24/michael-cohen-trump-tape-karen-mcdougal-payment

22 https://www.bbc.co.uk/news/world-us-canada-37982000

23 Hogg, M. A. (2010), 'Influence and leadership', in S. T. Fiske, D. T. Gilbert & G. Lindzey (eds), *Handbook of Social Psychology*, Hoboken, NJ: John Wiley & Sons, Vol. 2, pp.1166–1207.

24 Swire, B., Berinsky, A. J., Lewandowsky, S. & Ecker, U. K. (2017), 'Processing political misinformation: Comprehending the Trump phenomenon', *Royal Society Open Science, 4*(3), 160802.

25 https://news.gallup.com/poll/208640/majority-no-longer-thinks-trump-keeps-promises.aspx?g_source=Politics&g_medium=newsfeed&g_campaign=tiles

26 https://www.theguardian.com/commentisfree/2018/sep/05/trump-poll-ratings-macron-globalisation; https://www.ouest-france.fr/politique/emmanuel-macron/popularite-macron-son-plus-bas-niveau-en-juillet-selon-sept-instituts-de-sond-age-5904008?utm_source=dlvr.it&utm_medium=twitter

27 https://www.prri.org/research/prri-brookings-oct-19-poll-politics-election-clinton-double-digit-lead-trump/

28 https://www.nbcnews.com/think/opinion/trump-s-lying-seems-be-getting-worse-psychology-suggests-there-ncna876486; Gino, F. & Bazerman, M. H. (2009), 'When misconduct goes unnoticed: The acceptability of gradual erosion in others' unethical behavior', *Journal of Experimental Social Psychology, 45*(4), 708–19; see also Garrett, N., Lazzaro, S. C., Ariely, D. & Sharot, T. (2016), 'The brain adapts to dishonesty', *Nature Neuroscience, 19*(12), 1727–32.

29 (Spitzer): http://www.nytimes.com/2008/03/10/nyregion/10cnd-spitzer.html?pagewanted=all&_r=0; (Vaz): https://www.mirror.co.uk/news/uk-news/married-mp-keith-vaz-tells-8763805

30 Effron, D. A. & Monin, B. (2010), 'Letting people off the hook: When do good deeds excuse transgressions?', *Personality and Social Psychology Bulletin, 36*(12), 1618–34.

31 https://www.thecut.com/2018/11/how-did-larry-nassar-deceive-so-many-for-so-long.html

32 Cropanzano, R. & Mitchell, M. S. (2005), 'Social exchange theory: An interdisciplinary review', *Journal of Management, 31*(6), 874–900.

33 Flynn, F. J. (2003), 'How much should I give and how often? The effects of generosity and frequency of favor exchange on social status and productivity', *Academy of Management Journal, 46*(5), 539–53.

34 Diekmann, A., Jann, B., Przepiorka, W. & Wehrli, S. (2014), 'Reputation formation and the evolution of cooperation in anonymous online markets', *American Sociological Review, 79*(1), 65–85.

35 Lount Jr, R. B., Zhong, C. B., Sivanathan, N. & Murnighan, J. K. (2008), 'Getting off on the wrong foot: The timing of a breach and the restoration of trust', *Personality and Social Psychology Bulletin, 34*(12), 1601–12.

36 Bohnet, I. & Zeckhauser, R. (2004), 'Trust, risk and betrayal', *Journal of Economic Behavior & Organization, 55*(4), 467–84; Bohnet, I., Greig, F., Herrmann, B. & Zeckhauser, R. (2008), 'Betrayal aversion: Evidence from Brazil, China, Oman, Switzerland, Turkey, and the United States', *American Economic Review, 98*(1), 294–310.

37 Fetchenhauer, D. & Dunning, D. (2012), 'Betrayal aversion versus principled trustfulness – How to explain risk avoidance and risky choices in trust games', *Journal of Economic Behavior and Organization, 81*(2), 534–41; Schlösser, T., Mensching, O., Dunning, D. & Fetchenhauer, D. (2015), 'Trust and rationality: Shifting normative analyses of risks involving other people versus nature', *Social Cognition, 33*(5), 459–82.

38 Sally, D. (1995), 'Conversation and cooperation in social dilemmas: A meta-analysis of experiments from 1958 to 1992', *Rationality and Society, 7*, 58–92.

39 Balliet, D. (2010), 'Communication and cooperation in social dilemmas: A meta-analytic review', *Journal of Conflict Resolution, 54*(1), 39–57.

40 Roghanizad, M. M. & Bohns, V. K. (2017), 'Ask in person: You're less persuasive than you think over email', *Journal of Experimental Social Psychology, 69*, 223–6.

41 Oosterhof, N. N. & Todorov, A. (2008), 'The functional basis of face evaluation', *Proceedings of the National Academy of Sciences, 105*(32), 11087–92.

42 Duarte, J., Siegel, S. & Young, L. (2012), 'Trust and credit: The role of appearance in peer-to-peer lending', *The Review of Financial Studies, 25*(8), 2455–84; see also Linke, L., Saribay, S. A. & Kleisner, K. (2016), 'Perceived trustworthiness

is associated with position in a corporate hierarchy', *Personality and Individual Differences, 99*, 22–7.

43 Todorov, A. (2017), *Face Value: The irresistible influence of first impressions*, Princeton, NJ: Princeton University Press.

44 Bond Jr, C. F. & DePaulo, B. M. (2006), 'Accuracy of deception judgments', *Personality and Social Psychology Review, 10*(3), 214–34; Ekman, P. & O'Sullivan, M. (1991), 'Who can catch a liar', *American Psychologist, 46*(9), 913–20.

45 Wilson, J. P. & Rule, N. O. (2017), 'Advances in understanding the detectability of trustworthiness from the face: Toward a taxonomy of a multifaceted construct', *Current Directions in Psychological Science, 26*(4), 396–400.

46 Butler, E. A., Egloff, B., Wilhelm, F. H., Smith, N. C., Erickson, E. A. & Gross, J. J. (2003), 'The social consequences of expressive suppression', *Emotion, 3*(1), 48–67.

47 Decety, J. & Chaminade, T. (2003), 'Neural correlates of feeling sympathy', *Neuropsychologia, 41*(2), 127–38.

48 Van 't Veer, A. E., Gallucci, M., Stel, M. & Beest, I. V. (2015), 'Unconscious deception detection measured by finger skin temperature and indirect veracity judgments – results of a registered report', *Frontiers in psychology, 6*, 672.

49 Williams, K. D., Bourgeois, M. J. & Croyle, R. T. (1993), 'The effects of stealing thunder in criminal and civil trials', *Law and Human Behavior, 17*(6), 597–609; Dolnik, L., Case, T. I. & Williams, K. D. (2003), 'Stealing thunder as a courtroom tactic revisited: Processes and boundaries', *Law and Human Behavior, 27*(3), 267–87; Combs, D. J. & Keller, P. S. (2010), 'Politicians and trustworthiness: Acting contrary to self-interest enhances trustworthiness', *Basic and applied social psychology, 32*(4), 328–39; Fennis, B. M. & Stroebe, W. (2014), 'Softening the blow: Company self-disclosure of negative information lessens damaging effects on consumer judgment and decision making', *Journal of Business Ethics, 120*(1), 109–20.

50 Hamilton, R., Vohs, K. D. & McGill, A. L. (2014), 'We'll be honest, this won't be the best article you'll ever read: The use of dispreferred markers in word-of-mouth communication', *Journal of Consumer Research, 41*(1), 197–212.

51 https://www.bbc.co.uk/news/av/world-us-canada-44959340/donald-trump-what-you-re-seeing-and-what-you-re-reading-is-not-what-s-happening

52 Scott, M. B. & Lyman, S. M. (1968), 'Accounts', *American Sociological Review, 33*(1), 46–62.

53 Brühl, R., Basel, J. S. & Kury, M. F. (2018), 'Communication after an integrity-based trust violation: How organizational account giving affects trust', *European Management Journal, 36*, 161–70.

54 Schweitzer, M. E., Brooks, A. W. & Galinsky, A. D. (2015), 'The organizational apology', *Harvard Business Review, 94*, 44–52.

55 https://www.theguardian.com/news/2018/mar/17/data-war-whistleblower-christopher-wylie-faceook-nix-bannon-trump

56 https://www.theguardian.com/news/2018/mar/17/cambridge-analytica-facebook-influence-us-election

57 https://www.theguardian.com/technology/2018/mar/21/mark-zuckerberg-response-facebook-cambridge-analytica; https://www.businessinsider.com/facebook-ceo-mark-zuckerberg-responds-to-cambridge-analytica-scandal?r=US&IR=T

58 https://www.bloomberg.com/news/articles/2018-07-10/facebook-faces-u-k-privacy-fine-over-cambridge-analytica-probe; https://www.independent.co.uk/news/business/news/facebook-share-price-stock-market-value-crash-bad-results-mark-zuckerberg-a8464831.html

59 Schweitzer, M. E., Brooks, A. W. & Galinsky, A. D. (2015), 'The organizational apology', *Harvard Business Review*, *94*, 44–52.

60 Haselhuhn, M. P., Schweitzer, M. E. & Wood, A. M. (2010), 'How implicit beliefs influence trust recovery', *Psychological Science*, *21*(5), 645–8.

61 Mallea, R., Spektor, M. & Wheeler, N. J. (2015), 'The origins of nuclear cooperation: a critical oral history between Argentina and Brazil'. Retrieved from: https://www.birmingham.ac.uk/Documents/college-social-sciences/government-society/iccs/news-events/2015/critical-oral-history.pdf; https://www.americasquarterly.org/content/long-view-how-argentina-and-brazil-stepped-back-nuclear-race

Chapter 8: Charisma

1 For more on John Marks, see his autobiography: Marks, J. (2008), *The NHS: Beginning, Middle and End? The Autobiography of Dr John Marks*, Oxford, UK: Radcliffe Publishing.

2 Antonakis, J., Bastardoz, N., Jacquart, P. & Shamir, B. (2016), 'Charisma: An ill-defined and ill-measured gift', *Annual Review of Organizational Psychology and Organizational Behavior, 3*, 293–319.

3 https://blogs.wsj.com/law/2007/09/27/the-origins-of-justice-stewarts-i-know-it-when-i-see-it/

4 Tskhay, K. O., Zhu, R., Zou, C. & Rule, N. O. (2018), 'Charisma in everyday life: Conceptualization and validation of the General Charisma Inventory', *Journal of Personality and Social Psychology, 114*(1), 131–52.

5   Weber, M. (1978), *Economy and Society: An outline of interpretive sociology* (G. Roth & C. Wittich, eds), Berkeley, CA: University of California Press.

6   DeGroot, T., Kiker, D. S. & Cross, T. C. (2000), 'A meta-analysis to review organizational outcomes related to charismatic leadership', *Canadian Journal of Administrative Sciences*, *17*(4), 356–72.

7   Pillai, R. & Meindl, J. R. (1998), 'Context and charisma: A "meso" level examination of the relationship of organic structure, collectivism, and crisis to charismatic leadership', *Journal of Management*, *24*(5), 643–71.

8   Whitney, K., Sagrestano, L. M. & Maslach, C. (1994), 'Establishing the social impact of individuation', *Journal of Personality and Social Psychology*, *66*(6), 1140–53.

9   Hogg, M. A. (2010), 'Influence and Leadership', in S. T. Fiske, D. T. Gilbert & G. Lindzey (eds), *Handbook of Social Psychology*, Hoboken, NJ: John Wiley & Sons, Vol. 2, pp.1166–1207. See also, Conger, J. A. & Kanungo, R. N. (1987), 'Toward a behavioral theory of charismatic leadership in organizational settings', *Academy of Management Review*, *12*, 637–47.

10   Piff, P. K., Dietze, P., Feinberg, M., Stancato, D. M. & Keltner, D. (2015), 'Awe, the small self, and prosocial behavior', *Journal of Personality and Social Psychology*, *108*(6), 883–99.

11   https://www.nytimes.com/1993/01/21/us/the-inauguration-we-force-the-spring-transcript-of-address-by-president-clinton.html

12   https://www.nytimes.com/1996/02/19/opinion/l-cap-over-wall-joined-political-lexicon-055735.html

13   Heffer, S. (2014), *Like the Roman: The life of Enoch Powell*, London: Faber & Faber.

14   Mio, J. S., Riggio, R. E., Levin, S. & Reese, R. (2005), 'Presidential leadership and charisma: The effects of metaphor', *The Leadership Quarterly*, *16*(2), 287–94.

15   https://www.london.gov.uk/city-hall-blog/good-relationships-are-vital-our-mental-health-and-wellbeing

16   Paharia, N., Keinan, A., Avery, J. & Schor, J. B. (2010), 'The underdog effect: The marketing of disadvantage and determination through brand biography', *Journal of Consumer Research*, *37*(5), 775–90; Staton, M., Paharia, N. & Oveis, C. (2012), 'Emotional Marketing: How Pride and Compassion Impact Preferences For Underdog and Top Dog Brands', *Advances in Consumer Research*, *40*, 1045–6; Paharia, N. & Thompson, D. V. (2014), 'When Underdog Narratives Backfire: the Effect of Perceived Market Advantage on Brand Status', *Advances in Consumer Research*, *42*, 17–21.

17 Buss, D. M. (1991), 'Evolutionary personality psychology', *Annual Review of Psychology, 42*, 459–91.

18 Sy, T., Horton, C. & Riggio, R. (2018), 'Charismatic leadership: Eliciting and channeling follower emotions', *The Leadership Quarterly, 29*(1), 58–69; Wasielewski, P. L. (1985), 'The emotional basis of charisma', *Symbolic Interaction, 8*(2), 207–22; Bono, J. E. & Ilies, R. (2006), 'Charisma, positive emotions and mood contagion', *The Leadership Quarterly, 17*(4), 317–34.

19 Doherty, R. W. (1997), 'The emotional contagion scale: A measure of individual differences', *Journal of Nonverbal Behavior, 21*, 131–54; Readers interested in assessing their own susceptibility can find the Emotional Contagion Scale at: http://www.midss.org/content/emotional-contagion-scale

20 Kenny, D. A., Horner, C., Kashy, D. A. & Chu, L. C. (1992), 'Consensus at zero acquaintance: replication, behavioral cues, and stability', *Journal of Personality and Social Psychology, 62*(1), 88–97.

21 Koppensteiner, M., Stephan, P. & Jäschke, J. P. M. (2015), 'From body motion to cheers: Speakers' body movements as predictors of applause', *Personality and Individual Differences, 74*, 182–5.

22 https://www.ted.com/talks/fields_wicker_miurin_learning_from_leadership_s_missing_manual/

23 https://www.ted.com/talks/simon_sinek_how_great_leaders_inspire_action

24 https://www.huffingtonpost.com/vanessa-van-edwards/5-secrets-of-a-successful_b_6887472.html?guccounter=1

25 An entertaining take on Governor Kasich's hand-gestures comes in the form of an adaptation of the popular video game Fruit Ninja: https://www.youtube.com/watch?v=VqgkNtYbwwM

26 Antonakis, J., Bastardoz, N., Jacquart, P. & Shamir, B. (2016), 'Charisma: An ill-defined and ill-measured gift', *Annual Review of Organizational Psychology and Organizational Behavior, 3*, 293–319.

27 https://www.nytimes.com/2018/08/25/opinion/sunday/college-professors-experts-advice.html

28 Figlio, D. N., Schapiro, M. O. & Soter, K. B. (2015), 'Are tenure track professors better teachers?', *Review of Economics and Statistics, 97*(4), 715–24.

29 von Hippel, W., Ronay, R., Baker, E., Kjelsaas, K. & Murphy, S. C. (2016), 'Quick thinkers are smooth talkers: Mental speed facilitates charisma', *Psychological Science, 27*(1), 119–22.

30 Tskhay, K. O., Zhu, R., Zou, C. & Rule, N. O. (2018), 'Charisma in everyday life: Conceptualization and validation of the General Charisma Inventory', *Journal of Personality and Social Psychology, 114*(1), 131–52. Interested readers can

take the test by visiting: https://www.businessinsider.com/how-to-measure-charisma-2017-11?r=US&IR=T

31 Antonakis, J., Fenley, M. & Liechti, S. (2011), 'Can charisma be taught? Tests of two interventions', *Academy of Management Learning & Education*, *10*(3), 374–96.

32 Ambady, N. & Rosenthal, R. (1993), 'Half a minute: Predicting teacher evaluations from thin slices of nonverbal behavior and physical attractiveness', *Journal of Personality and Social Psychology*, *64*(3), 431–41.

Conclusion

1 https://api.parliament.uk/historic-hansard/commons/1981/nov/26/civil-defence-1

2 Garthwaite, C. & Moore, T. J. (2012), 'Can celebrity endorsements affect political outcomes? Evidence from the 2008 US democratic presidential primary', *The Journal of Law, Economics, & Organization*, *29*(2), 355–84.

3 https://losangeles.cbslocal.com/2018/11/06/tennessee-election-blackburn-taylor-swift/ and https://eu.tennessean.com/story/entertainment/music/2018/11/07/taylor-swift-bredesen-endorsement-tennessee-senate-race-political-post/1918440002/

4 https://eu.tennessean.com/story/news/politics/tn-elections/2018/10/07/marsha-blackburn-holds-8-point-lead-over-phil-bredesen-new-cbs-poll-tennessee-us-senate-race/1562109002/

5 https://www.vox.com/2018/10/9/17955288/taylor-swift-democrat-conservative-reaction-blackburn

6 https://nypost.com/2018/11/06/tennessee-voting-numbers-surge-after-taylor-swift-post/

7 Marks, J., Copland, E., Loh, E., Sunstein, C. R. & Sharot, T. (2018), 'Epistemic spillovers: Learning others' political views reduces the ability to assess and use their expertise in nonpolitical domains', *Cognition*, *188*, 74–84.

8 Thorndike, E. L. (1920), 'A constant error in psychological ratings', *Journal of Applied Psychology*, *4*(1), 25–9.

9 Wang, J. W. & Cuddy, A. J. C. (2008), 'Good traits travel: The perceived transitivity of traits across social networks', in *9th Annual Meeting of the Society for Personality and Social Psychology, Albuquerque, NM*.

10 Walther, E. (2002), 'Guilty by mere association: Evaluative conditioning and the spreading attitude effect', *Journal of Personality and Social Psychology, 82*(6), 919–34. See also Hebl, M. R. & Mannix, L. M. (2003), 'The weight of obesity in evaluating others: A mere proximity effect', *Personality and Social Psychology Bulletin, 29*(1), 28–38.

11 Vosoughi, S., Roy, D. & Aral, S. (2018), 'The spread of true and false news online', *Science, 359*(6380), 1146–51.

12 Pennycook, G. & Rand, D. G. (2019), 'Fighting misinformation on social media using crowdsourced judgments of news source quality', *Proceedings of the National Academy of Sciences, 116*(7), 2521–6.

13 Pennycook, G. & Rand, D. G. (2018), 'Lazy, not biased: Susceptibility to partisan fake news is better explained by lack of reasoning than by motivated reasoning', *Cognition, 188*, 39–50.

14 https://www.cambridgeassessment.org.uk/Images/518813-uptake-of-gcse-subjects-2017.pdf
https://c0arw235.caspio.com/dp/b7f930000e16e10a822c47b3baa2

15 https://www.apa.org/monitor/2017/11/trends-popular

16 Amos, C., Holmes, G. & Strutton, D. (2008), 'Exploring the relationship between celebrity endorser effects and advertising effectiveness: A quantitative synthesis of effect size', *International Journal of Advertising, 27*(2), 209–34.

17 Dolan, P., Hallsworth, M., Halpern, D., King, D., Metcalfe, R., & Vlaev, I. (2012), 'Influencing behaviour: The mindspace way', *Journal of Economic Psychology, 33*(1), 264–77.

18 Sznycer, D., Al-Shawaf, L., Bereby-Meyer, Y., Curry, O. S., De Smet, D., Ermer, E. & McClung, J. (2017), 'Cross-cultural regularities in the cognitive architecture of pride', *Proceedings of the National Academy of Sciences, 114*(8), 1874–9; Sznycer, D., Xygalatas, D., Alami, S., An, X. F., Ananyeva, K. I., Fukushima, S. & Onyishi, I. E. (2018), 'Invariances in the architecture of pride across small-scale societies', *Proceedings of the National Academy of Sciences, 115*(33), 8322–7.

19 Re, D. E. & Rule, N. (2017), 'Distinctive facial cues predict leadership rank and selection', *Personality and Social Psychology Bulletin, 43*(9), 1311–22.

20 Fiske, S. T. (2010), 'Interpersonal stratification: Status, power, and subordination', in S. T. Fiske, D. T. Gilbert & G. Lindzey (eds), *Handbook of Social Psychology*, Hoboken, NJ: John Wiley & Sons, pp.941–82.

21 Wang, A. C., Tsai, C. Y., Dionne, S. D., Yammarino, F. J., Spain, S. M., Ling, H. C. & Cheng, B. S. (2018), 'Benevolence-dominant, authoritarianism-dominant, and classical paternalistic leadership: Testing their relationships with subordinate performance', *The Leadership Quarterly, 29*(6), 686–97.

22 Aronson, E., Willerman, B. & Floyd, J. (1966), 'The effect of a pratfall on increasing interpersonal attractiveness', *Psychonomic Science*, 4(6), 227–8.

23 Brescoll, V. L., Okimoto, T. G. & Vial, A. C. (2018), 'You've come a long way ... maybe: How moral emotions trigger backlash against women leaders', *Journal of Social Issues*, 74(1), 144–64; Eagly, A. H. (2018), 'Some leaders come from nowhere: Their success is uneven', *Journal of Social Issues, 74*(1), 184–96; Brescoll, V. L. & Uhlmann, E. L. (2008), 'Can an angry woman get ahead? Status conferral, gender, and expression of emotion in the workplace', *Psychological Science, 19*(3), 268–75; Meaux, L. T., Cox, J. & Kopkin, M. R. (2018), 'Saving damsels, sentencing deviants and selective chivalry decisions: Juror decision-making in an ambiguous assault case', *Psychiatry, Psychology and Law, 25*(5), 724–36; Leinbach, M. D., Hort, B. E. & Fagot, B. I. (1997), 'Bears are for boys: Metaphorical associations in young children's gender stereotypes', *Cognitive Development, 12*(1), 107–30.

24 Cuddy, A. J., Fiske, S. T. & Glick, P. (2004), 'When professionals become mothers, warmth doesn't cut the ice', *Journal of Social Issues*, 60(4), 701–18.

25 McArthur, L. Z. & Resko, B. G. (1975), 'The portrayal of men and women in American television commercials', *The Journal of Social Psychology*, 97(2), 209–20; Knoll, J. & Matthes, J. (2017), 'The effectiveness of celebrity endorsements: A meta-analysis', *Journal of the Academy of Marketing Science*, 45(1), 55–75.

26 Ward, L. M. (2016), 'Media and sexualization: State of empirical research, 1995–2015', *The Journal of Sex Research*, 53(4–5), 560–77; Wirtz, J. G., Sparks, J. V. & Zimbres, T. M. (2018), 'The effect of exposure to sexual appeals in advertisements on memory, attitude, and purchase intention: A meta-analytic review', *International Journal of Advertising, 37*(2), 168–98.

27 Vaes, J., Paladino, P. & Puvia, E. (2011), 'Are sexualized women complete human beings? Why men and women dehumanize sexually objectified women', *European Journal of Social Psychology, 41*(6), 774–85.

28 Grabe, S., Ward, L. M. & Hyde, J. S. (2008), 'The role of the media in body image concerns among women: A meta-analysis of experimental and correlational studies', *Psychological Bulletin, 134*(3), 460–76.

29 Meltzer, A. L. & McNulty, J. K. (2015), 'Telling women that men desire women with bodies larger than the thin-ideal improves women's body satisfaction', *Social Psychological and Personality Science, 6*(4), 391–8.

30 Pinker, S. (2018), *Enlightenment Now: The case for reason, science, humanism, and progress*, New York, NY: Viking.

31 Fragale, A. R. (2006), 'The power of powerless speech: The effects of speech style and task interdependence on status conferral', *Organizational Behavior and*

Human Decision Processes, 101(2), 243–61; Torelli, C. J., Leslie, L. M., Stoner, J. L. & Puente, R. (2014), 'Cultural determinants of status: Implications for workplace evaluations and behaviors', *Organizational Behavior and Human Decision Processes, 123*(1), 34–48.

32 Kitayama, S., Markus, H. R., Matsumoto, H. & Norasakkunkit, V. (1997), 'Individual and collective processes in the construction of the self: Self-enhancement in the United States and self-criticism in Japan', *Journal of Personality and Social Psychology, 72*(6), 1245–67.

33 Fu, G., Heyman, G. D., Cameron, C. A. & Lee, K. (2016), 'Learning to be unsung heroes: Development of reputation management in two cultures', *Child development, 87*(3), 689–99.

34 Rule, N. O., Ambady, N., Adams Jr, R. B., Ozono, H., Nakashima, S., Yoshikawa, S. & Watabe, M. (2010), 'Polling the face: prediction and consensus across cultures', *Journal of Personality and Social Psychology, 98*, 1–15.

35 Hofstede, G. (1997), *Cultures and Organizations: Software of the mind*, New York, NY: McGraw Hill.

36 Abir, Y., Sklar, A. Y., Dotsch, R., Todorov, A. & Hassin, R. R. (2018), 'The determinants of consciousness of human faces', *Nature Human Behaviour, 2*(3), 194–9.

37 Tsikandilakis, M., Bali, P. & Chapman, P. (2019), 'Beauty Is in the Eye of the Beholder: The Appraisal of Facial Attractiveness and Its Relation to Conscious Awareness', *Perception, 48*(1), 72–92.

INDEX

Stephen Martin is CEO of Influence at Work UK and visiting professor of Behavioral Science at Columbia University's Graduate School of Business. His work has featured in the national and international press including the *New York Times, MSNBC, Time*, the *Harvard Business Review* and the *BBC*. He is coauthor of the Royal Society–nominated international bestseller, *Yes! 60 Secrets from the Science of Persuasion*, and a guest lecturer at Harvard and the London School of Economics.

Joseph Marks is a doctoral researcher at University College London and visiting researcher at the Massachusetts Institute of Technology. His research has been published in academic journals and the *New York Times, Guardian*, and the *Harvard Business Review*.

PublicAffairs is a publishing house founded in 1997. It is a tribute to the standards, values, and flair of three persons who have served as mentors to countless reporters, writers, editors, and book people of all kinds, including me.

I. F. STONE, proprietor of *I. F. Stone's Weekly*, combined a commitment to the First Amendment with entrepreneurial zeal and reporting skill and became one of the great independent journalists in American history. At the age of eighty, Izzy published *The Trial of Socrates*, which was a national bestseller. He wrote the book after he taught himself ancient Greek.

BENJAMIN C. BRADLEE was for nearly thirty years the charismatic editorial leader of *The Washington Post*. It was Ben who gave the *Post* the range and courage to pursue such historic issues as Watergate. He supported his reporters with a tenacity that made them fearless and it is no accident that so many became authors of influential, best-selling books.

ROBERT L. BERNSTEIN, the chief executive of Random House for more than a quarter century, guided one of the nation's premier publishing houses. Bob was personally responsible for many books of political dissent and argument that challenged tyranny around the globe. He is also the founder and longtime chair of Human Rights Watch, one of the most respected human rights organizations in the world.

· · ·

For fifty years, the banner of Public Affairs Press was carried by its owner Morris B. Schnapper, who published Gandhi, Nasser, Toynbee, Truman, and about 1,500 other authors. In 1983, Schnapper was described by *The Washington Post* as "a redoubtable gadfly." His legacy will endure in the books to come.

Peter Osnos, *Founder*